# *The Common T.H.R.E.A.D Method*

### A Proven Approach to Raising Capital
### Through Authentic Connections

**ANDREW BORSES**

# Table of Contents

# Praise for The Common T.H.R.E.A.D Method

"The Common Thread Method" isn't just another book—it's a blueprint for clarity, action, and real transformation. I've spent years helping people build businesses, manage money, and reach their goals, but what Andy Borses has done with the T.H.R.E.A.D. Method is next level. This isn't just a framework; it's a holistic guide that brings together key principles in a way that's actionable, relatable, and designed to deliver real, lasting results.

The T.H.R.E.A.D. Method is built on six powerful principles: Trust, Human Connection, Rapport, Emotional Intelligence, and Dedication to Growth. Each of these is critical not only for achieving success but for doing so in alignment with your values and purpose. It's rare to find a method that seamlessly emphasizes both personal and professional growth.

What stands out in Andy's approach is its practicality. He doesn't just talk about these ideas in theory—he shows you exactly how to apply them to your life and business, step by step. I've seen firsthand the breakthroughs that come from focusing on your 'common thread,' and with the T.H.R.E.A.D. Method, you have a clear path to building trust, strengthening relationships, and growing in meaningful ways.

If you're serious about making a shift, both personally and professionally, this book is a must-read. Andy Borses has created something truly special with "The Common Thread Method." It is the roadmap you've been searching for, and I can't recommend it highly enough."

Brad Hart,
Brad Hart /Founder - Make More Marbles / Author of The 8 Minute Mastermind and The 8 Minute Money Manager

*"In the tapestry of life, we are all connected. Each one of us is a gift to those around us, helping each other be who we are, weaving a perfect picture together."*

**ANITA MOORJANI**

# Dederications

**To my mother, Carol who is no longer with us,**

*You taught me to always look deeper, to see the common threads that connect us all, even in the most unexpected places. Your strength, wisdom, and ability to find light in every situation shaped the way I view relationships and life. This book, and everything it stands for, is a reflection of the values you instilled in me—thank you for being the ultimate guide through every twist and turn.*

**To my grandfather, Joe,**

*You had a gift for spotting the threads that tie people together. From you, I learned that life isn't just about what's on the surface, but about finding those deeper connections that make us truly relate to one another. Your stories, your patience, and your unwavering belief in the power of human connection live on in these pages. This is for you, with all my love and gratitude for showing me how to see the bigger picture.*

**To my wife, Maureen,**

*Your unwavering belief in me has been my rock through every twist and turn. You've taught me to always see the world through others' eyes and to reflect the kindness and empathy we all need. This book, and the journey behind it, wouldn't be possible without your love and constant support. Thank you for standing by me every step of the way.*

THE COMMON T.H.R.E.A.D METHOD

### To Jen,

*You have been a beacon, always pushing me to challenge myself and go beyond what I thought was possible. Where others saw dead ends, you created a roadmap, guiding me with your insight and showing me the power of seeing and connecting the common threads. Your mentorship has transformed not only this book but my entire journey. I'm forever grateful for your unwavering support and belief in me.*

### To Stacy,

*Your wisdom and knowledge in the world of real estate investing have been invaluable, but it's your heart that truly sets you apart. I call you "Mama Bear" because of the fierce way you protect your students and ensure their success within the academy. Your dedication, patience, and no-nonsense guidance have shaped not just my approach to investing, but how I view success as a whole. Thank you for always having our backs and for being the incredible leader you are.*

# *The Common T.H.R.E.A.D Method:*

A Proven Approach to Raising Capital
Through Authentic Connections

# *Foreword*

## BY JEN CONKEY

In the vast and often tumultuous ocean of raising capital, navigating the waters requires not just a keen understanding of the financial landscape but a profound connection with the people who inhabit it. This dual insight is what Andy Borses brings to the fore in his groundbreaking work. As someone privileged to have journeyed with Andy as his Mindset Coach, I've witnessed an evolution not just of a financial strategist, but of a person who embodies the very essence of transformation, and growth.

Andy's journey is one that many can relate to but few have the courage to undertake. The transition from a place of fear and embarrassment—feelings that often accompany the act of "asking for money"—to a position of strength and pride in offering genuine opportunities for investment is nothing short of remarkable. It's a testament to Andy's character and his unwavering commitment to not just personal development but to creating value for others.

What sets Andy apart is his gifted attention to detail and an innate ability to understand what's most important to people. This skill has not only been instrumental in his personal growth but has become the cornerstone of his T.H.R.E.A.D methodology—a revolutionary approach to raising capital. This methodology is not just a set of strategies; it's a philosophy that champions the building of long-term relationships, recognizing that true success in capital raising is as much about the people you serve as it is about the funds you secure.

The T.H.R.E.A.D methodology, detailed in this book, is Andy's gift to those who dare to dream big and are ready to change the narrative around capital raising. It's a method that promises to eliminate the scramble for capital by laying down a blueprint for sustainable growth and meaningful connections.

As you delve into the pages of this book, remember that you're not just learning a methodology; you're embarking on a journey of transformation.

Andy's personal journey of growth and transformation naturally led to the creation of the T.H.R.E.A.D methodology, a system that encapsulates his approach to building meaningful, trust-based relationships.

His story and his approach are a beacon for anyone looking to make a significant impact in the world of finance and beyond. The T.H.R.E.A.D methodology isn't just a testament to Andy's genius; it's a legacy that will stand the test of time.

To Andy, I extend my deepest gratitude for allowing me to be a part of your journey. To the reader, I offer this assurance: by embracing the principles laid out in this book, you're not just raising capital; you're elevating your entire approach to business and life.

*Welcome to a new era of capital raising.*

—JEN CONKEY

# *Prologue*

## BY
## SANYIKA "THE FIRESTARTER" STREET

**Here's a question...**

Would you let Bernie Madoff, the NY Stock juggernaut and mastermind of the largest Ponzi scheme in history—defrauding investors of over $65 billion—babysit your 401k and investment portfolio if he promised, "I'll be good this time"?

**Probably not.**

Here's another question...

Would you let Samuel Bankman-Fried, founder of the bankrupt cryptocurrency exchange FTX, recently convicted on seven counts of fraud and conspiracy for misappropriating nearly $2 billion, become CFO of your company if he said, "I'm a new man"?

**Again, probably not.**

Despite their obvious financial expertise, you wouldn't let Bernie Madoff or Samuel Bankman-Fried near your money or lead your company's finances. Why? Because they've lost the single most important factor when it comes to managing or raising capital: **they lost our trust**.

When it comes to managing money, stewarding wealth, or scaling revenue, you only get one shot—and they blew it. This book will give you the tools so when you get **your** shot, you'll win the game.

But Bernie and Sam are only human. We're all human. I'm human. Do we really only get one shot?

Yes, we are human
Yes, we make mistakes.
And yes, **you still only get one shot**.

It's unfair, I know. But when it comes to managing or scaling money, you need people who treat your hard-earned wealth like it's their one shot.

One big financial mistake means your life savings are **gone**. One major misstep could wipe out your retirement account. One serious error could put your portfolio in the IRS's hands **tomorrow**. It's critical to handle other people's money like you'd want them to handle yours—like they've only got **one shot** to get it right.

Getting it right doesn't mean every move makes millions. It means every move is grounded in principles. It means you and the person you're managing money for have a clear agreement: what's happening, what the upside is, what the risks are, and what the steps are. In my view, there's only one way to get it right when it comes to managing, stewarding, or scaling capital: **The Common T.H.R.E.A.D. Method**. Here's why...

The Common T.H.R.E.A.D. Method isn't about what you do—it's about **who you are**. People don't come to The Common T.H.R.E.A.D. to get money from you. **I am the Common Thread**, which makes me a safe place for people to invest, manage, and steward their capital. I am the Common T.H.R.E.A.D. because I live these principles:

- **T**rust
- **H**uman Connection
- **R**apport Development
- **E**motional Intelligence
- **A**uthentic Engagement
- **D**edication to Growth

The goal of this book isn't to give you tricks to "get money"—it's to help you **become the kind of person** people trust to steward their money. Whether you're managing, scaling, or investing capital, the aim is to become the person who protects the hearts and minds of those you serve.

I wish I had these tools growing up. I made plenty of mistakes, though fortunately, none were catastrophic. But the mistakes I did make cost me millions. My goal is for you to learn from the millions I lost by not living this method.

It's crucial that you read this book not just as advice for others, but as the manual for **your one shot** at the big time. It will empower you to become the person you've always wanted to be.

I'm grateful Bernie Madoff isn't managing my portfolio, and I'm equally relieved Samuel Bankman-Fried isn't the CFO of my company. But most of all, I'm excited to see you become the kind of person who will usher in a new era of financial stewards who understand the power of **The Common T.H.R.E.A.D. Method**. I look forward to seeing you become someone I'd trust with all my investments and the investments of those I serve.

As a business and leadership mentor for men, my mission has always been about empowering men to step into integrity, power, and purpose. Whether stewarding money or stewarding hearts, the common thread remains the same: **I must become the person** I am guiding others to be.

Similarly, **you** must become the person worthy of the trust of others, and this is a powerful method to do so. This isn't just about managing capital; it's about becoming the kind of leader others trust with their most valuable resources—be it money, their dreams, or their hearts. When you lead with trust, you create a ripple effect that transforms the world around you. That's the real work. That's the fire I'm here to ignite.

I'm looking forward to seeing the leader you become.

*From trust, with trust.*

SANYIKA "THE FIRESTARTER" STREET

# *Introduction*

## THE BLUEPRINT FOR BUILDING TRUST: *THE T.H.R.E.A.D METHOD*

L et's get real. In the cutthroat world of raising capital, it's not just about numbers or slick pitches. It's about people. It's about the connections you make and the trust you build. The *Common T.H.R.E.A.D Method* is your secret weapon. It's not just another method; it's the game-changer you've been waiting for. This framework is all about taking ordinary conversations and turning them into extraordinary opportunities.

So, what's the deal with T.H.R.E.A.D?

- **T: Trust**

  If you don't have trust, you don't have anything. Trust is the foundation of every successful relationship, period. You want people to take you seriously? You want them to invest in you? Then you need to show them you're the real deal. Consistency, reliability, and integrity—these are your new best friends.

- **H: Human Connection**

  Forget about the scripts and the templates. People want to connect with other people, not robots. This isn't about transactions; it's about relationships. See the human being across the table. Get to know them. Understand them. That's where the magic happens.

- **R: Rapport Development**

Building rapport isn't just a nice-to-have; it's a must-have. You've got to create that vibe where people feel comfortable opening up to you. It's about mutual respect and understanding. You do that, and you'll find that doors start opening for you in ways you never imagined.

- **E: Emotional Intelligence**

  Know yourself and know your audience. If you can't read the room, you're lost. Emotional intelligence is your compass. It helps you navigate the highs and lows of every interaction. When you get this right, you connect on a level that goes way beyond business.

- **A: Authentic Engagement**

  Here's the deal: People can smell BS from a mile away. Authenticity is everything. Show up as your true self, every single time. Be genuine, be real, and watch how people start gravitating toward you. Authentic engagement isn't just about being honest; it's about being YOU.

- **D: Dedication to Growth**

  You've got to be in it for the long haul. This isn't about quick wins or overnight success. It's about committing to constant improvement—personally and professionally. If you're not growing, you're dying. Keep learning, keep adapting, and keep pushing the limits.

These are the building blocks of the T.H.R.E.A.D method. It's not just a set of rules; it's a way of life. By mastering these principles, you'll turn potential investors into lifelong partners and partners into raving fans. This book is going to take you step-by-step through the T.H.R.E.A.D method, showing you exactly how to build connections that matter and raise capital with confidence.

This isn't just about business—it's about life. It's about making every interaction count. So, if you're ready to transform the way you connect, to turn relationships into your biggest asset, then buckle up. Your journey to success starts now. Let's go!

Throughout this book, we'll explore how each element of the T.H.R.E.A.D Method can be woven into your everyday interactions, turning casual conversations into opportunities for building trust, creating lasting partnerships, and, ultimately, raising capital effectively.

By mastering the T.H.R.E.A.D Method, you'll learn to weave these principles into every conversation, turning potential investors into partners, and turning partners into advocates.

This book will guide you through each step of the T.H.R.E.A.D framework, equipping you with the skills to connect on a deeper level and raise capital with confidence.

# COMMON T.H.R.E.A.D'S: THE FABRIC OF LIFE

*"When you can't reinvent the wheel… put your own spin on it."*

## —GARRETT SHIKUMA

We are like T.H.R.E.A.D's in a vast, beautiful tapestry, each T.H.R.E.A.D contributing its unique color and texture, yet all interwoven to form a greater design. These common T.H.R.E.A.D's are what bring us together. They are the shared experiences, the common values, and the mutual aspirations that bind us. When we recognize these T.H.R.E.A.D's in our conversations, we are not just connecting on a surface level; we are connecting heart to heart, soul to soul.

And when such genuine connections are made, money flows naturally. You see, money flows where there is harmony, where there is trust, and where there is true connection.

# How I Stumbled into Raising Capital

Have you ever found yourself in a room full of people, searching for that one thing that could break the ice and spark a genuine conversation? Or maybe you've been in a meeting, struggling to find common ground with potential investors, clients, or even colleagues?

What if I told you there's a way to effortlessly connect with others, no matter the situation?

Finding a common T.H.R.E.A.D with others often seems daunting in a world where meaningful connections can feel rare and elusive, especially in the high-stakes realms of business and personal relationships. Whether you're trying to raise capital for a real estate deal, build a new network, or simply foster deeper connections with those around you, the challenge remains the same: how do you bridge the gap and establish a real, authentic connection?

This book tackles that very challenge head-on.

It delves into the struggles many of us face when trying to connect with others, be it in professional settings or our personal lives. The Common T.H.R.E.A.D Method, which I learned from my own experiences and honed over the years, is not just a strategy—it's a mindset. It's about recognizing the shared inter-ests, experiences, or passions that can transform a simple conversation into a meaningful exchange.

The goal of this book is to equip you with the tools and insights to uncover and leverage these common T.H.R.E.A.D's, helping you navigate through conver-sations and interactions with ease and confidence. It's about more than just talking to people; it's about truly connecting with them. Through personal stories, practical examples, and actionable steps, I want to share with you the secrets of making every interaction count.

Connecting with others doesn't have to be a daunting task, nor does it require you to be a natural extrovert. It's about being present, listening, and finding that one thing you both care about.

Whether you're at a networking event, pitching to investors, or simply trying to deepen your relationships, this book will guide you in using The Common T.H.R.E.A.D Method to its fullest potential.

Together, we'll explore how these connections can open doors, create opportunities, and enrich your life in ways you might not have imagined. By the end of this journey, you'll not only be better at connecting with others but also more attuned to the subtle yet powerful ways these connections shape our lives.

The journey to writing this book has been a deeply personal one, shaped by my own life experiences and the lessons I've learned along the way.

Through these stories, I hope to inspire others to recognize and appreciate the common T.H.R.E.A.D's that weave through their own lives, understanding how these connections can lead to unexpected opportunities and profound relationships. It's a celebration of the resilience and interconnectedness that define our human experience.

What I learned from these experiences is that at the heart of every successful interaction, whether personal or professional, lies a COMMON T.H.R.E.A.D – a shared interest, experience, or goal that binds two people together. In real estate, where relationships are as crucial as the properties themselves, this method is particularly potent.

## Realizing the Power of The Common T.H.R.E.A.D

When I first entered the real estate world, I couldn't have imagined raising capital, let alone handling over 4.9 million dollars. Coming from a lower-middle-class background, it felt surreal and intimidating. I often felt like an imposter, as I was more familiar with making ends meet than with big investments and high stakes.

I frequently questioned whether I had what it took to succeed in this field because before venturing into the world of multifamily real estate investment, I spent over two decades immersed in the dazzling yet demanding TV and film industry, where every day was a whirlwind of creative chaos.

It was a career filled with its own kind of magic, complete with dramatic plot twists, compelling characters, and the occasional diva meltdown – and that was just off-camera! The industry was as demanding as it was dazzling, offering me a life that was anything but mundane.

**Then came the plot twist no scriptwriter could have foreseen:**

In the director's chair of my life's epic, "The Perfect Storm," I found myself orchestrating a narrative that was as tumultuous as it was transformative. The opening scene is set against the backdrop of 2008, a year that would mark the beginning of a personal and financial maelstrom.

This wasn't just any storm; it was my perfect storm, a confluence of personal and financial turmoil that tested every facet of my resilience. The economic downturn known globally as the Great Recession was merely the dark clouds gathering on the horizon.

The real tempest was the unraveling of my life as I knew it—losing my job was the first gust of wind, a harbinger of the chaos to follow.

The plot thickens as, guided by misguided advice, my wife and I lost the family home. This wasn't just a set piece; it was the heart of my story, a symbol of the journey from sharing a bed with my sisters in New Jersey to what I thought was the pinnacle of success. The next scene painfully unfolds with my car being towed away, a casualty not of the storm itself but of a legal oversight, leaving us adrift without anchor or sail. Our descent into financial ruin forced us to seek refuge in a smaller, humbler abode, our lives a stark contrast to the dreams we once harbored.

Act Two is a decade-long odyssey of redemption and resilience. With no script to guide us, my family and I navigated through the aftermath, determined to rebuild from the wreckage. The resolve to never face such devastation again was my driving force, a promise to myself and to those I held dear.

As the narrative arcs towards its climax, a second storm looms—this time in the form of a pandemic.

And the sequel is always worse than the original movie.

COVID-19, that unforeseen antagonist, threatened to rerun the tragedy of our past.

The industry that was my livelihood, my daily dose of creative chaos, hit the pause button. Suddenly, I found myself staging one-man shows in our living room, turning from a seasoned professional to an amateur performer overnight.

My wife, ever the supportive audience, watched with a mix of amusement and concern as I acted out my frustration, looking for a solution to our new reality.

She was there through every improvised scene and unrehearsed monologue, a silent reminder that we were in this script rewrite together.

It was during this pause that the reality of our financial foundation – or the lack thereof – started to sink in.

The pandemic continued its unwelcome extended cameo, and then came the kicker: my wife's business, her own masterpiece two decades in the making, was also given the 'cut' signal.

My wife's business, a casualty of the pandemic's relentless spread, forced us to adapt once more, taking on freelance work to supplement our dwindling income. The vow to avoid the snares of bankruptcy was a line I was determined not to cross again, even if it meant delivering pizzas to keep the storm at bay.

Our professional lives were starting to resemble one of those indie films where nothing goes as planned and you are always over budget.

But hey, every crisis is just an opportunity in a really, really good disguise, right? I chose to see this period as the universe's way of yelling…

"Cut! Let's take it from the top, but this time with more feeling… and maybe a different script."

It was a stark realization that no job, no matter how award-winning it may be, comes with a guarantee.

The hard truth hit us like a poorly timed slapstick gag – without a diverse income source or a substantial financial safety net, we were all treading water in the same unpredictable storm.

Desperation has a way of sharpening focus, of making you seek answers in places you'd never thought to look. We were no different. Like so many others, we turned to the wisdom of Robert Kiyosaki, diving into the pages of his books, hoping to find a roadmap to financial security. We scoured YouTube, hungry for guidance, latching onto every word from self-proclaimed gurus. But it all felt like chasing shadows, like Hansel and Gretel following crumbs through the forest, leading us in circles but never to the gingerbread house.

We were seeking more than crumbs; we hungered for the secret sauce, the substantial, tangible guidance that seemed to be just out of reach. And then, like a beacon in the dense fog, we found Jen and Stacy Conkey. It was my wife who, after those long, grueling months of searching, decided to take a leap of faith with them.

We started cautiously, barely dipping our toes in the water, thinking their group mentorship calls and Stacy's meticulously crafted videos would be enough. We didn't opt for the one-on-one coaching initially, because we were afraid to make a bigger financial commitment and made the decision to navigate these uncharted waters with a weekly call and training videos.

We rolled up our sleeves, put on our producer hats, and got to work. The mission? To build a stream of passive income sturdy enough to weather any storm. And our chosen vehicle for this epic production? Real estate. It wasn't just about investing; it was about rewriting our story, about taking the director's chair in our financial future.

This shift wasn't just a plot twist; it was a full-blown genre change, a leap from drama to action-adventure, and a decision that has since turned every 'No' into a note, every challenge into a plot development, and every success into a scene worth replaying.

When we made that decision, the world of multifamily real estate investment was as foreign to me as quantum physics. I remember sitting at my desk, flipping through a finance magazine, and reading about investment moguls who'd built empires out of apartment complexes and sprawling residential units.

It was fascinating, sure, but it might as well have been a story from another planet. My understanding of investments was pretty basic, mostly limited to what I'd seen in movies or overheard in conversations I barely grasped.

I could tell you how to produce a film or switch cameras for a live event, but on a caching call when I was asked what the ARV was on a property I was looking at I told the coach that I hoped to have a couple of ATVs in my garage one day.

She laughed and said not ATV!

ARV!...After Repair Value.

OMG, I have to remember another acronym I thought how many more are there?

Back then, if you'd told me that I'd be where I am today, knee-deep in the world of multifamily investments, I'd have laughed and handed you a beer, thinking you were pulling my leg. Real estate, to me, was about owning a home, maybe two, and that was the extent of it. The idea of owning, managing, and investing in properties where numerous families lived, shared, and built their lives was beyond my realm of imagination.

But there was this nagging feeling, a quiet whisper at the back of my mind that started as I mentioned during the pandemic – isn't there more to life than this? More to explore, more to achieve, more to create?

That whisper turned into a conversation, a loud one, the kind you can't easily ignore. It was a mix of curiosity and, I'll admit, a bit of envy. How were these investors doing it?

What did they know that I didn't? And then, the real kicker – could I do it too? Could I step into this world, so alien and intimidating, and carve a place for myself?

The challenge was daunting, almost laughably so. I mean, I was no financial guru. Sure, I'd done well enough for myself, but this? This was a different ball game.

So, that's where it all started. From the comfort of my predictable life, I peered into the vast, uncharted waters of multifamily real estate investment. Little did I know, that peek would soon turn into a plunge, a dive into depths I'd never explored. But every journey starts with a single step, right? Or in my case, a single, tentative peek.

For nine long months, we treaded water, making little to no progress. It was frustrating to feel so close yet so far from our goals. And that's when we realized—if we were going to swim, we couldn't just paddle in the shallow end. We had to dive in, headfirst, into the deep. We bit the bullet and invested in the full mentorship experience, putting all our hopes, dreams, and the last of our financial security on the line.

What I've come to understand, and believe me, this was a tough pill to swallow, is that even the world's best mentorship program won't mean a thing if you're not willing to walk the path laid out for you. It's a path that's been smoothed by the trials, errors, and hard-earned wisdom of those who've walked it before you. Ignoring that is like setting yourself up for a fall, like trying to build a house starting with the roof. I learned that the hard way.

You see, I was that guy, the one trying to find shortcuts, thinking I could cherry-pick my way through the process. If there was a 'Skip' button, you bet I'd hit it, convinced I could outsmart the system much like Captain Kirk rigging the Kobayashi Maru training exercise in Star Trek yes I am a geek at heart. Looking back, I realize that's been my approach to, well, pretty much everything.

It's a Capricorn thing, I guess – always aiming for the peak, sometimes forgetting about the climb that gets you there. But here's the thing – that's just an excuse, a way to shrug off the real issue.

My mentors, Jen and Stacy Conkey, saw through my excuses. When I blamed the system for my failures, they gave me a reality check: the problem was my ego. I was always looking for shortcuts, avoiding the necessary steps. They made me realize that my ego was a major obstacle, constantly shifting blame and resisting steady progress. The real work began with confronting this part of myself, learning to set it aside, and embracing the process instead of trying to skip ahead. This was the true game-changer.

And patience, oh boy, patience. That's not a word we New Yorkers are too fond of, right? But it was exactly what I needed. It wasn't just about learning to wait; it was about understanding the value of each step, of the grind, the learning, the slow but sure progress.

And once that clicked, once I embraced patience, things started to shift. Doors began to open, and opportunities started to unfold. It was like the universe was saying,

"Finally, you get it."

As my real estate journey progressed, I realized it's not a 'get rich quick' scheme—anyone claiming that is selling a fantasy.

Real estate is a marathon with hurdles, testing endurance, grit, and patience. Our early investments, like the duplex in Indianapolis, were full of unexpected lessons. For instance, we discovered the seller had used old clothes as insulation. These surprises highlighted the unpredictable nature of the business and the need for resilience.

Then came the second deal, a duplex we meticulously transformed from a caterpillar to a butterfly, only to have it trashed by tenants who seemed to have taken a page out of a con artist's handbook. Discovering the tenant was a bipolar drug dealer was the cherry on top of this stress sundae. Talk about a patience killer!

But the real test came with a triplex, affectionately dubbed 'the gift that keeps on giving.' After almost a year of battling these relentless challenges, my patience and mindset were stretched thinner than I thought possible. It was a grueling, eye-opening period, but it also sparked a pivotal decision. If we were going to pour our blood, sweat, and tears into this venture, we needed to level up.

With our mentors' guidance, we cautiously entered the world of apartment building investments. The training was rigorous, and the stakes were high, but we were determined.

We soon secured our first apartment in Chicago and raised nearly seven hundred thousand dollars for the deal, showcasing techniques I'll discuss in this book. However, the broker we worked with didn't have our best interests in mind. Thanks to our mentors' wisdom, we were able to avoid a potential disaster, highlighting the invaluable role of mentorship in our journey.

Instead, we redirected those funds and joint-ventured into a 31-unit apartment, a decision that reinvigorated my patience and reignited my ambition. After that, I believe the Universe took notice of our unwavering tenacity to keep going and never quit until we reached our goals.

That's when things started to shift. I got a call from my now business partner who little did I know was watching my growth from the sidelines with an intriguing proposition if he found the properties, would I be interested in raising the capital for them?

I had only raised capital once in this arena, but I wasn't about to let that deter me. Knowing his expertise and track record, I didn't hesitate. "LFG," I said, or to put it more formally, I gave a BIG YES!

That conversation sparked a significant change. I immediately got to work, using

The Common T.H.R.E.A.D Method to build a solid network of potential investors.

Our first project was a 14-unit apartment building in Tampa, Florida. It wasn't the grand, high-end "A" Class property I had initially envisioned, but it was a crucial first step.

I was excited to be actively engaging with investors, offering them a chance to grow their wealth. The method was effective, helping me identify what mattered to each investor.

Sure, there were plenty of 'No's, but that's the nature of the game.

Real estate investment is like a menu – some prefer the filet mignon, while others are content with a hamburger. And that's perfectly fine.

We closed on that Tampa deal, and I celebrated that victory, knowing it was just the beginning. The sky was the limit with my mentors and partners by my side. We soon took on a larger project in Cincinnati, each deal growing in size and complexity. But the real test came with a phone call from my partner, a call that challenged every ounce of self-belief I had. He had a unicorn of a deal in the works, and he wanted to know if I thought I could raise close to three million dollars for it.

I took a deep breath, feeling the weight of imposter syndrome creeping in. But then I remembered where I came from the challenges I'd already overcome.

I grew up in a lower-middle-class family and experienced the struggles of a household held together by a single parent. There were days when cornflakes were the meal of the day. But this deal, this opportunity, it was a chance to change the game. So, I told that nagging voice of doubt to take a back seat and watched as I dove headfirst into the challenge.

I became a man on a mission. My Excel spreadsheet became my constant companion, and LinkedIn and Facebook turned into my hunting grounds. I set up webinars, made countless calls, and pursued every lead relentlessly.

The Common T.H.R.E.A.D Method wasn't just a theory; it became my playbook, and it was effective. But it wasn't without challenges—like losing a $500,000 investor a week before closing.

Yet, when you set your intentions, the Universe responds. Our mentors, Jen and Stacy Conkey, stepped in as co-GP partners, leveraging their network to fill the gap. Together, we successfully closed the 96-unit deal.

With each hurdle, my resilience grew, and so did my hunger for the next deal. I began to see the journey not just as a series of investments but as an evolving narrative. The smaller properties were like children in kindergarten, each with its unique quirks and lessons.

The larger Multi-Family Apartments?

They were the college kids, more complex, more demanding, but also more rewarding. As you can see, humor became my ally in this journey, a way to lighten the load and keep perspective. It's a trait I've woven into the fabric of my investment philosophy, a reminder that while the road may be rocky, the journey is also rich with lessons, laughter, and the unwavering belief that the dream of my 'WHY' is not just a possibility, but a reality waiting to be seized.

As I continued to navigate the world of real estate and capital raising, another transformative moment came when Jen, someone who saw potential in me even when I couldn't, offered me an incredible opportunity. She invited me to take the stage as the master of ceremonies for the Warriors of Wealth (WOW) at their WOWCON events.

It was an honor I never expected, and frankly, one that I initially felt unworthy of. The imposter syndrome crept in again, whispering doubts about whether I was really the right person to lead such a prestigious event.

But Jen believed in me, and that belief pushed me to step out of my comfort zone. Standing on that stage, facing an audience eager to learn and grow, was both exhilarating and nerve-wracking.

I decided to share my story, to be open and honest about my journey—from the humble beginnings of layaway gifts to raising millions in capital. I spoke about the doubts I had faced, the lessons I had learned, and the pivotal moments that shaped my path.

As I poured my heart out, something incredible happened.

People connected with my story.

After the session, attendees walked up to me, not just to congratulate me, but to thank me for sharing my experiences.

They told me how much they could relate to my story, how they, too, had struggled with feelings of inadequacy and the fear of not belonging in the world of wealth and investment.

One person said, "Your story reminded me that we all start somewhere, and it's okay to have doubts. What's important is pushing through them." Another mentioned, "Hearing you talk about overcoming imposter syndrome gave me the courage to start working on raising capital for my own deals."

These conversations were eye-opening. It was humbling and deeply moving to realize that my journey, with all its ups and downs, could inspire others.

It was then that I fully understood the power of storytelling and The Common T.H.R.E.A.D Method. It wasn't just about connecting with investors or closing deals; it was about connecting with people on a fundamental level, sharing our struggles and triumphs, and encouraging each other to grow.

Jen's faith in me and the platform she provided were pivotal. They not only helped me overcome my own insecurities but also showed me the impact my story could have on others.

The feedback and gratitude I received from the WOWCON audience were affirmations that I was on the right path. It was a reminder that vulnerability and authenticity are powerful tools for connection and inspiration.

This experience solidified my commitment to writing this book. I wanted to share these insights and stories with a wider audience. Let others know that no matter where they come from or their doubts, they have the power to connect, inspire, and succeed. The Common T.H.R.E.A.D Method, which had guided me through so many challenges, could be a beacon for others navigating their own journeys.

A friend of mine, whom I was chatting with about writing this book, posed an interesting question: "Can a small start-up use the tactics in this book, or is it just for real estate investors?"

You know, that's a great question and one I've thought a lot about. Here's the thing: while this book is focused on real estate, the principles and tactics I share in this book aren't confined to any one industry. The Common T.H.R.E.A.D Method is really about connecting with people on a human level, finding shared interests, and building genuine relationships.

Whether you're raising capital for a multi-million-dollar real estate deal or pitching your first start-up idea to potential investors, the core idea remains the same: people invest in people.

It's about understanding the person on the other side of the table, relating to them, and finding that common ground that makes them say, 'Hey, I get where you're coming from.'

In fact, I'd argue that these tactics are even more crucial for small start-ups. When you're just starting out, you might not have a track record or big numbers to impress potential partners or investors. What you have, though, is your story, passion, and ability to connect. The Common T.H.R.E.A.D Method helps you leverage these personal elements to create strong, meaningful connections that can open doors and create opportunities.

So, whether you're a real estate investor, an entrepreneur, or just someone looking to build better relationships, the strategies in this book are for you.

They're about finding and weaving those common T.H.R.E.A.D's that make connections not just possible, but powerful. It's about showing up with a purpose.

This book is my way of paying forward the support and opportunities I've been given. It's about sharing the lessons I've learned, the strategies that have worked for me, and the belief that everyone has a story worth telling.

My story of "The Perfect Storm" is more than a tale of survival against economic and personal upheaval. It's a narrative of resilience, a testament to the human spirit's capacity to weather any storm. As the credits roll, it's clear that this journey, with all its trials and triumphs, is not just my story—it's a universal saga of overcoming adversity, a narrative that resonates with anyone who has faced their own perfect storm.

So, whether you're just starting out or are well into your journey, this book encourages you to embrace your own story, find your common T.H.R.E.A.D' s, and use them to connect with others and achieve your goals.

In writing this book, I aim to empower readers to face their own imposter syndrome, push through self-doubt, and confidently step into their potential. Just as Jen saw something in me and helped me rise to the occasion, I want this book to be a guide and a source of inspiration for anyone looking to make their mark, connect with others, and build a life of purpose and connection.

Now that you understand the foundation of the *T.H.R.E.A.D. Method*, let's begin by exploring the most fundamental aspect of relationship-building: resilience. In the next chapter, we'll uncover how personal resilience shapes the connections you build and the opportunities that follow.

# CHAPTER 1

# The Fabric of Relationships: *A Lesson in Resilience and Understanding*

*"The fabric of human life is woven with relationships. Once we thematize the importance of dialogue, the multiplicity of ongoing and created situations in which dialogical skills can be nurtured abound. As we have seen, this requires us to slow down and turn toward each other, having a clear sense of the relationship between our current footing in dialogue with one another and the future we are trying to create. The nurture of dialogical capacities is essential to human liberation."*

—MARY WATKINS,
Toward Psychologies of Liberation

As we dive deeper into the THREAD method, it's crucial to understand that the fabric of all successful capital-raising efforts is woven through relationships. In my own journey, I found this to be profoundly true.

So now you know how I managed to raise over four million dollars in a year, especially with little prior experience in capital raising, I know, it sounds wild, especially since I was pretty green in the whole capital-raising game when I started my real estate investing quest to find a better way to create the life I knew I was destined to live.

But here's the kicker – the real secret sauce behind it wasn't some high-end finance strategy; it was something way simpler and way more personal.

# Finding the Common Thread

In the complex world of raising capital, success is not just about crunching numbers or closing deals! It's rooted in the relationships we build and the connections we nurture. The Common T.H.R.E.A.D Method is more than a title; it's a strategic framework designed to unlock powerful connections through meaningful conversations. This method is all about identifying and leveraging shared experiences and values, transforming ordinary interactions into extraordinary opportunities.

# The Power of Trust

Every successful relationship, especially in business, is built on trust. Trust is the foundation that holds everything together. My journey into the world of capital raising began with an unexpected lesson in trust during a pivotal moment in my life.

## A Stormy Night and a Lesson in Trust

The year was 1970. My family was in the midst of upheaval. After my parents divorced, my mom decided to move my sisters and me from Florida to New York, seeking a fresh start.

My dad, in contrast, was on a quest to "find himself," caught up in the self-discovery wave of the late 60s and early 70s. While we were driving away from Florida, he remained behind, focusing inward on his personal journey.

On the first night of our journey, we were caught in a fierce thunderstorm. Visibility was zero, and we ended up sliding into a ditch right outside a gas station. The gas station owner, initially reluctant to help, wore a New York Mets cap.

My mom, ever resourceful, started talking about the Mets—a simple yet profound connection. This shared interest broke the ice, and the owner not only helped us out of the ditch but also invited us to stay in his garage for the night. That night, with hot chocolate in hand, we learned that finding common ground, no matter how small, could transform a potentially negative situation into a positive one.

**Lesson:** This experience taught me that trust begins with showing genuine interest in others and finding common ground, even in challenging circumstances.

# Resilience in the Face of Adversity

My mother's decision to uproot our lives and start over in New York was not just a physical journey; it was a testament to her resilience. Leaving everything behind, including my father, who was more focused on his personal quest than on providing for his family, was a daunting task. But my mother's determination to create a better life for us was unwavering.

## Starting Over: From Switchboard Operator to Social Worker

Upon arriving in New York, my mother had to start from scratch. With little money and no job prospects, she found work as a telephone switchboard operator. It wasn't glamorous, but it was a job that provided for her family. Watching her navigate this role, I saw firsthand what resilience looked like—never giving up, even when the odds were against her.

Over time, my mother transitioned from working at a switchboard to becoming a social worker. This wasn't a path laid out for her; it was a road she carved out through sheer determination and hard work. She had an incredible ability to connect with people, which she used to build a network of support and opportunities.

Despite the hardship, she remained focused on one thing: our family's well-being. She often told us, "It's not about how many times you fall, but how many times you get back up." This was her mantra, and it became mine too.

**Lesson:** Resilience is about finding the strength to start over, to build anew when everything falls apart. It's about maintaining hope and determination, no matter the obstacles.

# Building Human Connections

While my father focused inwardly, trying to understand his own path, my mother looked outward, focusing on building connections and ensuring our survival. Her approach to life was about reaching out and finding common threads with others, even in the midst of adversity. This principle became clear to me later in life, especially during my transition from the TV and film industry into real estate.

## From Film Sets to Real Estate: The Art of Genuine Connection

Before diving into real estate, I spent over two decades in the TV and film industry, where every day was a whirlwind of creativity and chaos. The transition wasn't easy, especially after facing the "perfect storm" of the 2008 financial crisis and personal setbacks, including losing our family home. It was a period of profound uncertainty, but it also forced me to re-evaluate my priorities and relationships.

In the aftermath, I realized that my success was tied not to the flashy success of the entertainment industry but to the genuine relationships I built. My ability to connect with people, understand their needs, and work together towards common goals became my most valuable asset.

**Lesson:** In real estate and beyond, success is about more than just closing deals. It's about building relationships that matter, based on mutual respect and understanding.

# Developing Rapport: The Role of Emotional Intelligence

Creating strong rapport lays the foundation for mutual respect and understanding essentials for any partnership. Emotional intelligence plays a significant role in this, as I learned from observing my grandfather, Joe.

## Grandpa Joe: The Original T.H.R.E.A.D Wizard

Growing up, I spent a lot of time with my grandfather, Joe, a man who owned a store in Patterson, New Jersey. Despite his rough exterior, Grandpa Joe had an incredible ability to connect with people. He remembered everyone's name, asked about their families, and made each person feel like they were the most important person in the room.

Watching him, I realized that his success wasn't just about business acumen; it was about making people feel seen and valued. He had a knack for finding common ground, whether it was through shared experiences or simply remembering small details about someone's life. These were his threads, weaving connections that lasted a lifetime.

**Lesson:** Building rapport is about more than just being friendly. It's about genuinely understanding and valuing others, using emotional intelligence to create lasting connections.

# Authentic Engagement: The Key to Meaningful Relationships

Being truly present and sincere in interactions fosters deeper, more meaningful relationships. This principle was a core part of my upbringing, thanks to my mom's resilience and empathy.

### Lessons from My Mother: The Power of Authenticity

My mother's journey from a telephone switchboard operator to a social worker taught me invaluable lessons about authentic engagement. Despite the challenges of raising three children on her own, she always found time to connect with others. Her job was more than just connecting calls; it was about connecting with people. She listened, empathized, and offered genuine support, often without expecting anything in return.

Even when our lives were turned upside down, she made sure that we never lost our sense of connection to others. She organized community events, volunteered at local charities, and was always the first to offer a helping hand. Her empathy wasn't just a personal trait; it was her way of surviving and thriving despite the odds.

These interactions weren't just transactions; they were opportunities to build trust and understanding. Watching her, I learned that being authentic and present in every interaction, no matter how small, could lead to meaningful, lasting relationships.

**Lesson:** Authentic engagement means being genuinely interested in others and present in every conversation. It's about connecting on a human level, beyond business or transactions.

## Dedication to Growth: Evolving Through Relationships

Commitment to continuous improvement, both personally and professionally, ensures that relationships are not just maintained but also evolved. This mindset has been crucial in my journey, especially during times of adversity.

## Navigating the Challenges of Real Estate

Entering the real estate world was a significant shift from my previous career. I faced numerous challenges, from understanding complex financial terms to raising significant amounts of capital. However, each challenge was an opportunity to grow, learn, and improve.

One of the key lessons I learned was the importance of resilience. In real estate, as in life, not everything goes as planned.

Deals fall through, markets shift, and setbacks happen. But by staying dedicated to growth, learning from every experience, and continuously improving, I was able to turn challenges into opportunities.

My mother's journey from loss to rebuilding was a constant source of inspiration. Watching her face adversity with courage taught me that success is not about never failing—it's about being willing to start over and keep pushing forward, no matter what.

**Lesson:** Dedication to growth means constantly seeking to improve and evolve. It's about using every experience as a steppingstone toward greater understanding and success.

# Weaving the T.H.R.E.A.D

The journey to success in capital raising is not a straight path. It's a series of connections, each one a thread that weaves together to create a strong, resilient fabric. By focusing on trust, human connection, rapport development, emotional intelligence, authentic engagement, and dedication to growth, we can build relationships that not only support our business goals but enrich our lives.

**Key Takeaway:**

As you move forward, remember that every interaction is an opportunity to weave a new thread into your fabric of relationships. The T.H.R.E.A.D method is not just a strategy; it's a mindset and a way of life that can transform how you connect, communicate, and succeed.

### Practical Application: Building Trust and Resilience

1. **Identify Trust Gaps**: Make a list of any relationships (personal or professional) where trust feels shaky. What's causing the trust issues? Write it down.

2. **Action Plan**: For each trust gap, identify one action you can take this week to rebuild or strengthen trust. Maybe it's a simple check-in or a more significant gesture.

3. **Resilience Booster**: Think of a recent setback. Write down three ways you handled it well and one area where you could improve your resilience next time.

Now that we've seen how resilience strengthens relationships, it's time to explore the mindset needed to apply this principle daily.

In Chapter 2, Jen will dive into the *T.H.R.E.A.D. Mindset* and learn how shifting from transactional to relational thinking can transform your business and personal life.

### Ready to Build Stronger, More Resilient Relationships?

Chapter 1 of *The Common T.H.R.E.A.D Method* teaches how resilience shapes lasting connections. But there's more to learn!

Head to www.commonthreadmethod.org and download your **FREE workbook** to explore deeper strategies for strengthening your relationships.

# T.H.R.E.A.D Mindset:
## *The Secret Key to Success*

*The Most Powerful Questions for Success:*
*"It's not what we do once in a while that shapes*
*our life, but what we do consistently."*

—TONY ROBBINS

Okay, it's time to give your future self a gift. Go grab a pen and get ready to go "inside" and find the leverage you need.

This exercise will help you dig in and get the clarity you need to stay motivated and...

**NEVER GIVE UP !**

### *Instructions:*

1. *Find a quiet place where you won't be interrupted.*
2. *Put on some calming music if it helps you think (I always search YouTube for Shamanic Drumming for exercises like these).*
3. *Take your time to think through each question. Start writing whatever comes to mind.*
4. *If the answers don't come right away, that's okay. Do your best and come back to your notes later if needed.*

I want you to answer the following questions.

## QUESTION #1–What do you REALLY want?

Example: "I want to achieve financial independence so that I can spend more time with my family and travel the world without worrying about money."

_____

_____

_____

_____

_____

_____

_____

_____

_____

_____

_____

## QUESTION #2–What will you gain once you have it?

Example: "Gaining financial independence will allow me to quit my 9-to-5 job, giving me the freedom to pursue my passion projects and spend quality time with my loved ones."

_____

_____

_____

_____

_____

_____

_____

_____

_____

_____

_____

_____

_____

_____

_____

_____

_____

_____

## QUESTION #3–What will it cost you NOT to achieve it?

Example: "Not achieving financial independence means I'll continue to be stuck in a job I dislike, missing out on precious moments with my family and not living life on my own terms."

_____

_____

_____

_____

_____

_____

_____

_____

_____

_____

_____

_____

_____

_____

_____

_____

_____

**QUESTION #4–What are two actions that you have been putting off, that if you did them, you would be one step closer to achieving the results you desire?**

Example: 1. Creating a detailed budget to track my expenses and identify savings opportunities.

Example 2. Reaching out to potential mentors or joining a mastermind group to gain insights and accountability.

_____

_____

_____

_____

_____

_____

_____

_____

_____

_____

_____

_____

_____

_____

_____

Answering these questions will help you connect with your WHY. When you are connected to your WHY, you have the leverage you need to stay motivated, take action, and NEVER quit.

Having the right mindset is crucial but maintaining it in the face of challenges is even more important in the next chapter we will dive into the T.H.R.E.A.D methodology with Andy. and explore some common pitfalls and understand why so many give up before they reach their goals.

**Key Takeaway**: The T.H.R.E.A.D mindset is your roadmap for building meaningful relationships. Yet, as straightforward as it sounds, many people struggle to maintain this mindset. Why? Because the road is long, and challenges often tempt us to quit.

**Mindset Shift Challenge:**

For the next 5 days, focus on shifting from a transactional mindset to a relational one. Each day, identify one interaction (personal or professional) where you can apply the *T.H.R.E.A.D. Mindset*. Be intentional about building a relationship rather than seeking an immediate result.

At the end of each day, reflect on the interaction. Did you notice a difference in how the conversation went? What were the outcomes?

Share your experience in the community group, and let's discuss how small mindset shifts can lead to bigger connections!

In Chapter 3, Jen will uncover the most common reasons people give up and, more importantly, how to overcome those barriers to achieve lasting success.

# T.H.R.E.A.D Mindset:
## *The Secret Key to Success*
## *The 5 Most Common*
## *Reasons People Quit*

*"A black belt is just a white belt that never gave up."*

—UNKNOWN

**B**efore we dive into the nitty-gritty of raising capital, it's important to understand the role mindset plays in your journey to success. In this chapter, we'll explore the importance of mindset so that you understand and overcome the obstacles that cause many people to quit.

Now, if you don't ever experience self-doubt, worry, fear, anxiety, or self-sabotaging behavior, then by all means, skip this segment of the book and get straight into the raising capital content.

If you're like me, and most other human beings on the planet, we have a tendency to get in our own way sometimes. Especially when learning a new skill and wanting to master it OVERNIGHT, so that we can just get some damn results, right?

If only we could plug a cable into the back of our heads to download the playbook on multifamily, similar to the way Neo mastered Kung Fu.

The reality is, we are not in the matrix, and learning a new skill requires us to show up with a different expectation. The challenge is that we have become a society obsessed with instant gratification, so most people give up WAY too soon.

Despite the best intentions, many people quit their journey before realizing their full potential. By understanding the five most common reasons people quit, you can identify and address these challenges head-on, helping you stay the course and succeed.

### *Most Common Reasons People Quit #1–Wrong Motivation*

You need to stay positive. You need to stay motivated. This is a challenging business at times, so having a solid mental game will make ALL the difference in whether you dig deep and get to see what you're made of or if you throw in the towel at the smallest challenge.

So how can you get a solid mental game?

For starters, you must have a compelling why. It seems like motivational speakers say that all the time, so it's easy to dismiss it.

In this business, you either have a strong association to your WHY, your reason for doing this, or you'll cut bait and run at the earliest sign of struggle.

If you're going to give up THAT easily, why even start?

Instead, quiet your mind and think about what is driving you to step into this world of raising capital.

What is important enough to you to deal with the uncomfortable segments of your life, where you don't understand all the pieces, you don't know how to sound knowledgeable, you don't know what questions to ask...

That is a hard period for overachievers who are used to being a badass in their current world.

What is your underlying motivation for sticking with it, even when you feel like there's just so much to learn and I'm never gonna get there?

In an interview with one of my students Brad, he said, *"Raising three kids I can never put myself in a position where someone else is deciding my income. No more. I cannot do that anymore. You can work your entire life and think you have it made and someone else can change it all just like that. I told myself, never again. I'm not putting all my eggs in one basket. A W-2 job can never be something that is hung over my head that I have to have that's out of my control and my choice. That's my number one reason. I want to be in the driver's seat in my life."*

Another student of mine, Kaycie said, *"I was tired of struggling, I was tired of working three different jobs that were barely covering what my family needed. And I wanted to move to Colorado, and I wanted to figure out how to do it. And during that process, I wanted to support my family if my kids needed something one day when they were older. I had a cancer scare a year ago, if something were to happen to me who's going to take care of my kids? And what means are they going to have to do that? So, it was kind of a really long process that led me to making the decision. I want to diversify myself and have a backup plan. And this was my backup plan."*

Can you relate to either of those?

It's terrifying to have all your eggs in one basket. Sometimes you don't think of it or realize it until someone tips your basket over and you realize...it's time to take control of your future.

Another student of mine, Teresa said, *"I have one child with special needs. And I wanted to be home with him. My goal was always to be a stay-at-home mom. So, I always look for things that are remote. I'm sure most people are envisioning sitting on the beach with a margarita doing business. But I'm picturing myself in my backyard with my son playing, while I still do business."*

It's so common for marketers to use all of the flashy lifestyle pictures...the sports cars, yachts, private planes, vacations...to show you what's possible.

Those things are great!

But they don't land with everyone.

I like them too, but it's not a big driver for me.

There is more to life.

And once you've had all of that (and I have), you just long for something deeper—true freedom. Happiness. The ability to have no money worries so you can do whatever you are meant to do.

And if you're meant to have a Lambo, by all means, GO FOR IT!

And if you're meant to hang out with your special needs kid in your backyard and enjoy just being present instead of leaving for a J-O-B, then by all means, GO FOR IT!

There are no rules here.

The point is to have options.

## *Most Common Reasons People Quit #2-Lack of Enjoyment*

If you're not enjoying the process, it's almost impossible to maintain the drive you'll need to succeed.

So, what can you do to increase your love of raising capital?

A lot of people make the mistake of thinking that this is a solo gig.

It can be...but that'll get you more frustrated than a crackhead without a lighter.

Too dark?

Doing this business solo gets old faster than trying to brush your teeth while eating Oreos!

Decide early on that this can be fun...but you'll need to find a partner who loves doing the stuff you find tedious or torturous. For example, building a website, landing page, or lead magnets...OMG, I'd rather stab myself in the face than do any of that. Andy, on the other hand, creates gorgeous digital assets and gets amped up about investor portals and creating email templates.

I am better at interacting with people and leaving technology to the experts!

When each member of the team focuses on the areas of the business that we (1) enjoy and (2) excel at, we can extract maximum enjoyment while we are building our wealth.

If you are going to be working solo, look for opportunities to delegate or outsource the things you find tedious or overwhelming.

## *Most Common Reasons People Quit #3-Lack of Support*

You MUST surround yourself with people who will encourage and support you.

All entrepreneurs struggle with this in the beginning.

You're excited about your new venture. You've figured out something that can change your financial future and naturally, you want to share that with everyone you care about!

Have you ever heard the phrase "Your Network is Your Net Worth"?

How does that apply here?

When you surround yourself with people who tear you down, discourage you, plant seeds of doubt in your mind, tell you how unrealistic or risky your dreams are...IGNORE them! They're fighting for their own fears, and you need to minimize that influence input, so that you do not adopt the fears or limiting beliefs of those around you.

I'm not saying to kick them out of your life. Just don't talk about what you're doing with them. Protect your psyche as you're learning and growing.

One of the most incredible things the students in my Academy get to experience is being surrounded by so much positivity, and encouragement, being a part of a network of people who have also said: "YES! I want more too...and I'm willing to engage in the journey to make it happen!". There is no scarcity mentality, no "I'm awesome and you suck". It's a pretty freaking magical experience being around a group of investors who end up becoming your lifelong friends, who celebrate with you at every step, and who feel your pain when you have a disappointment.

It's like you end up leveling up your friends while growing your wealth...and then you end up growing together and doing deals together.

Make sure you're doing something to minimize your time around the nay-sayers and get yourself around the go-getters, the ones who are willing to GO FOR IT with you!

## Most Common Reasons People Quit #4-Wrong Expectations

This one kills me because so many people are looking for "get rich quick" solutions and that silver bullet simply does not exist.

Success takes time, effort, resiliency, and patience.

Be prepared to face setbacks and challenges.

If your expectation is that it's going to be overnight or "get rich quick", just save yourself the mental time and effort and move on.

If your expectation is that this business is easy peasy lemon squeezy (you can thank my kids for that phrase), don't bother. Just go back to watching Netflix for 3-4 hours a night.

This business isn't rocket science once you learn the ins and outs, but there's nothing "common sense" about the ins and outs and it takes time to learn it.

And for those cowboys who want to skip the process of learning it, you'll be paying for a Ph.D. from the School of Hard Knocks. And then you'll still have to learn how to do it right.

You need to align your expectations to know that you're going to be uncomfortable for a period of time. You'll be learning something new. It's like nothing you've ever done before, so you're not able to draw on your years of work experience. That's frustrating for the overachiever.

So, if you can just get square with it now...prepare yourself for an epic adventure. An epic journey. One where you're going to be stretched. You're going to grow (in ways you can't even fathom yet). It's not always fun and it's definitely not comfortable.

But the rewards?

OH BABY!!

A life with the three freedoms–location freedom, time freedom, and financial freedom...that's what is waiting for you.

It just doesn't come overnight. And you WILL grow.

Fast forward 3-5 years after you get started...you'll look back and barely recognize your old self.

I seriously get goosebumps just thinking about what is ahead for you.

In the Academy, we say "DO EPIC SH!T"...when you start DOING epic sh!t, you start moving into a new realm of BEING epic too... and eventually, HAVING epic sh!t!

## Most Common Reasons People Quit #5–Lack of Time

Time management and learning to "bend time" is one of the skills you have to master when you're getting started and still balancing a job while you are growing your new business.

Everyone has the same 24 hours in the day.

It's how you structure your day, and how you plan your weeks and months that will separate success from stagnation.

EVERYONE struggles with this. Even me. And I'm pretty damn good at it.

# Epic Points from This Chapter (And How to NOT QUIT!)

**1**

### Importance of mindset:

Developing a strong mental game is crucial for success. A compelling "why" or reason for entering this field will help you persevere through challenges and setbacks.

**2**

### Finding enjoyment and the right partner:

Enjoying the process and focusing on your strengths is key to staying motivated. Partnering with someone who compliments your skillset can make the journey more enjoyable and productive.

**3**

### Building a supportive network:

Surrounding yourself with like-minded individuals who encourage and support you is essential. This positive environment fosters growth and helps you stay on track.

**4**

### Setting realistic expectations:

Success takes time, effort, and patience. Be prepared for setbacks and challenges and recognize that growth and rewards come with time and persistence.

**5**

### Time management:

Learning to manage your time effectively is vital, especially when balancing a job and family. Planning and organizing your days, weeks, and months will help separate success from stagnation.

**Key Takeaway**: Once we understand why people quit, we can better prepare ourselves to avoid these pitfalls. One of the biggest challenges many face is balancing multiple responsibilities.

**Stay the Course Challenge:**

Over the next 7 days, identify one challenge or frustration that has been holding you back in your personal or professional life. Break it down into manageable steps and focus on overcoming one small piece each day.

Track your progress in a journal, and if you feel stuck, reach out in the community group for advice and encouragement. At the end of the week, reflect on how breaking the problem down helped you move forward, and share your biggest takeaway in the group.

Ready to dig deeper into the mental game of success?

Get your **FREE workbook** now at www.commonthreadmethod.org and learn how to push past the urge to quit.

In the next chapter, Jen will explore practical strategies for managing work, family, and business without sacrificing what matters most.

# T.H.R.E.A.D Mindset:
## *The Secret Key to Success*

### BALANCING WORK, FAMILY & YOUR BUSINESS

*"Most of us spend too much time on what is urgent
and not enough time on what is important."*

—STEPHEN COVEY

L ook, I don't have a full-time job anymore, but up until 2015, I did. And for two years leading up to my grand departure, not only did I have a job working 80 hours a week, I was a single mom with twin three-year-olds. Sometimes I look back at that period in my life and I seriously have no idea how I survived.

WAIT.

Yes, I do.

My WHY (and A LOT of Monster energy drinks).

Even now, I am pretty solid at planning my weeks, months, and quarters to fit in everything that I want to. But I am not perfect. I get frustrated that something is taking longer than it should. I get ticked off that things aren't happening in the right order.

Fill in the blank.

We are all human beings going through the experience of life.

On a regular basis, I am figuring out the balance of having four kids, managing our existing real estate portfolio, running and growing the Remote Multifamily Investing Academy, and growing my personal network to continue acquiring larger deals. Oh, and of course I can't forget to spend time with my spouse, focusing on our relationship, dating each other, and just enjoying being in each others' presence outside of business.

It's a lot to balance. And it's all important.

Building my network of private investors helps me build my real estate empire.

There are days when the TV never goes on. At all. There's just no time between everything else.

Do I like to Netflix and chill like everyone else?

Hell yes!!

Do I do it occasionally?

Absolutely.

But if I want something different in life than what everyone else has...I have to be willing to do different things.

I have to be willing to make some sacrifices.

I am.

And because of that, I have location, time, and financial freedom.

If I want to take a 3-month cross-country trip in my RV with the kids, showing them all the cool things, instead of just having them read about them...I can.

Why?

Because I have decided that discomfort for a few years is worth it to have comfort for a lifetime!

And you can too.

Before you get too far into this business, take a hard look at how you spend your time and figure out what things you're willing to put on pause in order to create a compelling future for yourself.

Your future self will thank you!

**Epic Points from This Chapter:**

- Prioritizing what matters: Balancing work, family, and a business requires prioritizing relationships, personal growth, and investment goals while making necessary sacrifices to achieve long-term success.
- Embrace temporary discomfort: Accepting discomfort and making sacrifices in the short term can lead to a lifetime of financial freedom and flexibility, allowing you to create a fulfilling future for yourself and your family.

**Balance Breakthrough Challenge:**

Take the next 7 days to restructure your time and priorities to create better balance between work, family, and business. Each day, commit to spending at least 30 minutes on an important activity you've been neglecting, whether it's personal time, family connection, or a passion project.

At the end of the week, share your insights in the group: What was the hardest part of maintaining balance? What did you notice about your productivity and sense of well-being when you prioritized your time differently?

**Key Takeaway**: Achieving balance is one part of the equation, but living with purpose is what will truly drive your success.

Want to master the art of juggling it all?

Download your **FREE workbook** at www.commonthreadmethod.org and start living a balanced, fulfilled life!

In Chapter 5, we'll delve into the concept of *Ikigai*, helping you discover your 'reason for being' and align your life and business with your purpose

## CHAPTER 5

# The Essence of This Book

FIND your Ikigai

**I**n the world of raising capital and building businesses, it's easy to get lost in the hustle and chase of numbers, deals, and profits. But real success goes deeper—it's about finding your Ikigai, your reason for being.

This Japanese concept, Ikigai (生き甲斐), first popularized by Japanese psychiatrist and academic Mieko Kamiya in her 1966 book "On the Meaning of Life" is all about discovering that sweet spot where what you love, what you're good at, what the world needs, and what you can be paid for intersect.

For me, Ikigai has been the guiding thread throughout my journey, shaping my decisions and keeping me aligned with my purpose. It's about more than just making a living; it's about making a life that's meaningful and fulfilling. Let's explore how the principles of Ikigai connect to the T.H.R.E.A.D method and how you can find and follow your own Ikigai.

## Finding Your Ikigai: A Personal Journey

Discovering your Ikigai is a deeply personal journey, and it's different for everyone. For me, it began with a series of questions. What am I truly passionate about? What are my natural talents? How can I use these to make a difference in the world? And, crucially, how can I make a living doing what I love?

These questions guided me as I transitioned from the TV and film industry to real estate. I realized that my true passion wasn't just about being in the spotlight; it was about connecting with people, understanding their needs, and helping them achieve their dreams. My natural talent for building relationships and my desire to make a positive impact became the foundation of my work.

Finding your Ikigai means taking a step back from the daily grind to reflect on what truly matters to you. It's about aligning your passions, talents, and values with the needs of the world and finding a way to create value through that alignment.

# The Four Elements of Ikigai
# (生き甲斐)

**1** **What You Love**: This is the work that excites you, that makes you want to jump out of bed in the morning. For me, it's the thrill of meeting new people, understanding their stories, and finding ways to help them. In capital raising, this passion translates into building meaningful connections with investors, partners, and clients.

**2** **What You Are Good At (Profession)**: These are the skills and talents you bring to the table. Over the years, I've honed my ability to communicate, negotiate, and build trust. These skills are not just useful—they're essential in the world of business. Knowing your strengths and leveraging them is key to success.

**3** **What The World Needs (Mission)**: This is where you make a difference. It's about understanding the problems and challenges people face and finding ways to solve them. In real estate, the need might be for affordable housing, sustainable development, or creating opportunities for investors. Understanding these needs allows you to align your work with a greater purpose.

**4** **What You Can Be Paid For (Vocation)**: Let's be honest, we all need to make a living. But finding your Ikigai means finding a way to do what you love and what you're good at in a way that also provides financial security. For me, this has meant finding a niche in real estate where I can use my skills and passions to create value for others while also building a sustainable business.

The intersection of these four elements is where your Ikigai lies. It's not always easy to find, and it might take some trial and error, but when you do, it becomes a powerful source of motivation, fulfillment, and success.

## Aligning Ikigai with the T.H.R.E.A.D Method

The T.H.R.E.A.D method is all about building trust, human connection, rapport, emotional intelligence, authentic engagement, and dedication to growth. These principles align perfectly with the concept of Ikigai. When you're operating in your Ikigai, you're naturally more authentic, more engaged, and more connected to others. You're not just going through the motions—you're living your purpose.

- **Trust**: When you're living your Ikigai, trust comes naturally. People can sense your passion and authenticity, and they're more likely to trust you. This trust is the foundation of all successful relationships and business ventures.

- **Human Connection**: Ikigai is about finding meaning through connection. It's about understanding that success is not just about what you achieve, but about the impact you have on others.

  The T.H.R.E.A.D method emphasizes the importance of human connection, of seeing the person behind the deal, and of building relationships that go beyond transactions.

- **Rapport Development**: When you're in tune with your Ikigai, building rapport is easier. You're more genuine, more present, and more empathetic. This helps you create strong, lasting connections with others.

- **Emotional Intelligence**: Understanding your own emotions and the emotions of others is key to finding and following your Ikigai. It helps you navigate the ups and downs of life and business with grace and resilience.

- **Authentic Engagement**: Ikigai is about being true to yourself and showing up authentically in everything you do. This authenticity is at the heart of the T.H.R.E.A.D method, and it's what makes your connections with others meaningful and powerful.

- **Dedication to Growth**: Living your Ikigai is a journey, not a destination. It's about constantly growing, learning, and evolving. The T.H.R.E.A.D method encourages this dedication to growth, both personally and professionally.

By aligning your work with your Ikigai, you're not just achieving success—you're creating a life that's meaningful, fulfilling, and in harmony with your values and passions.

# Embrace Your Ikigai

Finding and living your Ikigai is one of the most powerful things you can do for yourself and your career. It's about more than just making a living; it's about making a life that's worth living. It's about waking up every day excited to do the work you love, confident in your abilities, and connected to a purpose greater than yourself.

As you move forward in your journey, remember that your Ikigai is your guiding thread. It's what gives your life and work meaning. It's what connects you to others, to opportunities, and to the world around you. So embrace your Ikigai, align it with the T.H.R.E.A.D method, and watch as your relationships, your career, and your life flourish.

**Instructions: Fill out each section with your thoughts and ideas. Where the circles overlap, you may discover your Ikigai—your reason for being.**

## What You Love

List your passions and interests.

_____

_____

_____

_____

_____

_____

_____

_____

_____

## What You Are Good At

List your skills and talents.

_____

_____

_____

_____

_____

_____

_____

_____

_____

_____

_____

## What The World Needs

List problems you care about solving or ways you can contribute to society.

_____

_____

_____

_____

_____

_____

_____

_____

_____

## What You Can Be Paid For

List potential ways to monetize your skills and passions.

_____

_____

_____

_____

_____

_____

_____

_____

_____

_____

# Ikigai Overlap Areas

### Passion (What You Love + What You Are Good At):

- Write down areas where your passions and skills intersect.

_____

_____

_____

_____

_____

_____

_____

_____

_____

**Mission (What You Love + What The World Needs):**

- Write down areas where your passions and the needs of the world intersect.

_____

_____

_____

_____

_____

_____

_____

_____

_____

_____

**Profession (What You Are Good At + What You Can Be Paid For):**

- Write down areas where your skills and potential income sources intersect.

_____

_____

_____

_____

_____

_____

_____

_____

### Vocation (What The World Needs + What You Can Be Paid For):

- Write down areas where the world's needs and potential income sources intersect.

_____

_____

_____

_____

_____

_____

_____

# LISTENING FOR IKIGAI: THE KEY TO UNCOVERING COMMON T.H.R.E.A.D's

Nicholas Kemp founder of Ikigai Tribe, often emphasizes that finding one's Ikigai is not merely about introspection, but about interaction—engaging deeply with others to uncover shared values and aspirations.

When you sit down with a potential investor, your primary goal should be to listen for their Ikigai. This involves tuning into the cues and signals that reveal their passions, strengths, needs, and financial goals.

### Listen for Passion and Purpose:

**1**

Investors, like anyone else, have dreams and ambitions that drive them. By listening attentively to their stories and what excites them, you can identify what they are truly passionate about. This might be a desire to make a positive impact through sustainable housing, or a keen interest in revitalizing urban spaces. Understanding their passion allows you to align your investment opportunities with their personal mission.

### Recognize Their Strengths and Expertise:

**2**

Everyone has unique skills and expertise that they bring to the table. By asking insightful questions and paying close attention to their experiences and successes, you can gauge their strengths. This knowledge helps you tailor your pitch to highlight how their skills can be an asset to your project, creating a sense of mutual benefit and collaboration.

**3**

### Identify Their Needs and Challenges:

Investors are looking for opportunities that meet their needs and address their challenges. Whether they seek steady returns, tax advantages, or portfolio diversification, understanding these needs is crucial. By listening carefully to their concerns and requirements, you can present your real estate deals as solutions that fulfill their specific financial objectives.

**4**

### Align Financial Goals with Investment Opportunities:

Ultimately, the goal is to find the intersection where your investment opportunities meet the investor's financial goals. This is where the concept of Ikigai shines. When you present an investment opportunity that aligns with their passion, utilizes their strengths, meets their needs, and offers financial returns, you create a compelling case that resonates on a deeper level.

# Listening for Cues in Conversations

When you listen for cues in conversations, you are essentially looking for recurring themes, interests, and needs that align with your own purpose and expertise. This is crucial in identifying the "Common T.H.R.E.A.D" that connects your passions and skills with the needs and desires of others.

# Application to Raising Capital for Real Estate Investments

1. **Identifying Investor Needs (What the World Needs)**:
   - Engage in conversations with potential investors to understand their motivations, concerns, and long-term goals.
   - Look for common themes, such as a desire for stable returns, interest in sustainable properties, or portfolio diversification.

2. **Matching Your Offerings (What You Can Be Paid For)**:
   - Present your real estate projects in a way that aligns with the identified needs and interests of the investors.
   - Highlight how your projects meet these needs through detailed market analysis, projected returns, and unique selling points.

3. **Leveraging Your Passion and Expertise (What You Love & What You Are Good At)**:
   - Share your personal story and passion for real estate to build trust and authenticity.
   - Demonstrate your expertise and track record in successfully managing and developing real estate projects.

# Creating the Connection: Ikigai in Real Estate Investment Conversations

**By listening for cues and identifying a common T.H.R.E.A.D in your conversations, you can align your real estate investment opportunities with the Ikigai concept. This alignment helps in:**

- Building a compelling narrative that resonates with investors on a deeper level.
- Ensuring that your projects not only fulfill your professional and financial goals but also meet the investors' needs and passions.

**Practical Steps:**

1. **Active Listening**: Pay close attention to what potential investors are saying in meetings, calls, and networking events.
2. **Note Common Themes**: Record recurring topics and concerns that investors express.
3. **Align Your Pitch**: Customize your investment pitch to address these common themes, highlighting how your projects align with the investors' goals and values.
4. **Build Relationships**: Foster long-term relationships based on shared values and mutual benefit.

By integrating the principles of Ikigai into your approach to raising capital, you can create a more meaningful and effective strategy that appeals to investors' deeper motivations, ultimately leading to successful real estate investments.

**Ikigai Discovery Challenge:**

For the next 5 days, spend 15 minutes each day reflecting on one of the four Ikigai elements: *What you love, what you're good at, what the world needs, and what you can be paid for.*

Write down your thoughts and see where these elements overlap.

At the end of the 5 days, put it all together: What have you discovered about your Ikigai?

How does it align with your personal and professional goals? Share your Ikigai journey in the community, and let's discuss how it connects to your broader purpose!

**Key Takeaway**: With a clear sense of purpose, it's time to apply the *T.H.R.E.A.D. Method* to your relationships. In the next chapter, we'll connect the dots between your personal mission and how to build strong, meaningful connections in the world of business.

# CHAPTER 6

# Connecting Dots:
## *How the T.H.R.E.A.D Method Works*

### Unveiling the Framework for Success in Real Estate Networking

**Your Role in This Story is to have an Abundance Mentality**

*"An abundance mentality springs from internal security, not from external rankings, comparisons, opinions, possessions, or associations."*

—STEVEN COVEY

Alright, now that you've got the success mindset locked in, it's time to get real. Let's talk about how you can actually use the THREAD method to crush it in real estate. This is where you take those principles and put them to work.

In the dynamic world of real estate, the ability to build and sustain meaningful relationships is as crucial as having a keen eye for property or an understanding of market trends.

The COMMON T.H.R.E.A.D METHOD is a comprehensive framework designed to enhance these relationships imagine each potential investor as a unique tapestry, rich with experiences, interests, and aspirations.

Your goal is to find a strand, a common T.H.R.E.A.D, that connects you to them. This book uses the 'common T.H.R.E.A.D' metaphor to illustrate the art of building relationships in the world of real estate investment. This method, grounded in the concept of finding and nurturing common T.H.R.E.A.D's, serves as a guide to weaving stronger, more resilient networks in real estate.

# Step-by-Step Guides to Applying the T.H.R.E.A.D Method

## 1. Building Trust in Every Interaction

**Objective**: Establish and maintain trust with clients, investors, and partners.

**Step-by-Step Guide:**

1. **Be Consistent**: Show up when you say you will. Consistency builds reliability, and reliability builds trust.
2. **Communicate Openly**: Be transparent about your intentions, plans, and any challenges you foresee. Open communication prevents misunderstandings.
3. **Follow Through**: If you commit to something, make sure you deliver. Honor your promises, no matter how small.
4. **Show Respect**: Value others' time, opinions, and contributions. Acknowledge and appreciate the people you work with.
5. **Admit Mistakes**: If you make a mistake, own it. Apologize, correct it if possible, and learn from it. Accountability enhances trust.

**Checklist:**

- ☐ Consistent presence in meetings/calls
- ☐ Transparent communication about plans and challenges
- ☐ Fulfillment of commitments and promises

☐ Display of respect towards others

☐ Admission and correction of mistakes

## 2. Creating Human Connections Beyond Business

**Objective**: Build genuine relationships that go beyond mere transactions.

**Step-by-Step Guide:**

1. **Be Genuine**: Show real interest in the person, not just the business opportunity. Ask about their interests, hobbies, and family.

2. **Find Common Ground**: Look for shared interests or experiences. This could be sports, travel, books, or even favorite foods.

3. **Listen Actively**: Pay attention to what they're saying, and respond thoughtfully. Show that you value their perspective.

4. **Share Personal Stories**: Open up about your own experiences. This creates a sense of shared humanity and vulnerability.

5. **Stay in Touch**: Follow up after meetings, not just to talk business but to check in on how they are doing.

**Checklist:**

☐ Engage in conversations about interests and hobbies

☐ Identify common interests or experiences

☐ Practice active listening during discussions

☐ Share personal stories and experiences

☐ Regularly follow up and check in on the person

## 3. Developing Rapport with New Contacts

**Objective**: Establish a foundation of mutual respect and understanding with new contacts.

### Step-by-Step Guide:

1. **Do Your Homework**: Learn about the person before meeting them. Find out about their background, interests, and recent achievements.

2. **Start with a Compliment**: Begin conversations by acknowledging something positive about them, like their work or a recent accomplishment.

3. **Mirror and Match**: Subtly mirror their body language and tone to create a subconscious connection.

4. **Ask Open-Ended Questions**: Encourage them to talk about themselves. Questions like "What inspired you to get into this field?" help open up conversations.

5. **Find and Highlight Common Goals**: Identify shared objectives or values and use them to strengthen your connection.

### Checklist:

- ☐ Research background and interests of new contacts
- ☐ Start conversations with genuine compliments
- ☐ Practice mirroring body language and tone
- ☐ Use open-ended questions to facilitate conversation
- ☐ Identify and highlight common goals or values

## 4. Using Emotional Intelligence in Negotiations

**Objective**: Leverage emotional intelligence to understand and manage emotions during negotiations.

### Step-by-Step Guide:

1. **Prepare Emotionally**: Before entering negotiations, take a moment to calm yourself and set a positive mindset.

2. **Observe and Recognize Emotions**: Pay attention to both verbal and non-verbal cues to gauge the emotions of others.

3. **Stay Calm and Composed**: Even if the negotiation becomes tense, maintain your composure. Your calmness can defuse tension.

4. **Empathize**: Acknowledge the emotions of others. Statements like "I understand that this is important to you" show empathy.

5. **Respond, Don't React**: Take a moment to think before responding to emotional statements. This prevents escalation and keeps the discussion productive.

**Checklist:**

- ☐ Prepare mentally and emotionally before negotiations
- ☐ Observe and recognize the emotions of others
- ☐ Maintain calmness and composure
- ☐ Use empathetic statements to acknowledge emotions
- ☐ Respond thoughtfully rather than reacting impulsively

## 5. Engaging Authentically with Clients and Investors

**Objective**: Foster authentic engagement to build stronger, more genuine relationships.

**Step-by-Step Guide:**

1. **Be Yourself**: Don't try to put on a façade or act like someone you're not. Authenticity resonates more than perfection.

2. **Share Your Vision**: Be open about your goals, vision, and what drives you. This helps others connect with you on a deeper level.

3. **Admit What You Don't Know**: It's okay to not have all the answers. Admitting this shows honesty and a willingness to learn.

4. **Be Present**: Give your full attention in conversations. Avoid distractions, and focus on the person you're speaking with.

5. **Express Appreciation**: Show genuine gratitude for their time, support, and contributions. People appreciate being valued.

**Checklist:**

- ☐ Present yourself authentically in all interactions
- ☐ Clearly share your vision and goals
- ☐ Be honest about areas where you lack knowledge
- ☐ Give full attention in conversations
- ☐ Regularly express appreciation and gratitude

## 6. Demonstrating Dedication to Personal and Professional Growth

**Objective**: Commit to continuous improvement for yourself and your relationships.

**Step-by-Step Guide:**

1. **Set Personal Development Goals**: Identify areas where you want to grow and set specific, measurable goals.
2. **Seek Feedback**: Regularly ask for feedback from colleagues, clients, and mentors. Use it to improve your skills and approach.
3. **Invest in Learning**: Attend workshops, read books, and participate in courses that enhance your knowledge and skills.
4. **Reflect Regularly**: Take time to reflect on your experiences, successes, and failures. Use these reflections to guide your growth.
5. **Adapt and Evolve**: Be open to change and willing to adapt your strategies as you learn and grow.

**Checklist:**

- ☐ Set and track personal development goals
- ☐ Seek and act on feedback from others
- ☐ Continuously invest in learning and education
- ☐ Regularly reflect on personal and professional experiences
- ☐ Adapt and evolve strategies based on learning and feedback

## 7. Crafting a Compelling Personal Narrative

**Objective**: Use storytelling to create a compelling narrative that resonates with others.

**Step-by-Step Guide:**

1. **Identify Key Life Experiences**: Reflect on pivotal moments in your life that have shaped who you are.
2. **Connect Experiences to Your Work**: Show how these experiences have influenced your career choices and business philosophy.
3. **Highlight Challenges and Growth**: Share stories of challenges you've faced and how you overcame them. This shows resilience and relatability.
4. **Illustrate Successes**: Use examples of success to demonstrate your skills and credibility.
5. **End with a Vision**: Conclude your story with your vision for the future, and how others can be part of that journey.

**Checklist:**

- ☐ Reflect on and identify key life experiences
- ☐ Connect personal experiences to professional work
- ☐ Share stories of overcoming challenges
- ☐ Use success stories to demonstrate credibility
- ☐ Conclude with a compelling vision for the future

## 8. Networking Effectively Using the T.H.R.E.A.D Method

**Objective**: Build and maintain a strong professional network.

**Step-by-Step Guide:**

1. **Be Strategic**: Identify key people in your industry who align with your values and goals.

2. **Reach Out with Purpose**: When contacting someone, have a clear reason for reaching out. Whether it's to seek advice, explore partnerships, or share ideas, be specific.

3. **Add Value**: Before asking for something, think about what you can offer. This could be knowledge, introductions, or support.

4. **Follow Up Consistently**: Keep the conversation going by regularly following up. Share updates, articles of interest, or just check in.

5. **Maintain Relationships**: Networking isn't a one-time event. Invest time in maintaining relationships, even when you don't need anything.

**Checklist:**

- ☐ Identify key people to network with
- ☐ Reach out with a clear purpose
- ☐ Offer value before asking for help
- ☐ Consistently follow up to keep the conversation going
- ☐ Regularly invest time in maintaining relationships

**Connection Challenge:**

For the next 5 days, practice connecting the dots between your purpose and your relationships. Each day, have one conversation where you consciously apply the *T.H.R.E.A.D. Method* to strengthen trust and rapport. Focus on finding common ground with the other person, whether it's through shared values, interests, or goals.

At the end of the week, reflect on how the *T.H.R.E.A.D. Method* changed your interactions. Post about your most meaningful connection in the group and share what you learned from the experience.

**Key Takeaway**: The T.H.R.E.A.D method provides a practical framework for building strong, authentic relationships that lead to success. At the core of the THREAD method is trust. Trust is the invisible force that binds relationships and fuels successful partnerships.

In Chapter 7, we'll explore why trust is the invisible force that fuels all relationships, and how to build and maintain it in every interaction.

# T = Trust–The Invisible Force

*"It takes 20 years to build a reputation and five minutes to ruin it."*

—WARREN BUFFETT

The concept of trust having a specific frequency is more metaphorical than literal, as it originates from the idea that everything, including emotions and values like trust, vibrates at certain energy levels. In this metaphorical sense, trust is associated with positive, high-vibration frequencies. These frequencies are characterized by feelings of safety, calmness, authenticity, and openness.

Trust is like the foundation of a grand building; without it, everything collapses. We rely on trust in our relationships, in our business dealings, and in our day-to-day lives. Whether in personal life or in business, trust is essential. Especially when we ask someone to invest their hard-earned money with us, trust is the currency we must value above all else.

But how do we build this trust? How do we make investors feel safe and confident in our partnership? It all starts with understanding the frequency at which trust vibrates.

# The Energy of Trust

Trust has a frequency, an energy that resonates with consistency, sincerity, and care. It's like a warm, gentle hum, creating an environment of safety and peace. But how do we create this frequency in our interactions? By recognizing that trust-building happens in the little things, the everyday gestures that show we value people for who they are, not just for what they can offer us.

Imagine this: A quick phone call to share a relevant market update, a congratulatory message for a personal achievement, or simply remembering to ask about their family. These small gestures are like T.H.R.E.A.D's in the fabric of trust. They show that we are genuinely interested in the person, not just the business they bring. They send a clear message: "I value you beyond the transactions."

# The Power of Personal Touch

I've found that a little personal touch goes a long way. Remembering their birthday, celebrating their favorite sports team's big win, or even asking about how their children are doing in school—these may seem like small details, but they are powerful. They show that we are paying attention, that we care about them as people.

And it is this care that resonates at the frequency of trust. When we remember these personal details, we are saying, "You matter to me." And trust, my friends, is built on the foundation of knowing that we matter.

# Weaving the Fabric of Trust

Building trust is like weaving a robust and resilient fabric. It's done T.H.R.E.A.D by T.H.R.E.A.D, interaction by interaction. Each time we show up authentically, each time we keep our word, and each time we show that we care, we add another T.H.R.E.A.D to the fabric. This fabric becomes strong, resilient, and capable of withstanding the challenges that come our way.

Think of it as a continuous process, an ongoing effort. Trust is not built overnight, nor is it built with a single act. It is the accumulation of many small, consistent actions. It is about being genuine, consistent, and truly interested in the people we are connecting with.

Every interaction is an opportunity to strengthen the fabric of trust.

# The "T.H.R.E.A.D" of LinkedIn: Harnessing "T"–Trust

In today's world, much of our networking happens online, and platforms like LinkedIn have become the new meeting grounds. On LinkedIn, the "T" for Trust is particularly relevant. This platform is where professionals seek reliable, credible connections and content. Trust on LinkedIn is not just about having a well-polished profile; it's about showing up consistently, engaging genuinely, and sharing valuable insights.

Trust can be effectively cultivated on LinkedIn through simple, yet powerful actions. Start by being authentic in your posts and interactions. Share insights and updates that are meaningful and relevant. Congratulate your connections on their achievements, endorse their skills, and offer thoughtful comments on their posts. These actions may seem small, but they are the T.H.R.E.A.D's that weave the fabric of trust online.

By showing that you are genuinely interested in the success and well-being of your connections, you create an environment of trust. This trust not only strengthens your relationships but also attracts potential investors who are looking for reliability and credibility. Remember, on LinkedIn, as in life, trust is the bridge that connects you to opportunities.

# Authenticity: The Key to Trust

When it comes to investors, authenticity is crucial. Think of it this way: an investor is like a buyer at a market. They are looking for something real, something trustworthy. If we put up a façade or try to pretend, it's like offering fake fruits— they may look good from afar, but once tested, they crumble. Authenticity, on the other hand, is the real, fresh fruit that people can trust. By being genuine, by showing our true selves, we send out a clear, honest signal. Investors are drawn to this because it resonates with the frequency of trust. They know that what they see is what they get, and this transparency builds confidence.

## Vulnerability: The Strength in Openness

Many people think that showing vulnerability in business is a weakness. But in reality, vulnerability is a powerful strength. When we are vulnerable, we are honest about our challenges, our limitations, and our fears. We are not pretending to be invincible. When asking an investor to invest, showing vulnerability means being honest about the risks, about what we don't know, and about the challenges ahead. This honesty doesn't scare investors away; it draws them closer.

It shows that we have nothing to hide and that we are prepared to face challenges with integrity. This openness and honesty resonate with the frequency of trust, creating a strong, meaningful connection.

## Trust through Actions, Not Just Words

Trust is not built by words alone; it is built through actions. Imagine someone who talks a lot but doesn't follow through—would you trust them with your money? Trust is about showing up, doing what we say we will do, and being consistent. When we ask an investor to invest, we need to demonstrate through our actions that we are trustworthy. This means delivering results, being accountable, and showing reliability. Actions speak louder than words, and it is through our actions that we show that we can be trusted with an investor's money.

## Creating a Trusting Relationship with Investors

Building trust with investors is about more than just securing funds; it's about building a partnership. It's about understanding their needs, their concerns, and their aspirations. It's about listening without judgment, showing empathy, and being transparent. When we build a trusting relationship with investors, we are not just asking for money; we are offering a partnership. A partnership built on trust, mutual respect, and shared goals. This partnership is like a dance, where both parties move in harmony, creating a flow that leads to success and abundance.

## TRUST - The Trust Equation: Steve Jobs' Secret to Apple's Succes

When it comes to building trust in business, few people understood it better than Steve Jobs. He didn't just focus on making great products; he focused on creating experiences that people could believe in, time and time again. Trust is everything. It's not something you can fake or gloss over. You've got to earn it—one product, one interaction, one moment at a time.

Jobs wasn't obsessed with packing as much tech as possible into every device. No. He knew that what mattered most was how that technology served the customer. He wasn't about showing off what engineers could do; he was about showing customers what Apple could do for them.

That's why he said:

*"One of the things I've always found is that you've got to start with the customer experience and work backwards to the technology. You can't start with the technology and try to figure out where you are going to sell it. And as we have tried to come up with a strategy and a vision for Apple, it started with 'What incredible benefits can we give to the customer?' 'Where can we take the customer?' Not starting with 'Let's sit down with the engineers and figure out what awesome technology we have and then how are we going to market that.' And I think that's the right path to take."*

Jobs got it. He understood that trust comes from delivering what people need, even before they know they need it. You start with the customer, and everything else follows. Apple didn't become Apple by accident—it became Apple because they put the customer at the center of every decision. They designed products so reliable and seamless that people didn't just want them—they trusted them.

Look, here's the thing. People trust Apple because it doesn't compromise. EVER. And you know why that works? Because they sweat the details. Apple isn't out here cutting corners just to save a few bucks or speed things up. It's about making sure that when someone picks up an iPhone or a MacBook, they know it's gonna work. They TRUST it to work. No surprises. No BS.

You wanna know why Apple is a monster brand? Because they've built a relationship with their customers based on reliability. They don't need to flash you with ads all day long. They just deliver. Day in and day out. Every time. And when you do that, people will keep coming back, no matter what.

Let's face it: you screw up once, and you've probably lost a customer for life. Apple gets that. They're playing the long game. They're not just trying to sell you a phone—they're trying to get you locked into a lifetime of buying every new piece of tech they come out with because you TRUST them. And that's the secret sauce, man. It's all about trust. You build it, you keep it, and you win. Simple as that.

And that's why Jobs' approach was so powerful. He wasn't just building products; he was building relationships—relationships based on trust, reliability, and consistency. Apple's success? It's not magic. It's trust, earned over time by delivering real value. That's how you win.

## Conclusion: Living at the Frequency of Trust

Trust is not just a word; it is a way of living. It is a frequency that we can tune into, a vibration that we can create. When we live at the frequency of trust, we create a life that is rich in meaningful relationships, in peace, and in joy.

We attract people who are trustworthy, who are genuine, and who resonate with our own authenticity. Living at the frequency of trust means being true to ourselves, being honest with others, and showing up with integrity. It means nurturing our relationships, keeping our promises, and being a source of strength and support.

When we ask someone to invest their money with us, we are not just asking for financial support; we are asking for trust. And to earn this trust, we must live at the frequency of trust.

By doing so, we create a world where trust is abundant, where relationships are built on a foundation of honesty, integrity, and love.

This is the way to a life that is fulfilling, meaningful, and truly abundant.

## The Circle of Trust: The Three C's of Trust:

### Competence: Know Your Stuff and Show It Off

Let's talk about competence first. It's like being that friend who knows everything about everything real estate. You're the go-to for the latest trends, from fix-and-flips to those juicy, high-yield, cash-cow properties. It's not just about throwing around big words but showing you've got the chops to back it up. Think about it like this: you're at a conference, and someone asks about opportunistic investments. You dive into the nitty-gritty of wholesale, fix-and-flip, and why Class C properties can be hidden gems for the right investor. You're not just talking; you're educating with style.

**Character: Be the Good Guy in the Story** Character is all about being the good guy in the story of real estate investment. It's showing up as yourself, being honest about the risks, and not just the rewards. Your reputation is your currency.

When you're discussing potential investments, it's about being upfront, sharing a story or two about deals gone right (and wrong) and what you learned. It's about building trust through transparency. You're not just a capital raiser but a partner on this journey.

### Consistency: Be the Beat You Can Dance To!

Lastly, let's groove on consistency. This is about being the beat everyone can dance to—reliable, steady, and always on. Whether the market's up or down, you're there, offering solid advice, keeping your investors in the loop, and sticking to your investment philosophy.

Say you're big on opportunistic investments. You keep bringing those opportunities to the table, proving you're not a one-hit-wonder but a consistent hit machine.

Together, these three C's are like your playlist for hitting the right notes at real estate conferences or webinars. They're about showing you know your stuff, you're the real deal, and you're in it for the long haul. Plus, let's not forget, real estate's got its perks—passive income, tax breaks, and that sweet appreciation potential. It's about making those connections, sharing your tunes, and maybe, just maybe, making a few fans along the way.

**Trust-Building Challenge:**

For the next 7 days, commit to taking one trust-building action in both your personal and professional life. This could be through keeping promises, following up on commitments, or simply being more consistent and reliable in your daily interactions.

Track the responses you get from others and reflect on how these small actions enhance trust. At the end of the week, share in the group what specific action had the biggest impact on building trust in your relationships.

While trust lays the foundation, human connection is what brings that trust to life. It's time to explore how genuine human connections can bridge gaps and create deeper, more meaningful relationships

# H = Human Connection:
## *Bridging Hearts and Minds*

*"Connection is why we're here; it is what gives purpose and meaning to our lives."*

—BRENE BROWN

You know, in this fast-paced, digital world, it's easy to forget that at the core of everything are real, live human beings. That's where "H" comes in – Human Connection.

It's about seeing beyond the business facade and connecting heart-to-heart, person-to-person.

At the heart of every meaningful connection are the **T.H.R.E.A.D's** that bind us—our shared experiences, interests, and challenges. These **Common T.H.R.E.A.D's** do more than merely link us together; they create a rich tapestry of support, essential for our physical and emotional well-being.

Through these threads, we discover strength, understanding, and a deep sense of belonging. Just as fabric is made stronger by the individual threads woven together, our lives are enriched by the relationships we build and nurture.

The **frequency of human connection** is like tuning into a radio signal. When we align with the T.H.R.E.A.D's of others—whether through shared experiences, empathy, or common goals—our interactions harmonize, creating connections that resonate on a profound level. When we are misaligned, we experience disconnect and isolation. Yet, the beauty of human connection is that it can be consciously cultivated. By becoming aware of our shared T.H.R.E.A.D's, we can recalibrate our relationships and foster deeper, more authentic bonds.

The **Common Thread Method** is a guide for consciously identifying and nurturing these threads that unite us. At the center of this method are the key T.H.R.E.A.D's: **Trust, Human Connection, Rapport, Emotional Intelligence, Authenticity, and Dedication to Growth**. These elements are the foundation of meaningful relationships and the building blocks for strong connections. Each of these threads represents a frequency that we can consciously tune into, deepening our interactions and creating lasting bonds.

Through the **Common Thread Method**, we learn that relationships are not simply about communication but about being attuned to these shared threads. These T.H.R.E.A.D's are the invisible bonds that help us navigate life's complexities, bringing clarity, support, and a deeper connection to those around us. Each thread, when woven with intention, strengthens the larger tapestry of our lives, forming a foundation of trust, empathy, and shared growth.

That's why, in today's world, brands that understand human connection are the ones that thrive. Take Netflix, for example—a company that didn't just set out to deliver movies and TV shows. Netflix has mastered the art of connecting with people on a deeper level.

### "More Than Movies: The Netflix Formula for Human Connection"

When you look at **Netflix**, you don't just see a company that delivers movies and TV shows—you see a company that has mastered the art of **human connection**. From the very beginning, founders Marc Randolph and Reed Hastings didn't set out to create just another entertainment company. They wanted to create something that would change the way people experienced content. And they understood one thing: the key wasn't just in the content itself—it was in how they **connected** with their audience.

Marc and Reed knew that if you could truly understand what people want—before they even know it themselves—you could create something that goes beyond business. You could create a brand that people feel emotionally attached to. Reed Hastings once said:

**"I realized that if we could give people a better way to access entertainment—an experience that was faster, easier, and personalized—we could completely change how they connect with the content they love."**

And that's exactly what Netflix did. They didn't just offer movies; they offered **connection**. Their algorithms weren't about showing you what's popular—they were about showing you what speaks to **you**. It's that feeling of opening Netflix and seeing a show or movie that feels like it was handpicked just for you. That's human connection at scale.

Netflix isn't just in the content business—it's in the **relationship business**. They've built their platform around understanding what their audience wants, how they behave, and what makes them tick. And here's the thing: They made it personal. The more you watch, the more Netflix learns about what resonates with you. It's like they know you better than you know yourself.

But here's where they really nailed it: **Consistency.** They made sure that every time you logged in, it felt easy. It felt familiar. No friction, no headaches—just a personalized experience that speaks directly to your preferences. That's how you build long-term loyalty, and that's how you keep people coming back.

Think about it: People aren't just watching Netflix because it's convenient—they're watching because they feel connected to the content. It's personal. It's human. And Marc and Reed knew that from day one.

And here's the thing: The magic behind Netflix's success isn't just in what they offer, it's in how they connect with us as individuals. Their approach mirrors the Common T.H.R.E.A.D Method—deliberately fostering relationships, listening, and evolving with their audience.

In a world often marked by disconnection and division, the Common T.H.R.E.A.D Method reminds us of the frequencies that bring us together. When we consciously cultivate these T.H.R.E.A.D's, we not only enrich our own lives but contribute to a broader, more connected world.

This understanding became even more evident to me recently as I navigated through the bustling corridors of several Real Estate Conferences. For those of us familiar with these events, it's clear that the essence of connection isn't found in the endless cascade of PowerPoint presentations.

Rather, it blooms in the informal moments—the lobby exchanges, the bar-side chats, and the shared dinners. These spontaneous interactions are where the real connections are made, and where the T.H.R.E.A.D's of trust, rapport, and authenticity truly come to life.

But the question remains: How does one weave those genuine connections amidst such settings?

**By understanding the Rythm of Conversation:**

Think of a conversation like jamming out with your friends in a band. Each person's got their own instrument (or in this case, their voice), and together, you're trying to make this beautiful piece of music, aka a smooth chat.

We're going to dive deep into what makes a conversation really tick – think of it as getting the band to groove together perfectly. We'll look into how important it is to hit your cues at the right time, keep the tempo going just right, and really connect with the emotion of the piece.

By breaking down these parts, I want to help you become a master conversationalist, whether you're chatting it up at a coffee shop or sealing the deal in a boardroom. It's all about making those interactions count, making them memorable, and most importantly, making them feel good for everyone involved.

In any business, especially one as interactive as real estate, mastering this rhythm can be the difference between closing a deal or walking away empty-handed. It's not just about what you say; it's how and when you say it.

First things first: listening. As I have talked about in other chapters is the most underrated skill in conversation. When you're dealing with clients, investors, or even learning from a mentor, listening helps you catch the beat of the conversation. What are their needs? Their fears? Their aspirations? When you listen, really listen, you start to dance in sync with them.

Now, let's talk about timing. In a conversation, timing is everything. Knowing when to pitch your idea, when to ask a question, and when to just listen, can make all the difference.

It's like finding the right moment in a song to jump in. Good questions are your secret weapon. They're like the spotlight in a dark room, focusing the attention where you want it.

And not just any questions – open-ended ones that make people think and open up. Instead of asking a client, "Do you like this property?" try, "What excites you about this property?" See the difference? One is a dead-end, the other opens up a highway.

Now, let's add a layer–active listening. This is where you not only hear what's being said but also what's left unsaid. It's about reading between the lines, catching those subtle cues in tone, body language, and even what's not being said. In real estate, this can be the difference between understanding a client's true needs versus just hearing their surface-level requests.

But here's where it gets interesting – the art of mirroring. This doesn't mean you mimic the other person. It's about matching their energy, their pace of speaking, and their level of enthusiasm. It's like dancing – you move in sync. If they're excited, match that energy. If they're more reserved, tone it down. It's all about creating that comfortable rapport where real connections happen.

Finally, humor – Let's be honest, who doesn't like a good laugh? Used strategically. Humor breaks down barriers and lightens the mood, making complex or stressful topics like real estate investing more palatable. When we talk about the rhythm of conversation, remember, it's not a military march. It's more like a salsa dance – unpredictable, fun, and sometimes you step on a few toes. Oops!

So, how do you add humor to your conversation without turning it into a stand-up comedy show? Well, first, know your audience. Dropping a joke about cap rates might get you some chuckles in a room full of real estate pros, but might earn you blank stares at a kindergarten show-and-tell.

Timing is your best friend here, just like in any good joke. It's the pause before the punchline, the suspense before the surprise. And in business conversations, it's knowing when to lighten the mood or when to keep it serious. You don't want to crack a joke when discussing a sensitive topic. Trust me, it's like laughing at a funeral – not cool.

Let's talk about relatability. The best humor is the kind people can relate to. In real estate, it's those shared experiences – like the thrill of closing a deal or the frustration when things don't go as planned. Sharing a light-hearted comment about common struggles can build rapport faster than you can say "property management headache."

But here's the key – self-deprecation. Laughing at yourself shows you're human and not just a real estate robot. It's like saying, "Hey, I make mistakes too, but I'm cool with it." Just don't overdo it. You don't want to come off as the clown of the real estate circus.

Remember, the goal here is to make your conversations engaging and memorable, not to audition for a comedy club. A little humor goes a long way in making complex topics like real estate investing more approachable and enjoyable.

So, as you move forward, think about how you're engaging in conversations. Are you listening to the beat? Are you moving in time with the rhythm? This isn't just a skill; it's an art. And like all arts, it takes practice...

...and I practice all the time!

During one of these conferences, I engaged in a conversation with a woman in her late thirties. She was relatively new to the real estate scene, a mother of two boys, keen on mastering the art of raising capital—a common goal shared by many attendees, myself included.

As we delved deeper into the conversation, her initial response mirrored the rehearsed pitches that had become all too familiar within the conference halls. It felt like we were part of a live TV show where everyone recited from the same script.

**Encountering at least a thousand participants, it seemed as though we were all reading from identical cue cards. Her pitch unfolded predictably:**

"I am a multifamily investor seeking to raise capital for X number of doors, and we're just X amount short of closing."

In that moment, I yearned for an escape, as if wishing for a sudden commercial break during a live broadcast glitch. I halted the rehearsed dialogue, seeking a deeper connection. "That's not what I'm asking," I interjected, looking her squarely in the eyes.

"Who are you, beyond your professional facade, In other words, I want to know -

# "Who Are You, Not What Are You."

The woman immediately responded by telling me that my story was very similar to hers. She grew up in a Hispanic neighborhood and her family struggled financially. She wanted to create passive income to be able to come home to her two kids, and she chose real estate as the vehicle to achieve that.

However, she initially felt uncertain about which role to pursue. At first, she thought she would be an acquisition manager because of her background as a design engineer. Then, she considered asset management due to her experience as a project manager. Now, she believes she is suited for capital raising because she is very good with people, which is why she attended the capital raising conference.

My head was spinning from all the Avatars she was identifying herself with.

Ever noticed how your brain kinda goes into a freeze mode when you're staring at a gazillion flavors of ice cream? That's what happens when life throws too many choices at us. It's like, "Cool, options!" But then, it quickly turns into, "Oh no, which one do I pick?"

## THIS IS KNOWN AS "CHOICE OVERLOAD OR THE PARADOX CHOICE"

This concept suggests that while having options is generally considered a good thing, an excessive number of choices can lead to negative outcomes.

**Here's the lowdown on what goes down when we're swamped with choices:**

**Can't Make Up My Mind:** Suddenly, picking something feels like trying to solve a Rubik's cube blindfolded. Too many options just make us stand there, scratching our heads, unable to decide.

**The 'What If' Game:** After finally making a choice, there's this annoying little voice asking, "But what if the other one was better?" It's like no matter how good your pick is, you're left wondering about the road not taken.

**Sky-High Expectations:** With a boatload of choices, you'd think finding the perfect one would be a breeze, right? Wrong. It just makes us expect the moon, and then we're bummed out when we get, well, not the moon.

**Stress City:** Trying to pick the best out of a bazillion options is like trying to find a needle in a haystack. It's stressful, and honestly, who needs that kind of pressure?

**Satisfaction Dips:** Even if you end up loving your choice, just knowing there were a million other possibilities can make your happy bubble a bit less bubbly. It's weird how our brains work, isn't it?

**Brain Drain:** Making decisions is hard work for our noggin. And when it's bombarded with too many choices, it's like our brain runs out of juice, leading to not-so-great decisions because, well, mental exhaustion.

So, what's the trick to dealing with this? Keep it simple. Don't sweat the small stuff, and remember, chasing perfection in every choice is like trying to catch smoke with your bare hands. Focus on what really matters, and let the rest slide. Life's too short to get tangled up in decision paralysis.

So knowing that, I asked her did you ever read or watch Lewis Carroll's "Alice's Adventures in Wonderland" she said you mean "Alice in Wonderland" I said yes and then asked if she remembered the scene between Alice and the Caterpillar she said that she did but she never really quite understood it.

I said The encounter between Alice and the Caterpillar is a fascinating exploration of identity and the perplexities of understanding oneself, which resonated deeply with our topic of discovering

## "WHO ARE YOU, NOT WHAT ARE YOU"

I went on to explain that In that iconic scene, Alice meets the Caterpillar who is sitting on a mushroom and smoking a hookah.

The Caterpillar's first question to Alice is "WHO ARE YOU?"—a question that seems simple but is loaded with existential weight, especially in the context of Alice's ongoing transformations in Wonderland. Alice responds, somewhat perplexed and frustrated, that she cannot explain herself, mainly because she feels she has changed several times since that morning.

This exchange highlights the fluidity of identity and the struggle to define oneself in a constantly changing environment or, metaphorically, in a changing world.

Just like Alice, we often find our identities in flux, shaped by our experiences, roles, and the social contexts we navigate.

The question "Who are you?" is not static but evolves as we grow, learn, and change. This mirrors the journey of personal and professional development, where new experiences and roles offer opportunities to redefine ourselves.

Alice's difficulty in explaining who she is to the Caterpillar mirrors our own struggles in articulating our identities beyond the surface level.

It's one thing to list roles or job titles and another to delve into the essence of who we truly are—our values, passions, and the unique stories that define us.

Alice's journey is a quest for understanding in a world that seems to make little sense. Similarly, in our professional and personal lives, we seek clarity about our identities amidst change. The Common T.H.R.E.A.D Method encourages us to find continuity through our core values and interests, even when our external circumstances shift.

The conversation between Alice and the Caterpillar encourages us to embrace the complexity of our identities. Rather than seeking a fixed label, it's about appreciating the multifaceted aspects of self that contribute to who we are. This approach fosters a more nuanced and authentic connection with others, as we recognize and celebrate the diversity of experiences and perspectives that shape us.

The Alice-Caterpillar encounter, through the lens of The Common T.H.R.E.A.D Method, highlights the importance of introspection and dialogue in understanding identity.

It reminds us that the question of "Who are you?" is not just about seeking definitive answers but about engaging in a continuous process of self-discovery and expression. In our interactions, whether in Wonderland or the real world, embracing the complexity of our identities and the stories that define us can lead to deeper, more meaningful connections.

Imagine for a moment the last time you felt a deep connection with someone. Was it because you shared a similar interest, went through a similar experience, or faced a common challenge? These moments of connection are powerful because they remind us that we're not alone. They provide a mirror in which we see our reflections, validating our feelings and experiences.

The Common T.H.R.E.A.D Method emphasizes finding and nurturing these connections by actively seeking out shared experiences and interests. It's about being intentional in our interactions and recognizing the potential for connection in everyday moments.

Whether it's joining a community garden, participating in a support group, or simply sharing stories with a friend, these activities weave stronger bonds between us.

Now, let's connect the dots to health. Research has shown that strong social bonds are linked to a host of health benefits, from lower rates of heart disease and depression to longer lifespans.

But how does The Common T.H.R.E.A.D Method fit into this? It's simple, yet profound. By fostering connections based on shared experiences, we not only enrich our social network but also build a support system that can buffer against stress, enhance our resilience, and promote a sense of well-being.

Consider the power of a support group for those dealing with a specific health issue. The common T.H.R.E.A.D of their shared experience creates a space where members can offer understanding, empathy, and practical advice. This kind of targeted support can be incredibly healing, both emotionally and physically. It's a testament to how our social connections can directly impact our health.

So, what can we do to weave these common T.H.R.E.A.D's into our lives? Start by reflecting on what matters most to you, your passions, and your challenges. Then, seek out communities or individuals who share these T.H.R.E.A.D's. Be open to sharing your own experiences and listening to others. Remember, it's through vulnerability that we find our strongest connections.

Real estate is more than just transactions; it connects people to their dreams and aspirations. This aspect of the T.H.R.E.A.D method emphasizes the importance of humanizing business interactions recognizing and valuing the personal side of professional relationships.

The Common T.H.R.E.A.D of Humanity–Beyond Business Roles: When I meet someone, sure, I'm interested in what they do, but I'm more interested in who they are.

Like what makes them tick, what they're passionate about outside of work. It's about finding that common human T.H.R.E.A.D that ties us all.

Sharing personal experiences is key, I might talk about the challenges of balancing work and family life or the latest book that changed my perspective. Or have a conversation like this one I had at a conference.

Me: You know, when we talk about raising capital, we often get caught up in the mechanics—the pitches, the numbers, the strategies. But at its core, it's really about human connection, isn't it?

Lina: Absolutely, Andy. It's that human element that often gets overlooked. I'm curious, with your expertise, how do you see us reimagining this space?

Me: Well, let's think outside the traditional frameworks. For instance, consider the concept of 'emotional dividends.' What if we approached potential investors not just with the promise of financial returns but with the potential for emotional and societal returns as well?

Lina: Emotional dividends? That's intriguing. Can you expand on that?

Me: Sure. Imagine presenting a business model that not only forecasts profit margins but also maps out the emotional impact of the investment. This could include the joy derived from supporting a cause the investor cares deeply about or the satisfaction of contributing to a solution for a pressing societal issue. It's about quantifying the unquantifiable putting a spotlight on the emotional rewards of investment.

Lina: That's a powerful concept. It shifts the conversation from purely financial to deeply personal.

Me: Exactly. And it's about leveraging those deep, personal connections for mutual benefit. Another idea is 'connective storytelling.' This goes beyond traditional storytelling in pitches. It's about creating a narrative that weaves the investor's personal story with that of the business, highlighting shared values and visions.

Lina: So, it's not just telling the business's story but intertwining it with the investor's narrative?

Me: Precisely. It's a collaborative narrative that positions the investment as a shared journey towards a common goal. This approach fosters a deeper sense of partnership and commitment.

Lina: These ideas really flip the script on traditional capital raising. How do you see these concepts being received in the current climate?

Me: There's a growing appetite for meaningful investment opportunities, especially among the younger generations. They're looking for more than just financial gains; they want their capital to reflect their values and contribute to positive change.

By tapping into this desire for meaningful connection and impact, we can open new avenues for raising capital that resonate on a deeper level.

Lina: It sounds like we're on the cusp of a significant shift in how we approach business relationships and investments.

Me: Indeed, we are. And it's these human connections, grounded in shared values and emotional dividends, that will drive the future of capital raising. It's about creating a community of investors who are financially, emotionally, and socially invested in the ventures they support.

Lina: Andy, this conversation has been incredibly enlightening. Your perspective on leveraging human connection in new ways gives me hope for a more connected, impactful future in business.

Me: I'm glad to hear that. Remember, at the end of the day, business is about people. We can redefine success in capital raising and beyond by fostering genuine connections and aligning our efforts with our shared humanity.

This dialogue introduces fresh concepts like emotional dividends and connective storytelling, aiming to provide unique insights into the role of human connection in raising capital, setting your book apart with innovative ideas and perspectives.

It's these shared human experiences that deepen connections and make them more authentic.

In every interaction, I try to bring empathy to the table. Understanding someone's challenges, joys, and fears is what human connection is about. It's putting yourself in their shoes, even if just for a moment. Everyone's personal story is unique, and that's what makes connecting so exciting. I love learning about different cultural backgrounds, hobbies, or life philosophies. It's about celebrating our diversity and finding common ground in our shared humanity.

Human connection can happen anywhere—over a coffee, during a walk, or in a casual chat before a meeting starts.

It's about making those moments count, showing genuine interest and care. What we're creating here goes beyond networks—it's a community—a community where people feel seen, heard, and valued, where every interaction isn't transactional but transformational.

At the end of the day, human connections matter most. They make our professional and personal lives richer and more fulfilling. Remember, building human connections is a journey, not a destination. It's about being present, being real, and being open to the stories and experiences of others.

The "H" in our T.H.R.E.A.D method underscores the importance of Human Connection in every aspect of life. It's about fostering relationships rooted in empathy, understanding, and a celebration of our shared humanity.

In a world where business can often overshadow personal connections, remembering the "H" brings us back to what's truly important – the people behind the projects the stories behind the statistics.

**Human Connection Challenge:**

Spend the next 5 days deepening your human connections. Each day, have a meaningful conversation with someone in your network—whether personal or professional—where your only goal is to learn something new about them. Focus on truly listening and understanding their needs or experiences.

After each conversation, reflect on what you discovered and how this new information could strengthen your relationship. Share your most surprising or powerful connection in the community group and discuss how building deeper relationships is transforming your interactions.

Once a connection is made, the next step is to nurture and develop it. **Building Rapport** is essential to cultivating these connections naturally. In Chapter 9, we'll discuss techniques for rapid rapport development, helping you create strong connections in any environment.

# R = Rapport Development: *Cultivating Connections Naturally*

*"People will forget what you said, people will forget what you did, but people will never forget how you made them feel."*

—MAYA ANGELOU

WELCOME TO YOUR CRASH COURSE IN INSTANT RAPPORT-BUILDING.

Let's explore something that I hold close to my heart—building genuine rapport. You've heard people talk about networking and making connections, but I want to flip the script and get real about what building rapport truly means.

First, throw out the playbook. Authentic rapport doesn't come from a step-by-step guide; it comes from genuine interactions where you give more than you take. It's not about handing out your business card at a networking event; it's about creating real relationships.

And here's the thing—this idea of authentic rapport doesn't just apply to one-on-one relationships. It's the foundation of any successful business too. Take Amazon, for example. From day one, they weren't just focused on building a business—they built a relationship powerhouse. If you want to create something that stands the test of time, you need to crush one key thing: rapport.

## From Click to Connection: The Art of Building Rapport at Amazon

If there's one thing that sets **Amazon** apart, is they didn't just build a business—they built a relationship powerhouse. If you want to create something that stands the test of time, you need to crush one key thing: Rapport.

**Jeff Bezos?** He nailed this from day one. He didn't want people just dropping in for a quick buy and bounce—he wanted them to keep coming back like they're family. And the only way to pull that off is by connecting on a deeper level, making people feel like they're more than just numbers—they matter.

**Bezos once said:**

*"We see our customers as invited guests to a party, and we are the hosts. It's our job every day to make every important aspect of the customer experience a little bit better."*

And that's the key to building rapport. It's not about **selling**—it's about creating a relationship where the customer feels valued. You don't just provide a service; you make the entire experience **seamless** and **consistent**. From one-click ordering to fast delivery, Bezos knew that if Amazon could make life easier for customers, they'd build a level of trust that goes way beyond just selling products.

Let's get real for a second...Rapport? It's about showing up, every time. Not just once. Not when it's convenient. But consistently. Amazon isn't in the game just because they've got everything from A to Z. They win because they've mastered building relationships at scale. They deliver what people want before they even know they need it. Think about Prime: It's not just fast shipping, it's seamless convenience delivered to your door. And every single time they over-deliver, that bond gets stronger. It's not just shopping; it's trust.

Here's the punchline: Bezos understood something fundamental rapport isn't just about good customer service. It's about **predictability**.

People don't want surprises when they shop. They want to know that when they click "Buy Now," it's going to show up on their doorstep, on time, no problems. That's what creates **rapport**—the trust that Amazon has your back, no matter what.

And that's how you win. You build rapport by showing up consistently, by doing the little things that make people's lives easier, and by always putting the customer first. You make them feel like they're **part of the Amazon family**. And when you do that, they don't just shop they **stay**.

That same approach applies beyond just businesses like Amazon. Whether you're running a company or sitting across from a high-net-worth individual, it's all about creating genuine connections. It's not just about making the sale or getting a deal done—it's about making people feel understood and valued. And that's where the magic happens.

Imagine you're sitting down with a high-net-worth individual, and you want to make a connection. You know The Common T.H.R.E.A.D Method is gold for this—finding something you both love and chatting about it.

But here's the kicker: time. These folks are busy, and you've got to make your move quickly.

When you first meet, you've got maybe 2-3 minutes max to hook them with a shared interest. It could be anything—snowboarding, cooking, boating, or those epic vacations in Europe. The trick is not to get lost in it. You don't want to spend half your meeting talking about that time you hit the slopes in Aspen and totally wipe out on your chance to pitch.

Here's how you do it. You find that common ground fast, and then, bam, you pivot back to your pitch. Think of it like a smooth transition in a conversation. You start with snowboarding, but you quickly link it back to your business.

**Example Time:**

**You meet an investor who loves snowboarding as much as you do. Kick off with something like this:**

You: "I just got back from snowboarding in the Alps. Man, it was a rush! You know, it's a lot like planning a business strategy. Speaking of which, I've got this killer investment opportunity I think you'd really dig..."

Boom. You've built a connection, shown you're relatable, and moved straight into your pitch.

**Example Meeting Someone Who Loves Cooking:**

You: "Hey, I heard you're into cooking! I just tried this new recipe last week – a crazy good truffle pasta. Cooking is like running a business, don't you think? You need the right ingredients and timing to get everything just right. Speaking of which, I've got this business idea that I think you'd be interested in..."

Investor: "Oh, I love truffle pasta! What's your idea?"

You: "So, it's about creating a platform that connects local farmers with urban restaurants. It's all about fresh, high-quality ingredients delivered fast. Imagine the impact on the dining experience..."

**Example Connecting Over Boating:**

You: "I noticed you mentioned boating earlier. I'm a huge fan of sailing myself. Last summer, I took my boat out to the Bahamas, and it was incredible. Sailing really teaches you about navigating challenges, just like in business. By the way, that reminds me, I have an investment opportunity that's all about navigating new markets..."

Investor: "I love the Bahamas! Tell me more about your idea."

You: "Absolutely. It's a startup focused on leveraging AI to predict market trends. Just like how we read the wind and currents, our tech helps businesses read market shifts and adjust their strategies in real-time..."

**Example Shared Interest in Snowboarding:**

You: "I hear you're a big snowboarder! I just got back from a trip to Whistler, and the powder was insane. Snowboarding always makes me think about the rush of starting a new venture – the excitement, the challenges. Speaking of which, I'd love to share this new project I'm working on..."

Investor: "Whistler is amazing! What's your project about?"

You: "We're developing a wearable tech line that monitors athletic performance in real-time. Imagine having data on your form and speed while you're shredding the slopes, helping you improve instantly..."

**Example Talking Travel and Business:**

You: "You've been to Europe recently? That's awesome. I was just in Italy exploring the Amalfi Coast. Traveling gives you such a fresh perspective, doesn't it? It's a lot like business – seeing new opportunities and adapting. Speaking of which, I have a business proposition I think you'll find exciting..."

Investor: "Italy is beautiful! What's the proposition?"

You: "It's a travel app that curates personalized itineraries based on user preferences and real-time local events. Imagine getting insider tips and must-see spots tailored just for you..."

**Example Passion for Fitness:**

You: "I heard you're into fitness. I'm big on CrossFit myself. There's something about pushing your limits that translates directly to the business world, right? That reminds me, I've been working on something that could really revolutionize the fitness industry..."

Investor: "CrossFit is intense! What are you working on?"

You: "We're launching a new fitness platform that combines virtual coaching with AI-driven personalized workout plans. It's like having a personal trainer and a fitness tracker rolled into one..."

These examples showcase how to quickly establish rapport over shared interests and smoothly transition into discussing your business idea, all while maintaining a conversational and engaging tone.

**Three Key Moves:**
1. Find the Common T.H.R.E.A.D Fast: Use those first 2-3 minutes wisely. Nail down that shared interest quick.
2. Smooth Transition: Seamlessly connect the conversation back to your investment. Make it relevant.
3. Stay Focused: Keep your eye on the prize. Don't let the convo drift too far from your main goal.

Have you ever met someone who just has that magic touch when it comes to connecting with others? It's like they can strike up a bond with anyone, creating trust and understanding in no time at all.

Some might say being good at this is just a talent you're born with – you either have it, or you don't. But that's not the full picture. Sure, rapport can come naturally for some, but guess what? It's also a skill that can be honed and enhanced, just like any other ability.

Here's the deal: people are your most valuable asset. In the hustle of business, whether it's real estate, tech, or any field, the connections you make can define your path. But here's where most get it wrong – they focus on quantity over quality. They count connections instead of making connections count. Let's get one thing straight – building rapport is not about manipulating or schmoozing.

It's about listening, engaging, and adding value.

You want to know the quickest way to build rapport? Give without expecting anything in return. Provide value, whether it's an insight, a resource, or just a genuine compliment.

And listen, really listen. In a world where everyone's broadcasting their own message, the ones who listen, who can hear what's not being said, are the ones who stand out. That's how you build trust, and trust is the bedrock of every solid relationship. Now, you might be thinking, 'Andy, how do I do this authentically?' Here's the thing: be unapologetically yourself. People can smell fake a mile away. Be real, share your passions, your struggles, and your victories. When you're real, you attract people who resonate with your authentic self.

Alright, let's level up on this whole rapport thing with The Common T.H.R.E.A.D Method. This is where the real magic happens in building not just connections, but meaningful relationships.

Here's the deal: when you're talking to someone, whether it's in a business meeting, at a conference, or even in a casual setting, pay close attention.

Listen – and I mean really listen – to what they're saying. People often drop hints about their interests, their values, their experiences. These are your 'Common T.H.R.E.A.D's.'

Now, the trick is to pick up on these T.H.R.E.A.D's and weave them into the conversation. Let's say you're talking to someone, and they mention they love vintage cars. Boom – there's a T.H.R.E.A.D. If you share that interest, or even if you just know a bit about it, dive into that. Share your experiences, ask questions, get them talking more about it. This isn't just small talk; it's finding that mutual ground where genuine connections are made.

But it's more than just finding common interests. It's about identifying shared experiences, challenges, and ambitions. Maybe they talk about a challenge they faced in their career. If you've faced something similar, share that. It's about showing that you understand that you've been there too. This is how you go from surface-level chitchat to building a rapport that's based on real understanding and mutual respect.

And here's something crucial – authenticity. Don't fake it. Don't pretend to be interested in something just because they are... People can see right through that. Be genuine. If you don't know much about a topic they're interested in, be honest. Show interest. Ask questions. People appreciate sincerity, and they love to share their passions.

Remember, building rapport using The Common T.H.R.E.A.D Method isn't a tactic; it's a way to genuinely connect with people on a deeper level. It's about finding those T.H.R.E.A.D's that bind us, whether in business or life, and weaving them into conversations that matter. So next time you're talking to someone, look for those T.H.R.E.A.D's. Listen, engage, and watch how these shared connections can turn into long-lasting relationships."

Building rapport is like tending a garden. You can't just plant a seed and walk away. You nurture it, water it, give it sunlight. Follow up, keep in touch, and show that you care not just about the deal or the project, but about the person.

Rapport goes hand-in-hand with trust. Developing a genuine rapport with clients and peers in the real estate industry can open doors to opportunities that go beyond mere business dealings. This part of the method focuses on the art of building rapport through empathy, understanding, and shared experiences.

It's a Special Kind of Magic, So, when we talk about building rapport, we're diving into something that's both an art and a science. It's more than just making a connection; it's about creating a vibe, an understanding, that makes every interaction feel more like a conversation between old friends than a stiff business meeting. Building rapport is like tuning into someone's frequency. It's about syncing up your communication style, your energy, and even your humor with theirs.

**This is crucial.** Building rapport isn't just about being interesting; it's about being interested. I make it a point to really listen, ask follow-up questions, and show that I'm engaged. It's about valuing their input and making them feel heard. I use The Common T.H.R.E.A.D Method to build bridges, not just contacts, In the dance of relationships, especially in the realm of investing, building rapport is like learning the right steps to a great tune. It's not just about making contacts; it's about creating connections that resonate and last.

Rapport isn't one-size-fits-all. How I build rapport at a casual networking event versus a formal business meeting can vary. It's about reading the situation and adjusting your approach accordingly. While my approach might change based on the setting, being consistently friendly, open, and respectful doesn't. That consistency is key in maintaining rapport over time. Think of rapport as the rhythm that makes conversations and relationships flow smoother. It's about creating a comfortable space where ideas and stories can be shared freely and enthusiastically.

Rapport is the bridge that turns a simple connection into a lasting relationship.

Finding Shared Interests: Starting with shared interests is like finding a shortcut to rapport. It could be as simple as a mutual love for a particular cuisine, or a shared hobby like photography. These interests act as icebreakers and pave the way for deeper conversations."

The Art of Conversation: I like to keep conversations light but meaningful at first. Talk about a recent sports game, a new restaurant, or a movie that's got everyone talking. It sets a relaxed tone and shows that you're relatable and approachable.

Nurturing Rapport Through Genuine Interactions.

Consistent Engagement: Rapport isn't built overnight. It's about consistently showing up, being interested in what they have to say, and remembering little details from past conversations. It's these small things that make people feel valued and understood.

Authenticity is key; people can tell when you're being genuine. So, I'm always myself, whether I'm in a boardroom or at a casual meet-up. Authenticity builds trust and strengthens rapport in ways that nothing else can.

Building rapport doesn't have to be confined to business settings. Casual interactions, like a quick catch-up call or a friendly text, can reinforce the rapport you've built. It's about showing you care beyond the professional realm.

I use The Common T.H.R.E.A.D Method to encourage mutual sharing, It's a two-way street. The more they share, the more rapport we build. It's about creating a comfortable space for mutual exchange.

So, why is this whole rapport thing a big deal across the board, from cubicles to classrooms, and even in those high-stakes boardrooms? Rapport is about syncing up with someone, finding a rhythm that works for both of you. It's an essential component of any successful relationship, professional or personal.

Let's break it down, nice and easy, without all the formal fluff.

### In Business: It's Like Your Secret Handshake

Imagine walking into a room and, within minutes, you're no longer a stranger—you're the person everyone wants to know. That's rapport in the business world. It's like having a secret handshake that instantly makes deals smoother, conversations richer, and yes, opens doors you didn't even know existed. When people feel connected to you, they're more likely to want to work with you, share opportunities, or simply grab a coffee and brainstorm the next big thing.

### In Healthcare: More Than Just a Number

Ever felt like just another appointment on a doctor's busy schedule? Well, when healthcare pros get rapport right, you feel seen, heard, and genuinely cared for. It's not just about the stethoscope and prescriptions; it's about connecting on a human level. This trust can make all the difference in how patients follow advice, manage their health, and even how they recover. Plus, it makes those sterile exam rooms feel a bit warmer.

### In Education: From Eye Rolls to High Fives

Picture a classroom where the teacher's not just another adult laying down the rules but someone who really gets it. That's the magic of building rapport in education. Students are more engaged, willing to participate, and even excited to learn. It's about turning those eye rolls into high fives and creating an environment where learning feels more like discovery and less like a chore.

## In Real Estate: Beyond the Front Door

Now, real estate isn't just selling houses; it's selling dreams, right? A good rapport means agents and clients are on the same wavelength, making the hunt for the perfect home less about sales and more about shared visions. When clients feel understood, they're more likely to trust their agent's advice, making the whole process smoother and, dare we say, enjoyable.

Imagine a world where talking about real estate investments is as easy and engaging as chatting about your latest Netflix binge. That's the vibe one standout capital raiser brings to the table when diving into the multifamily real estate game. She's not just about the cold, hard numbers; she's all about building genuine connections with her potential investors.

Instead of launching straight into ROI, cap rates, and leverage points, she starts with a simple, "What's your dream scenario?" She really listens  nodding along, throwing in a "totally get that" now and then, making each investor feel like they're in a coffee shop chat rather than a stiff investment meeting.

Her secret sauce? She treats every investor like a new friend joining her on a thrilling real estate adventure. She's quick to share her own stories, the good, the bad, and the ugly, making her human and relatable. It's not just about finding investors; it's about inviting people to be part of something exciting, something bigger.

And she doesn't stop at the handshake. She keeps the conversation going, sending out casual updates, fun facts about the market, or even inviting investors over for a backyard BBQ. It's like being in a cool club where everyone's on a first-name basis, swapping stories and dreams.

This chill, friendly approach turns the traditional investor relationship on its head. Instead of a one-and-done deal, she's building a community, a family of sorts, who are all in on the journey with her. And guess what? It works. Her approach not only fills the funding pot but also builds a circle of investors who are ready to jump on the next deal she brings to the table. In the cutthroat world of real estate, she's proof that sometimes, a little warmth and friendliness can go a long way.

This casual twist on building rapport in the investment world highlights that success isn't always about being the most knowledgeable person in the room; sometimes, it's about being the most approachable

So, there you have it. Rapport is your Swiss Army knife in just about any field. It's about making genuine connections that can turn opportunities into successes, making every interaction a little more human and a lot more productive. And the best part? It's a skill that gets better with practice, just like your grandma's secret cookie recipe. The more you do it, the sweeter the results.

**Learning techniques to build rapport is essential for anyone looking to enhance their interpersonal skills. Here are some effective strategies to consider:**

1. **Active Listening:** This involves more than just hearing words. It's about understanding the message behind them. Show that you're engaged by nodding, maintaining eye contact, and offering verbal affirmations like "I see" or "That makes sense." Active listening makes the other person feel valued and heard.

> **➔ TIP:**
>
> If people know about body language, they'll pick up that you're mirroring and this might have an opposite effect to the one that you want.
>
> So, don't be mechanistic- be relaxed and appropriate.

2. **Mirroring and Matching:** Subtly mimic the other person's body language, speech patterns, and energy level. This doesn't mean copying every move they make but rather aligning with their general demeanor. This technique, known as mirroring, can help establish a subconscious sense of harmony and comfort between you and the other person.

> **→ TIP:**
>
> It's hard to establish rapport with someone who wants to talk only about themselves, so try to balance the conversation.
>
> Aim to share as much as the other person does. You both feel more comfortable as a result.

3. **Open-Ended Questions:** Ask questions that require more than a yes or no answer. This encourages the other person to share more about themselves, providing you with more opportunities to find common ground and deepen the connection.

4. **Empathy:** Try to genuinely understand and share the feelings of the other person. Showing empathy can break down barriers and create a strong emotional bond.

5. **Sharing Personal Stories:** Appropriately sharing something personal can make you seem more relatable and trustworthy. It shows vulnerability and openness, inviting the other person to lower their guard.

6. **Consistent Follow-Up:** Building rapport is not a one-time effort; it requires nurturing. Sending a thoughtful follow-up message or checking in periodically can reinforce the connection and show that you care.

7. **Positive Attitude:** A positive, upbeat demeanor is contagious and can set the tone for the interaction. People are naturally drawn to individuals who are optimistic and have a good energy about them.

8. **Respect for Boundaries**: While it's important to seek commonalities and shared interests, respecting the other person's boundaries is crucial. Pay attention to cues that indicate they may be uncomfortable or wish to change the subject.

By integrating these techniques into your interactions, you'll be well on your way to building stronger, more meaningful rapport with those around you. Remember, like any skill, building rapport takes practice and patience, so be persistent and genuine in your efforts.

So, here's the bottom line: flip the script. Instead of asking what someone can do for you, ask what you can do for them. Make every interaction count, and remember, in the long game of business and life, it's the relationships you build and nurture that make all the difference.

---

→ **More Key Advice:**

1.  **Read the Room:** Pay attention to your investor's body language and responses. Are they engaged? If they're leaning in and asking questions, you've hooked them. If they're checking their watch, it's time to speed things up.

2.  **Value Their Time:** High-net-worth individuals are often juggling a million things. Respect their schedule. Be concise, be clear, and be compelling. Don't waste a second.

3.  **Bring Energy:** Your passion is contagious. When you talk about that shared interest, let your enthusiasm shine through. Then, carry that same energy into your pitch. People invest in people as much as they invest in ideas.

4.  **Know Your Stuff:** Be prepared. Know your pitch inside and out. Anticipate questions and be ready with solid answers. Confidence comes from being well-prepared.

5.  **Be Authentic:** Don't force the connection. If you don't have a genuine common interest, don't fake it. Authenticity builds trust, and trust is the foundation of any successful pitch.

6.  **Follow Up:** The meeting doesn't end when you walk out the door. Send a follow-up email thanking them for their time, and briefly reiterate the key points of your pitch. Keep the lines of communication open.

---

Remember, the Common T.H.R.E.A.D Method is your opener, not the whole playbook. Use it to get in the door, then make sure you deliver your pitch before time runs out. Keep it tight, keep it focused, and you'll maximize your chances of success.

**However, success doesn't stop at getting in the door—it's about what you do once you're there. Developing rapport is crucial, but it must be underpinned by authenticity.**

**Practical Application: Building Rapport**

1. **Match and Mirror**: Practice matching the tone, pace, and body language of the person you're speaking with. This helps create a subconscious sense of similarity and rapport.

2. **Shared Stories**: Share a personal story that relates to the topic of conversation. Use storytelling to build connections and show vulnerability.

3. **Follow-Up**: After a meeting or networking event, follow up with a personal note or message. Mention something specific from your conversation to show you were genuinely engaged.

Developing rapport is crucial, but understanding emotions is equally important in any interaction. In Chapter 10, we'll explore emotional intelligence and how managing emotions can help you build emotional resonance in your conversations

# E = Emotional Intelligence:

*"Emotional intelligence, more than any other factor, more
than IQ or expertise, accounts for 85% to 90% of success
at work... IQ is a threshold competence. You need it, but it
doesn't make you a star. Emotional intelligence can."*

—PETER SALOVEY

## Tuning Into Emotional Intelligence

Have you ever walked into a room and felt the mood instantly? Sometimes there's a sense of calm, while other times, tension is so thick you could cut it with a knife. What you are sensing is the energy, the frequency of emotions that fills the space.

Emotions, like everything else, have a frequency, an energy that they carry. This energy can uplift us or bring us down. Emotional Intelligence is the ability to understand, manage, and respond to these emotions in a way that is positive and constructive. It's about tuning into the right frequency, the one that brings harmony, understanding, and compassion into our lives.

# Understanding the Frequency of Emotions

Every emotion vibrates at a certain frequency. Joy, love, and gratitude are high-frequency emotions. They are uplifting, bringing a sense of peace and happiness. On the other hand, anger, fear, and sadness are low-frequency emotions. They are heavy and can drain our energy. Emotional Intelligence is about recognizing these frequencies and choosing to align ourselves with the higher ones. It's about understanding that we have the power to change the energy around us by managing our own emotional state.

Think of it this way: Just as a radio can be tuned to different stations, we can tune our emotions to different frequencies. By tuning into the higher frequencies, we can create a positive and uplifting environment. This is the essence of Emotional Intelligence. It is not about denying or suppressing our emotions but about understanding them and choosing how to respond. It's about turning the dial to the station that brings peace, joy, and understanding.

# The Power of Self-Awareness

The first step to tuning into the frequency of Emotional Intelligence is self-awareness. It's about knowing ourselves, understanding our own emotions, and how they affect us and those around us.

Self-awareness is like a mirror that reflects our true selves. It shows us our strengths, our weaknesses, and our triggers. When we are self-aware, we can recognize when we are vibrating at a low frequency and take steps to shift to a higher one.

Imagine being aware that you are feeling stressed. Instead of letting that stress control you, you take a deep breath, pause, and choose to respond calmly. This shift in response changes the frequency from stress to calm. It's a simple act, but it has a powerful impact. This is the power of self-awareness. It allows us to take control of our emotions, rather than being controlled by them.

# Empathy: The Heart of Emotional Intelligence

Empathy is the ability to understand and share the feelings of others. It is the heart of Emotional Intelligence, and it vibrates at a high frequency of compassion and understanding. When we are empathetic, we connect with others on a deep level. We feel their joy, their pain, and their struggles. This connection creates a bond, a resonance that is powerful and healing.

Imagine a friend who is going through a tough time. Instead of giving advice or trying to fix their problems, you simply listen. You show that you understand and that you care. This simple act of empathy creates a safe space for them to express their feelings. It's like tuning into their frequency and resonating with their emotions. This resonance is powerful because it shows that we are not alone, that someone understands and cares. Empathy is a gift that we can give to others, and it is a key component of Emotional Intelligence.

# Managing Emotions: Choosing the Right Frequency

Managing emotions is like being a conductor of an orchestra. It's about knowing which emotions to amplify and which ones to quiet down. Emotional Intelligence is about choosing the right frequency, the one that will bring harmony and balance. This doesn't mean suppressing negative emotions, but rather understanding them and choosing how to respond.

Imagine a situation where you are feeling angry. Instead of reacting with anger, you take a moment to breathe and calm yourself. You choose to respond with kindness and understanding. This choice changes the frequency from anger to compassion. It transforms the energy and creates a positive outcome. Managing emotions is about being mindful, about making conscious choices that align with the higher frequencies of peace and understanding.

# The Common T.H.R.E.A.D Method: Weaving Emotional Intelligence

In the fabric of our lives, the Common T.H.R.E.A.D Method works in perfect harmony with Emotional Intelligence.

Both are essential for building strong, resilient connections. While Emotional Intelligence is fundamentally about understanding, using, and managing emotions in positive ways, the Common T.H.R.E.A.D Method focuses on finding and nurturing the T.H.R.E.A.D's that connect us with others. These two elements work together to create a beautiful tapestry of relationships, trust, and collaboration.

Think of Emotional Intelligence as the needle that guides the T.H.R.E.A.D. It helps us navigate the complexities of human emotions, enabling us to communicate effectively, empathize with others, overcome challenges, and defuse conflicts. When we are emotionally intelligent, we can identify the common T.H.R.E.A.D's that bind us to others. We can use these T.H.R.E.A.D's to build bridges, to connect on a deeper level, and to create a sense of unity and belonging.

In business, particularly in raising capital and attracting investments, this synergy is invaluable. Investors are not just looking for good returns; they are looking for partners who understand them, who resonate with their values, and who can manage challenges with grace.

And it's the same when you're raising capital or attracting investments. It's not just about the numbers—it's about building relationships that resonate on a deeper level. Investors want to work with people who get them, who can navigate challenges without losing that human touch.

The power of emotional intelligence goes beyond personal relationships and investor meetings—it's at the heart of some of the world's most successful companies. Take Airbnb, for example. They didn't just build a platform; they created an experience that taps into one of the most powerful human needs: the need to belong.

## Belong Anywhere: How Airbnb Masters Emotional Intelligence

When you think about **Airbnb**, it's not just a company that provides a place to stay. It's a company that understands how to make people **feel at home**, no matter where they are in the world. And this is where **emotional intelligence** comes into play. Airbnb didn't build its success solely on offering cheaper accommodations or unique places to stay—it built it by tapping into one of the most human desires: the need to **belong**.

**Brian Chesky**, one of Airbnb's founders, once said:

*"What I've learned from building Airbnb is that a brand is a feeling. It's not a logo or a website; it's the emotional connection people have with your company."*

That's where Airbnb shines. It uses **emotional intelligence** to create an experience where travelers don't just feel like they're renting a room—they feel like they're **welcomed into a community**. They feel understood. It's personal. It's human.

When you book an Airbnb, you're not just staying in someone's house. You're connecting with a local host, someone who can offer you a unique, authentic experience that a hotel just can't match. Airbnb didn't just build a platform; they built a **connection** between people from all corners of the world. And they did it by deeply understanding what travelers truly want: an experience that feels genuine, warm, and **emotionally meaningful**.

But here's the kicker: Airbnb's emotional intelligence isn't just about their hosts and guests; it's embedded in the entire brand. From the way they communicate with users, to how they handle customer support, to how they've adapted during crises like the pandemic—it's all about listening, understanding, and responding with empathy.

Think about it. Travelers want more than just a roof over their heads. They want **connection**. They want to feel like they're part of the culture and community they're visiting. And Airbnb nailed that. They took the cold, impersonal nature of traditional travel and turned it into something **deeply personal**. This is **emotional intelligence** in action: understanding people's emotions, predicting their needs, and then creating a product that fulfills those desires in a **meaningful** way.

You see, Airbnb doesn't just win because they have a great product. They win because they make people feel **seen**. They make them feel like they belong anywhere in the world. And that's emotional intelligence at its best.

Their approach isn't about making noise; it's about making meaningful connections. It's about listening—truly listening—not just to the words being said but to the spaces between those words, the pauses and breaths that reveal more than speeches.

Consider a scenario where an entrepreneur meets with potential investors. Rather than overwhelming them with data and enthusiasm, imagine starting the conversation with genuine curiosity about the investor's own journey and interests. By focusing on the subtle, non-verbal signals, such as a slight hesitation before answering a question, you show a level of care and attention that speaks louder than any sales pitch.

In our fast-paced, often overwhelmingly loud world, the power of that kind of quieter approach cannot be underestimated. Introverts, for example, naturally excel in these empathetic connections. This isn't just a tactical move; it's fundamentally about recognizing the person across from you as exactly that—a person, not just a means to an end.

Empathetic connections emphasize the strength found in vulnerability. Being open about challenges and uncertainties can resonate more deeply than showcasing only your successes.

This honesty invites reciprocal openness and builds deeper relationships. It's about showing genuine concern and responding in a way that demonstrates you truly understand where they're coming from.

## Using Emotional Intelligence to Read the Room

Emotional Intelligence acts like an internal compass, guiding you through the emotional landscapes of every interaction. This compass allows you to detect and interpret what's not being said aloud—the hesitations, the excitement, the reluctance, and the enthusiasm. It enables you to sense the mood and energy of the room, which is crucial when dealing with potential investors.

Imagine pitching an idea to a potential investor. If you possess a high level of Emotional Intelligence, you'll pick up on subtle cues in the investor's behavior and responses. This sensitivity can guide you in adjusting your pitch on the fly, aligning it more closely with what truly matters to the investor. For example, if you notice excitement when discussing the scalability of your project, pivot your focus to emphasize scalability, thereby aligning your pitch with the investor's interests.

Moreover, this emotional compass isn't just about reading others; it's also about understanding your own emotional state. Are you truly confident in what you're presenting, or are you feeling uncertain? Investors can sense these emotions, and this can influence their confidence in you and your proposal. By being aware of your own emotional state, you can manage and adjust your demeanor, ensuring you come across as composed and assured.

# Building Resilience and Navigating Setbacks

Emotional Intelligence also equips you to handle rejections and setbacks with greater resilience. When employing The Common T.H.R.E.A.D Method, not every interaction will result in success. Investors may have reservations or disagree with certain aspects of your proposal.

Here, Emotional Intelligence comes into play by enabling you to manage your own emotions and respond constructively. Instead of showing frustration or disappointment, use these moments as opportunities to ask for feedback, understand the investor's perspective better, and refine your approach for future discussions.

## TikTok: Embracing "E"–Engagement

In today's digital age, platforms like TikTok have become powerful tools for connection and engagement. Emotional Intelligence is not just relevant in face-to-face interactions but also in the digital world. On TikTok, the "E" stands for Engagement, and it resonates with the frequency of Emotional Intelligence. Engagement is not just about getting likes and shares; it's about creating meaningful connections. It's about giving engagement to receive engagement.

Just as in real life, digital engagement begins with showing genuine interest in others. Commenting thoughtfully on someone's video, sharing content that resonates, or simply appreciating someone's creativity are ways to give engagement. These actions show that we value others, that we are not just seeking attention but are genuinely interested in connecting. When we give engagement, we create a positive energy, a frequency that attracts more engagement. It's a cycle of giving and receiving, of creating value and connection.

## Building Relationships Through Emotional Intelligence

Relationships are like bridges that connect us to others. Emotional Intelligence is the foundation of these bridges. It's about understanding and managing our own emotions, as well as being aware of and responding to the emotions of others. Whether in person or online, when we are emotionally intelligent, we create relationships that are strong, resilient, and fulfilling.

Think of a time when you felt truly understood by someone. It felt good, didn't it? That's because understanding and empathy create a connection that is deep and meaningful. Emotional Intelligence helps us build these connections. It helps us communicate effectively, resolve conflicts, and build trust. It's about creating a frequency of understanding and respect, one that brings people closer together.

## Living at the Frequency of Emotional Intelligence

Emotional Intelligence is not just a skill; it is a way of living. It is about tuning into the right frequency, the one that brings peace, joy, and understanding. It is about being self-aware, empathetic, and mindful. It is about managing our emotions in a way that creates positive and uplifting energy. By living at the frequency of Emotional Intelligence, we create a life that is rich in meaningful relationships, in peace, and in joy. We attract people who resonate with our own authenticity, who uplift us and bring out the best in us.

The Common T.H.R.E.A.D Method and Emotional Intelligence work together, weaving a fabric that is strong, resilient, and beautiful. Whether in raising capital, engaging on TikTok, or building personal relationships, these two elements are our greatest assets. They allow us to create connections that are built on trust, understanding, and respect. They allow us to present ourselves with confidence and integrity. And they allow us

Let's start by exploring how emotional intelligence can enhance the effectiveness of The Common T.H.R.E.A.D Method. When you identify commonalities with others, particularly investors, you're engaging in a form of **empathetic connection,** which is a core component of EI.

In our fast-paced, often overwhelmingly loud world, the power of a quieter approach—especially in the realm of emotional intelligence—cannot be underestimated. When we speak of empathetic connections, we delve into a realm where introverts naturally excel. It's about listening, truly listening, not just to the words being said but to the spaces between those words, the pauses and breaths that reveal more than speeches.

Empathetic connections are forged in these quiet moments. For instance, consider a scenario where an entrepreneur meets with potential investors. Rather than overwhelming them with data and enthusiasm, imagine instead a conversation that begins with genuine curiosity about the investor's own journey and interests. This isn't merely tactical; it's fundamentally about recognizing the person across from you as exactly that—a person, not just a means to an end.

This form of connection relies heavily on the ability to be present. In these interactions, it's important to create a space where silent cues are as important as spoken words. This might mean noticing a slight hesitation before answering a question, which could indicate concern or a need for clarification. Addressing these non-verbal signals shows a level of care and attention that speaks louder than any sales pitch.

Furthermore, empathetic connections emphasize the strength found in vulnerability—being open about challenges and uncertainties can often resonate more deeply than showcasing only your successes. This type of honesty invites a reciprocal openness and builds deeper, more meaningful relationships.

So, while the world often celebrates the loudest voices, remember the strength that lies in quiet connection. By fostering deep, empathetic engagements, you not only enhance your interactions but also align more closely with those values that call for a thoughtful, introspective approach to business and life.

This process not only helps in building rapport but also in fostering trust. By leveraging emotional intelligence, you can better interpret the emotional states and needs of investors, allowing you to tailor your communication in a way that resonates deeply with them.

Imagine a scenario where you're pitching an idea to a potential investor. If you possess a high level of emotional intelligence, you'll be more adept at picking up subtle cues in the investor's behavior and responses. This sensitivity can guide you in adjusting your pitch on-the-fly, aligning it more closely with what truly matters to the investor, based on the emotional cues you've observed.

This could be anything from focusing on the financial security aspect of the investment if they seem risk-averse, to highlighting innovative elements if they show excitement about novel ideas.

Moreover, emotional intelligence allows you to handle rejections and setbacks with greater resilience. When employing The Common T.H.R.E.A.D Method, not every interaction will result in success. Investors may have reservations or disagree with certain aspects of your proposal. Here, EI comes into play by enabling you to manage your own emotions and respond constructively.

Instead of showing frustration or disappointment, you can use these moments as opportunities to ask for feedback, understand the investor's perspective better, and refine your approach for future discussions.

Emotional Intelligence (EI) is like having an internal compass that guides you through the emotional landscape of every interaction.

You know how sometimes you just feel the vibe of a room or a person? That's your internal emotional compass at work. It's like this intuitive guide that helps you navigate through all sorts of conversations and relationships.

Let me break down how this works for me.

Think of your internal emotional compass as this intuitive sixth sense that not only picks up on the undercurrents of an interaction but also guides you through the emotional landscapes of others, almost like navigating a map of hidden sentiments and reactions.

This emotional compass allows you to detect and interpret what's not being said aloud—the hesitations, the excitement, the reluctance, and the enthusiasm. It enables you to sense the mood and energy of the room, which is crucial when dealing with potential investors. This capability is especially important in high-stakes environments where understanding subtle dynamics can make or break a deal.

For instance, during a meeting with an investor, while you're employing The Common T.H.R.E.A.D Method to establish common ground, your EI compass might alert you to a shift in the investor's enthusiasm when certain topics are broached. Perhaps when discussing the scalability of your project, you notice a spark in their eyes or a lean-forward posture that wasn't present before. Recognizing these cues can lead you to pivot your focus more heavily on scalability, thereby aligning your pitch more closely with what excites your investor.

Moreover, this emotional compass isn't just about reading others; it's also about understanding your own emotional state and its influence on your interactions. Are you truly confident in what you're presenting, or are you feeling uncertain? Investors can sense these emotions, and this can influence their confidence in you and your proposal. By being aware of your own emotional state, you can manage and adjust your demeanor, ensuring you always come across as composed and assured.

In your discussions, this emotional awareness facilitates a deeper connection, as you're not only addressing what investors say but also responding to what they feel. This level of empathy and understanding can dramatically enhance the persuasiveness of your pitch, making it more than just a transaction—it becomes a meaningful interaction that respects and values the emotional inputs of all parties involved.

Think of your emotional compass as this sixth sense that picks up on the under-currents of an interaction. Like, I can usually tell if someone's enthusiastic or just going through the motions. It's about sensing those subtle emotional signals and adjusting your approach accordingly.

Have you ever walked into a room and immediately read the room? EI is all about picking up on the vibes in the room. It's like being a bit of a mind reader, but not in a creepy way. You sense the mood, the feelings, the unspoken concerns. This awareness helps you navigate conversations more thoughtfully.

Reading the room is about being emotionally intelligent you're not just hearing words; you're also tuned into the emotions behind them. It's about empathizing, showing genuine concern, and responding in a way that shows you truly get where they're coming from.

Emotional intelligence is key when dealing with tough conversations or nego-tiations. It's about staying calm, composed, and understanding, even when the situation gets a bit heated.

It's not just about keeping your cool; it's about helping others keep theirs too, and that's when you can build stronger bonds because using EI helps in building deeper connections.

It's not just about what you can do for them professionally. It's about connecting on a more personal level, showing that you care about their wellbeing as much as you care about the business.

Emotional intelligence isn't just for business meetings. It's for every interaction – with family, friends, colleagues. It's about being aware of your emotions and those of others in every situation, leading to more meaningful and authentic relationships. I like to create an environment where people feel comfortable expressing their feelings and thoughts. It's about mutual respect and under-standing, where emotional expression is seen as a strength, not a weakness.

If you're not paying attention to emotional intelligence in your interactions, you're leaving money on the table—it's that simple. Emotional intelligence? It's the game. It's not just some fluffy, feel-good skill to pat yourself on the back with. It's the secret weapon, the secret sauce that makes everything in business tick.

You want to make your conversations richer, your deals more effective, your relationships with investors not just good but freaking great? Then get this: emotional intelligence is your hook. It's about truly getting into the shoes of the person across from you, feeling their vibe, understanding what drives them—not just what they say, but what they **feel**.

You've got to be able to read the room like a book, my friends. See that hesitation? That excitement? That skepticism? That's your cue. Pivot, adapt, and connect. And it's not just about reading them—you've got to be in check with your own emotions too. Are you coming off too strong? Too desperate? Chill out, recalibrate, and go back in.

Here's the real talk: Business is no longer just business. It's personal. Every interaction, every meeting, every pitch—it's a chance to make a real connection. Do that effectively? You'll see your success skyrocket. Ignore it, and you're just another player in the game, not the one leading it.

So, lace up, equip yourself with emotional intelligence, and watch how you start changing the game. It's about making every single interaction count, turning them into opportunities not just for transactions, but for transformations. That's how you win big in this hustle.

## Emotional Intelligence Mastery Challenge:

For the next 5 days, practice managing your emotions and reading the emotions of others in your conversations. Each day, choose one key aspect of emotional intelligence to focus on: self-awareness, empathy, self-regulation, motivation, or social skills.

At the end of each day, journal about how you applied that focus in your interactions. Did it change the outcome of the conversation? Share your experiences in the group and discuss which aspect of emotional intelligence you found the most challenging—and rewarding.

While emotional intelligence helps you understand others, authenticity is what allows you to show your true self. In the next chapter, we'll explore the power of authenticity in business and how being genuine can build trust and engagement.

# CHAPTER 11

# A = Authentic Engagement:

*"Authenticity is the daily practice of letting go of who we think we're supposed to be and embracing who we are."*

—BRENÉ BROWN:

In a world overflowing with noise and distractions, authentic engagement stands out like a clear bell ringing through the chaos.

If you're not getting real in your conversations, you're not doing it right. Authentic engagement? It's everything. It's not just some nice-to-have; it's the oxygen for your business's survival. When you're authentic and showing up as yourself, you're not just talking; you're resonating. That's when the magic happens.

You want to create a space where ideas pop off like fireworks, where trust isn't just built, it's cemented, and where collaboration isn't a buzzword but the real deal?

Then start by being real yourself. Drop the act. Stop selling and start connecting. Share your doubts, your wins, your screw-ups. Trust me, it's liberating.

In a world full of scripted pitches and rehearsed speeches, genuine, heartfelt engagement is like a breath of fresh air, isn't it? Think about it. When was the last time you had a conversation that felt real, unscripted, and genuinely engaging? That's the kind of interaction we should strive for, whether we're talking with a client, an investor, or even a friend.

Authentic engagement isn't just about being honest or sincere; it's about creating a connection that's real and tangible. It's like when you're out on a boat. You're not just steering through the water; you're feeling the wind, watching the waves, and experiencing the moment in its purest form.

Listen, authentic engagement isn't just a nice-to-have—it's a must-have if you want to dominate. You want real connections? You've got to show up raw, real, and ready to deliver. When you listen, understand, and make people feel like they matter, that's when trust goes through the roof. And trust? That's the ultimate currency in business.

You want a prime example of this? Look no further than Patagonia.

## Walking the Talk: Patagonia's Blueprint for Authenticity

When you talk about **authenticity** in business, it's impossible to overlook **Patagonia**. Here's a brand that doesn't just say they care about the environment—they live it in every single decision they make. From the products they create to the activism they support, Patagonia is all about being **real** and staying true to their values, no matter the cost. Authenticity is the foundation of their brand, and that's why their customers trust them deeply.

### Patagonia's founder, Yvon Chouinard, famously said:

*"Patagonia exists to challenge conventional wisdom and change the way people think about business and the environment."*

And they've done just that. Think about their famous "Don't Buy This Jacket" campaign. Who does that? A company that's not just in the game to sell more products, but to **stand for something bigger**. That's authenticity. They encouraged customers to think twice before buying—urging them to repair and reuse instead of always buying new. This campaign wasn't just marketing—it was a bold statement that they're not going to compromise their values just to make a buck.

Here's the thing about Patagonia: They don't just talk the talk. When they say they're committed to **sustainability**, they back it up. From their **Fair Trade** practices to their **1% for the Planet** commitment, Patagonia proves that you can be both **profitable** and **purpose-driven**. They've earned their customers' trust because they're **transparent**, **honest**, and refuse to stray from what they believe in.

And people can smell inauthenticity from a mile away. In a world where brands are constantly trying to look like they care about causes, Patagonia actually does. They're not chasing trends—they're living their truth. They've been championing environmental sustainability long before it became cool, and that's why they've built such a loyal, passionate customer base.

Authenticity isn't just a buzzword at Patagonia—it's the core of who they are. They've built a brand that's real, trustworthy, and committed to a cause that goes beyond profit. And that's why Patagonia is more than just a brand—it's a **movement**. People don't just buy Patagonia gear because it's high-quality. They buy it because they believe in what the company stands for.

Patagonia's success isn't just about great products; it's about being unapologetically authentic. They've built a brand that stands for something bigger, and that's why people don't just buy from them—they believe in them. It's a movement, driven by trust and a shared purpose.

So, how do you bring that same level of engagement into your conversations?

First and foremost, forget the script. This doesn't mean you should be unprepared. On the contrary, know your stuff, but be ready to go off the beaten path. Listen more than you talk, and respond to what you hear, not what you planned to say.

When you lead with authenticity, you make it safe for everyone else to bring their A-game. They'll bring ideas to the table that are game-changers because they trust the environment. They trust you. You'll see innovation like never before because everyone's not just involved; they're invested.

And here's the kicker: when shit hits the fan, and it will—because that's business—your team won't just scatter. They'll rally. Why? Because real trust was built from real talks. You've shown your true colors, so they'll have your back.

Lastly, remember this: authentic engagement is a catalyst for growth. It makes feedback not just something you give, but something that everyone craves. It's about pushing each other, challenging the status quo, because everyone knows it's all in the name of getting better, together.

So, start getting real. The more authentic your engagements are, the more explosive your growth will be. This is the stuff that builds empires, that makes legends. Are you ready to be legendary?

Then let's get authentic. Let's get real and transform those ordinary interactions into extraordinary opportunities by using *Instagram* the best social media platforms for harnessing the power of ***Authenticity!***

**Among the elements of the "T.H.R.E.A.D." acronym, "A" for Authenticity stands out as particularly relevant to Instagram. Here's why Authenticity is key on Instagram and how it can be utilized:**

## Why Authenticity Resonates on Instagram:

You know, in this crazy, fast-paced world of filters, highlights, and sometimes, let's be real, straight-up fakery, there's one thing that cuts through all the noise—authenticity. That raw, unfiltered, genuine connection. It's not just about being real; it's about being YOU, and here's why that's the gold standard on Instagram.

First off, think about what grabs your attention. Is it the polished, perfect posts that look like a million other things you've scrolled past? Or is it the moments where someone shares a real struggle, a genuine laugh, or an honest insight? That's the stuff that sticks because it feels like a real human connection, not just another brand trying to sell you something.

Authenticity builds trust. When you're real with your followers, you're not just another influencer or brand; you're a voice they can trust. And in a world where trust is harder to earn than ever, that's priceless. It's about showing up, flaws and all, and saying, "Hey, this is me, take it or leave it." People respect that kind of honesty.

And let's talk about engagement. Authentic posts create conversations, not just likes and comments. Real talk sparks real talk. When you open up, your followers feel safe doing the same. It turns a post into a community, a dialogue, and that's where the magic happens. That's when you go from being a person on a screen to being a part of someone's day, someone's life.

So, why does authenticity resonate on Instagram? Because at the end of the day, we're all craving connection. We want to feel seen, heard, and understood.

And the only way to do that is to be unapologetically ourselves. It's about ditching the script, tearing down the facade, and just being real.

Remember, the beauty of social media, and Instagram in particular, isn't in the polished perfection; it's in the messy, beautiful reality of life. It's in sharing your journey, your passions, your failures, and your wins. That's what people want to see. That's what people want to connect with.

Let's dive deeper into the heart of Instagram and really unpack why being authentic isn't just good advice—it's the secret sauce to truly resonating and building an unbreakable bond with your audience. Focusing on weaving in those common T.H.R.E.A.D's that make authenticity not just a practice, but a powerful strategy.

Now, when I say "Common T.H.R.E.A.D's," I'm talking about those universal experiences, emotions, and truths that every single one of us can relate to. It's the struggles, the triumphs, the moments of doubt, and the flashes of pure joy. By sharing these parts of your journey, you're tapping into something much bigger than just your own story—you're tapping into the human experience.

Think about it. Why do stories of overcoming obstacles hit us so hard? Why do we get chills when someone shares a moment of vulnerability? It's because, deep down, we see ourselves in those stories.

We've all faced challenges, felt vulnerable, and fought to overcome our fears. And when you, as an influencer or brand, get real about these moments, you're not just sharing content; you're igniting a connection that's based on something real and shared.

Let's get tactical for a second. When you're creating content, think about those common T.H.R.E.A.D's in your life.

Maybe it's the grind of turning your passion into a business, the ups and downs of personal growth, or the simple moments that bring you joy. Whatever it is, share it. Share it with honesty, with passion, and without fear. Because guess what? That's what people are drawn to. They're drawn to the real you, the one that laughs, cries, fails, and gets back up again.

And here's where it gets really powerful. When you start weaving these common

T.H.R.E.A.D's into your content regularly, you're doing more than just building a brand; you're building a community. A community that's rooted in authenticity, shared experiences, and genuine engagement. You'll start to see your comments section light up not just with emojis and quick remarks, but with real stories, genuine questions, and heartfelt connections.

So, my challenge to you? Start looking for those common T.H.R.E.A.D's in your own life and in the world around you. Share them openly and watch as your authenticity transforms your Instagram from a platform into a community. Remember, the most powerful thing you can be on social media, and in life, is yourself. Authentic, unfiltered, and unapologetically you.

Keep crushing it, keep being real, and let's show the world the power of authenticity. Let's make those common T.H.R.E.A.D's the fabric of our community on Instagram.

So here's the challenge for you: Next time you're about to post something, ask yourself, "Is this me being 100% real?" If not, it might be time to rethink it. Because authenticity? That's the ultimate influencer.

Stay real, stay passionate, and keep crushing it.

Let's break it down further because I want you to really get this—authenticity isn't just about being nice or relatable; it's about building a freaking empire that lasts. So let's talk about how real engagement drives massive growth, shapes killer leaders, and forges a culture that beats any competition.

**Growth**: When you're genuine in your interactions, when you really listen and connect, you're not just building relationships—you're opening doors.

Every real conversation is an opportunity, a chance to spot trends, to pivot, to innovate ahead of the curve. Authenticity makes your clients, your partners, everyone feel they're part of the process, part of the success. This isn't just good morale—it's good business. It drives loyalty, referrals, and, yes, it boosts your bottom line.

**Empathy:** It's the cornerstone of authentic engagement. It's about truly under-standing where the other person is coming from, stepping into their shoes.

When you empathize, you don't just hear the words; you feel them. In the world of real estate, this could mean understanding an investor's fears and aspirations, not just their financial goals.

**Leadership:** Authentic leaders are gold—they're rare, they're valued, and they are damn effective. Why?

Because they lead by example. They show that they value honesty over perfec-tion. They make it okay to fail and learn. This doesn't just build better teams; it builds leaders at every level of your company. When you foster this kind of leadership, you're not just running a team; you're inspiring a movement. People want to follow, they want to give their best, and they want to be part of something bigger than themselves.

**Culture:** Culture is the secret sauce of your company. It's what makes people want to work for you or buy from you. And guess what?

Authenticity is at the heart of any great company culture. It's what creates an environment where people can be themselves, where their voices are heard, and their ideas matter. This kind of culture isn't just nice to have; it's a magnet for talent, for investment, for customer loyalty. It's what sets you apart from the noise, making your brand not just heard, but followed, admired, and preferred.

And let me tell you, in this digital age, authenticity is more critical than ever. People can spot a fake from miles away, and they're tired of corporate speak. They want real. They crave real. Give them that, and they'll give you their trust, their business, and their loyalty.

So, think about it—are you just talking at people, or are you really talking with them? Are you dictating, or are you listening?

The businesses that get this right, the ones that truly engage authentically, they don't just grow; they thrive. They don't just exist; they lead. They don't just compete; they dominate.

Get real with your engagement. Make authenticity the cornerstone of your business strategy, and watch as you not only meet your goals but blow them out of the water.

**That's how you make a mark. That's how you win!**

Here's where it gets really interesting. When we engage authentically, we create a space where ideas can flourish, where trust is built, and where real collaboration can happen.

It's like when you're trying to solve a complex problem – the solution often comes from a place of deep understanding and shared perspective

And remember, authenticity is contagious. When you're genuinely engaged, it encourages others to drop their guards and open up. It's a two-way street. You're not just sharing information; you're building a relationship. Here's something else to consider – vulnerability.

Yes, it can be scary, but sharing your own challenges, mistakes, and learnings can bridge gaps like nothing else. It shows you're human, just like your listener. And in those shared human experiences, real connections are formed.

Remember, authentic engagement isn't just a skill; it's a way of being. It's about showing up as your true self, ready to connect, ready to listen, and ready to share. And in this space of authenticity, who knows what amazing things we can achieve together?

So, next time you're in a conversation, ask yourself, 'Am I truly engaged? Am I listening, empathizing, and connecting on a human level?' That's what authentic engagement is all about.

It's not just good for business; it's good for the soul.

So now let's dive into what 'Authentic Engagement' means for us as real estate investors. It's not just about the properties or the numbers; it's about the genuine connections we forge along the way. Let me break it down for you. In the investment world, trust isn't just important; it's everything. Whether you're dealing with property sellers, buyers, or fellow investors, being genuine is key. No facades, no B.S., just the real you. Be transparent in your dealings. Whether it's a great investment opportunity or a risky venture, be upfront. That honesty? It builds lasting trust and respect.

Remember, you're not just investing in properties; you're investing in relationships. Get to know the people behind the deals. What drives them? What are their concerns? Connect on that human level.

# AND...BE EVERYWHERE!!!

# "BE BINGE-WORTHY"

*"Dude, **Breaking Bad** is such an amazing **show**. You should **watch it**. It's totally binge-worthy."*

*Cultural anthropologist Grant McCracken, is quoted as saying—"TV viewers are no longer zoning out as a way to forget about their day, they are tuning in, on their own schedule, to a different world. Getting immersed in multiple episodes or even multiple seasons of a show over a few weeks is a new kind of escapism that is especially welcomed today."*

Alright, let's get real for a second. You wanna raise capital? You want people to throw money at your deals like it's Black Friday? Then you better be thinking about one thing—being binge-worthy. Yeah, I said it. Binge-worthy.

Look, in today's world, people have the attention span of a goldfish. You've got seconds—SECONDS—to grab their attention, and if you're not delivering insane value right out of the gate, you're done. Game over. But here's the flip side: if you can hook them, if you can create content that people can't stop watching, you've won. They'll be glued to you like a damn magnet, and guess what? That's where the money is.

# Remember Content is the Currency of Connection

In today's fast-paced world, content has become the bridge that connects people, ideas, and brands. It's the narrative that pulls at our heartstrings, the story that makes us lean in, and the message that compels us to act. Content isn't just information; it's the currency of connection.

Your content becomes binge-worthy when you successfully combine episodic delivery with a great story, good storytelling techniques (which we will discuss in another chapter), and impeccable technical constructs.

Studies have shown that 92% of people say they're more likely to buy a product if they hear about it through a recommendation from a friend or family member, so creating valuable, binge-worthy content that viewers are excited to talk about can help get that flywheel going.

Use platforms like **Facebook, Instagram, LinkedIn, YouTube or even TikTok** to show who you really are.

Social media isn't just the backdrop of our digital lives; it's the vibrant tapestry where the art of marketing is being reimagined.

Platforms like TikTok, Instagram, Facebook, and YouTube are more than just stages; they're the spaces where your brand doesn't just broadcast but truly connects and blossoms alongside your audience. When you weave in The Common T.H.R.E.A.D Method, especially in the realm of raising capital, you're not just sharing content—you're crafting stories that resonate, creating bonds that last, and building a community that believes in your vision.

Imagine you're scrolling through your feed, and there it is: a piece of content about multifamily real estate that just grabs you. Not just any content, but something so engaging, so insightful, you can't help but dive deeper.

That's where we're heading—into the realm of Storytelling, which we will explore in a later chapter.

But not just any stories—stories that resonate, that hit home. When it comes to raising capital for multifamily real estate, it's not just about the numbers or the deals; it's about the dreams, the journeys, the impact. It's about painting a picture so vivid, so compelling, that your audience can't help but see themselves in it.

## So, how do we make this content binge-worthy?

## It starts with authenticity.

Be real about the challenges, victories, and rollercoaster ride of real estate investing. Share stories of real people, real investors, and real tenants whose lives have been changed through multifamily properties.

This isn't just about investment returns; it's about creating communities, building futures, and making a real difference.

# "Document, Don't Create!" (GaryV)

Show the behind-the-scenes of a deal from start to finish. Let your audience in on the search, the analysis, the negotiation, the renovation, and finally, the transformation. Make it a series, with each step having its own episode, so your audience is always waiting for the next installment.

This isn't just content; it's an adventure you're inviting them on.

But here's the crucial part: engagement. This content needs to spark conversations, encourage questions, and invite interaction. Why? Because when people talk, they get invested, and when they're invested, they're more likely to join you on this journey.

So, ask for their opinions, experiences, fears, and dreams. Make your platform a place for community, not just consumption.

And let's not forget about the value. Every piece of content should leave your audience with something: a piece of knowledge, a new perspective, a spark of inspiration. Whether it's understanding market trends, financial strategies, or the impact of design on tenant satisfaction, give them something that makes them smarter, more informed, and more ready to take the leap with you.

Make your content so good, so engaging, so full of value that missing out feels like a missed opportunity. It's about creating a compelling narrative that your audience wants to binge on it and be a part of it. That's how you turn content into capital, stories into investments.

This isn't about flooding feeds with content; it's about making every piece so compelling, so utterly engaging, that your audience can't help but crave more. It's storytelling with a hook, content that sticks, making your brand not just seen but eagerly anticipated.

This blend of the dynamic world of social media, the authentic, engaging approach of The Common T.H.R.E.A.D Method, and the irresistible allure of binge-worthy content not only elevates your brand's narrative but also transforms your capital-raising journey into an inspiring saga that captivates and convinces.

Embrace this evolution and watch your brand's story unfold in ways that truly connect, engage, and grow your venture, turning followers into fans. Fans into a community rallied around your cause.

In the vast, interconnected world of social media, the true art of capital raising transcends traditional boundaries, tapping into the rich tapestry of our passions and interests. "Visionary Vanessa," our trailblazing capital raiser, knows this all too well.

She's not just about numbers and returns; she's about connecting on a human level, finding those unique common T.H.R.E.A.D's that bind us all, whether it's our love for art, the thrill of travel, the rhythms of music, the excitement of sports, the adventure of skiing, the refinement of wine tasting, the freedom of boating, or the companionship of horses.

Vanessa uses these passions as the cornerstone of her strategy, crafting investment opportunities that resonate on a personal level with her audience.

When she embarked on her journey to transform a neglected property into a vibrant community hub, she knew she had to do more than just present a business plan. She had to tell a story. It is a story about renewal, community, and the potential for something greater. She crafted content that highlighted not only the financial opportunities but also the human impact. She shared testimonials from future residents, showcased her sustainable building practices, and painted a vivid picture of the thriving community she envisioned.

This content became the currency of her connection with investors. It turned abstract concepts into tangible, relatable stories. It allowed investors to see the project through her eyes and feel the passion and commitment driving her efforts. It wasn't just about showing potential returns; it was about making investors a part of a transformative journey.

The common T.H.R.E.A.D that ties all of this together is the consistency and authenticity of your content. Each piece, whether a social media post, a detailed blog, or a video testimonial, weaves into the larger narrative of our mission. This T.H.R.E.A.D is what makes your story cohesive and compelling. It's what transforms disparate facts and figures into a unified vision that investors can believe in and support.

Vanessa's projects are more than investments; they're invitations to be part of something that mirrors investors' own passions and dreams.

Through her social media channels, Vanessa shares stories that highlight these unique aspects. A post might feature an upcoming development that includes a state-of-the-art music studio, appealing to those who dream of blending their investment portfolio with their love for music. Another update could showcase a property designed with equestrian facilities, drawing in those who find joy and connection through horses.

But what truly makes Vanessa's approach stand out is her genuine engagement with her audience. She doesn't just broadcast; she converses, asking her followers about their latest travel adventures, their favorite wine regions, or their most memorable skiing experiences.

This authentic interaction not only strengthens the bond with her audience but also deepens the understanding of what they truly value in an investment.

In this narrative, "Visionary Vanessa" redefines the essence of capital raising. It's not just about finding investors; it's about connecting with fellow enthusiasts, sharing in their passions, and offering them a chance to invest in projects that reflect their personal interests and lifestyles. Vanessa's approach turns the investment journey into a shared adventure, one that's paved with the common T.H.R.E.A.D's of our diverse interests and passions.

Imagine weaving a tapestry, where each T.H.R.E.A.D represents a different facet of your brand's interaction with the world.

At the core of this intricate design is the creation of content that's not just seen but felt—content that's undeniably binge-worthy. This isn't about churning out what everyone else is; it's about embedding pieces of your authentic self into everything you share. Each post, video, or story becomes a reflection of your uniqueness, inviting people into a world only you can create.

Now, as you engage with your audience, you're not just speaking to them; you're speaking with them. This engagement is a two-way street paved with genuine exchanges and real connections. It's here, in the authenticity of these interactions, that the magic happens. People don't just see your content; they feel it, relate to it, and, most importantly, trust it. This trust is the golden T.H.R.E.A.D that strengthens the fabric of your community, making each member feel seen, heard, and valued.

But the beauty of this tapestry doesn't end with the borders of your existing audience. As you continue to weave your narrative with T.H.R.E.A.D's of authenticity and engagement, the tapestry grows, reaching out into the world. This expansion is fueled by word-of-mouth referrals, the age-old method of sharing that remains unbeatably powerful. When your content truly resonates, when it sparks joy, thought, or inspiration, people can't help but share it. And it's this sharing, this vocal advocacy from those outside your immediate circle, that extends the reach of your tapestry far beyond its original confines.

Each T.H.R.E.A.D—whether it's your binge-worthy content, your authentic engagement, or the word-of-mouth referrals it generates—interlocks with the others, creating a cohesive, vibrant, and expansive tapestry that is your brand's presence in the world.

This common T.H.R.E.A.D method doesn't just tie your efforts together; it amplifies them, ensuring that your message, your brand, and your impact resonate far and wide, touching lives and building a community that extends beyond any boundaries you once imagined.

In essence, by focusing on what makes your content truly binge-worthy and engaging with your audience authentically, you're not just creating a following; you're inspiring a movement. This movement, powered by the genuine connections and conversations you foster, naturally propels itself through word-of-mouth, weaving an ever-expanding tapestry that captures the essence of your brand and the heart of your mission.

Your reach goes way beyond just the folks already using your product, those who follow you on social media, or the ones signed up to your email updates. Let's not forget, the oldest trick in the book, word-of-mouth, still holds the crown as the most effective way to spread the word. By crafting content that's downright irresistible, you're essentially fueling a passionate squad of supporters outside your usual crowd. This is about making something so good, so binge-worthy, that people can't help but talk about it, turning them into your loudest cheerleaders without them even realizing it.

Think about it: your circle of influence isn't just limited to the folks who already know your brand, your social media admirers, or the names on your email list. Remember, in this vast world of connections, the power of a good old-fashioned recommendation hasn't lost its spark. It's still the golden key in spreading the word.

But here's the clincher: creating content that's so engaging, so authentically you, and so utterly binge-worthy can turn even the casual observer into a fervent advocate.

**But there's an even simpler reason behind why we enjoy binge-watching. Dr. Renee Carr, Psy. D, a clinical psychologist states-"To put it simply, it makes**

us feel good." In fact, according to one study, 73% of us have positive feelings about binge-watching binge-viewing–It produces a continuous stream of dopamine in our brains:

"[Dopamine] gives the body a natural, internal reward of pleasure that reinforces continued engagement in that activity. It's the brain's signal that communicates to the body—This feels good. You should keep doing this!"

This is about more than just catching eyes and getting a dopamine hit, it's about capturing hearts through genuine, real-deal connections. When your content resonates deeply, speaks your truth, and is consistently compelling, you're not just building an audience; you're nurturing a community of vocal supporters beyond your immediate circle. And that, my friends, is the secret sauce to spreading your message far and wide, powered by the most authentic engagement there is.

So, you're probably wondering,

# "How do you get started...What Makes Content Engaging?"

### Engagement is a two-way street

**1**

You want people to engage with your content? Start by engaging with theirs. Don't just post and ghost.

### Earn permission before you ask

**2**

Engagement comes from trust. First, give your audience something valuable – their attention is earned, not owed.

### Focus on connection, not attention

**3**

It's not about how many people see your content, but how many deeply connect with it. Be meaningful to the few, instead of superficial to the many.

### Create a tribe, not an audience

**4**

Engagement is about creating belonging. When you make your audience feel like part of a community, they engage naturally because they care.

### Use curiosity as a hook

**5**

Start with an intriguing question or an unexpected statement. People engage when they're curious and can't resist finding the answer.

Getting started on this journey of crafting binge-worthy content and engaging authentically with your audience is much like beginning a new adventure. It starts with a step, a leap of faith into expressing the true essence of your brand and yourself.

**Here's a roadmap to help you navigate this exciting path:**

Engaging content captures attention and encourages interaction. It is often visually appealing, emotionally compelling, and interactive.

**Defining Relevance in Content:** Relevant content meets the needs and interests of your audience. It aligns with their values and helps solve their problems.

**Balancing Engagement and Relevance:** Strive to create content that is both engaging and relevant. For example, an interactive quiz about sustainable fashion practices can be both fun and informative, aligning with your brand values while

1. **Find Your Voice:** Begin by discovering and fine-tuning your unique voice.

This isn't about echoing the trends or mimicking what's already out there; it's about digging deep to find what you're truly passionate about and how you can share that passion in a way that's uniquely yours. Ask yourself, what topics can you talk about endlessly?

## Find Your Unique Selling Proposition (USP)

Your USP differentiates you from competitors. It's the unique benefit that only your brand can offer. For a fashion brand, this could be a focus on bespoke tailoring or eco-friendly materials.

What perspective do you bring that's fresh and engaging?

Your voice is your signature; make it distinct and authentic.

2. **Understand Your Audience:** Knowing who you're talking to is just as important as knowing what you're talking about.

Spend time understanding your audience—their interests, challenges, and desires. Engage in conversations, ask questions, and listen. This understanding will guide you in creating content that resonates and connects on a deeper level.

3. **Create with Intention:** Every piece of content you create should serve a purpose.

Whether it's to inform, entertain, inspire, or provoke thought, ensure that there's a clear intention behind what you're sharing. This doesn't mean every post has to be profound, but it should be meaningful in its own right, contributing to the larger narrative you're weaving.

4. **Solve Your Audience's Problems:** Think about the problems your audience faces and how you can help solve them. Here's how you can do that:

Answer Common Questions: "How to Evaluate a Multifamily Investment Property" or "What to Look for in a Property Management Company."

Step-by-Step Guides: Provide comprehensive guides on topics like "The Beginner's Guide to Investing in Multifamily Real Estate" or "How to Finance Your First Multifamily Property."

5. **Create Compelling Headlines**: Headlines are the first thing your audience sees.

**Make them catchy, intriguing, and relevant to grab attention:**
- "Invest Smarter: How to Identify High-Value Properties"
- "From Desperation to Domination in Real Estate"
- "The Blueprint to Non-Stop Investor Interest"
- "Stop Waiting: Get into Real Estate Investing NOW!"
- "Turning Prospects into Profit: Here's How"
- "From Zero to Property Hero: Your Guide to Real Estate Investing"
- "From Drought to Downpour: Get Investor Leads Today"
- "Turn Desperation into Success – Find Investors Now!"
- "Scale Up: How Multifamily Properties Can Boost Your Portfolio"
- "Why Settle for One? Multiply Your Income with Multifamily Investments!"

- "Double the Doors, Double the Income: Start Your Multifamily Journey!"

## 6. Craft a Compelling Storyline–Create a Strong Narrative Arc

Every piece of binge-able content has a strong narrative arc that keeps the audience invested. Develop a storyline that is compelling, with clear beginning, middle, and end sections.

## Building Tension and Suspense

Introduce elements of tension and suspense to keep your audience on the edge of their seats. **Cliffhangers** are particularly effective in encouraging viewers to consume the next piece of content.

End each segment or episode with a teaser for the next one. This creates anticipation and encourages your audience to continue watching or reading.

## Crafting Suspenseful Endings

Design your endings to leave your audience wanting more. This could be through unanswered questions, unresolved conflicts, or exciting previews of what's to come.

7. **Use Emotional Triggers:** Visual: Emojis representing different emotions (happy, sad, surprised). Content that evokes strong emotions tends to be more engaging. Whether it's joy, surprise, or even a bit of controversy, make sure your content connects emotionally with your audience.

So how do you do it? Let me break it down for you with a few quick examples.

**Imagine this:**

**You're walking down the street, coffee in hand, phone in selfie mode. You look straight into the camera and BOOM—you hit them with this:**

*"Alright, here's the deal—if you're raising capital and still using old-school tactics, you're leaving stacks of cash on the table. I'm about to drop a 3-minute hack that's gonna change your game forever. Watch this!"*

**You see what I did there? Hooked 'em. But you don't stop there. Now you take them somewhere clean, professional—a boardroom, your office, whatever. And you lay it out:**

**Hook #1:** *"Here's the thing—raising capital isn't about the pitch, the numbers, the hard sell. It's about this."*

And then you draw two circles on a whiteboard—one's your values, the other's theirs, and right in the middle? That's the common T.H.R.E.A.D. That's where the magic happens.

Let me hit you with a real-world story. I'm in a meeting with an investor, and instead of jumping into the numbers, I start talking about architecture because this guy just got back from Italy and was hyped about the design there. That common T.H.R.E.A.D?

Locked in the deal before we even touched on ROI. Simple. As. That.

**Hook #2:** *Now, here's the kicker–"Next time you're pitching, don't be a sales-person. Be a storyteller. Find that common T.H.R.E.A.D. And hey, if this hits home, hit that follow button. I've got a ton more where this came from. We're just getting started, and if you're serious about raising capital, you're gonna want to be here for it."*

Another binge-worthy idea would be a series called *The Real Estate Deal Breakdown*. Each week, you take one of your real estate deals and break it down step by step—how you found it, negotiated it, financed it, and closed it. But you don't stop there. You also dive into the challenges, the mistakes, and what you learned from the deal.

Start each episode with a hook like: *"Alright, I'm about to take you behind the scenes of one of my latest deals. This isn't just a highlight reel; I'm talking about the good, the bad, and the ugly. You're gonna see exactly how I turned this property into a profit—and what almost killed the deal. Let's get into it."*

This series is binge-worthy because it's real, raw, and packed with value. People in real estate love to learn from someone who's been in the trenches, and when you show them the whole process, mistakes and all, they can't help but watch. Plus, by consistently delivering this kind of content, you position yourself as an authority who isn't afraid to show the reality of the business.

Another series can be called *Real Estate MythBusters*. In each episode, you tackle a common real estate or investment myth and break it down with data, examples, and real-life experiences. The goal is to help your audience avoid common pitfalls and make smarter investment decisions.

**Start the first episode with something like:**

**Hook:** *"Hey guys, it's _____, and today we're busting some real estate myths wide open. You've heard it all before...*

*"You need 20% down to buy a house,' 'Flipping homes is easy money,' 'Real estate is too risky.' But is any of this actually true? Let's break down the facts, the numbers, and the reality behind these myths so you can make smarter decisions with your money. Let's dive in."*

This series is binge-worthy because it cuts through the noise and gives viewers the truth. People love to learn what's really going on behind the scenes, especially when it comes to their money. By consistently delivering content that challenges conventional wisdom, you position yourself as a trusted source of information, keeping your audience coming back for more no-nonsense advice.

Or you can create a series called: *The Confidence to Get Started in Real Estate!*

Instead of advanced negotiation tactics, focus on building the confidence to take the first steps in real estate. This series would cover topics like overcoming fear, setting realistic goals, and how to present yourself confidently even if you're new to the game.

**Hook:** *"Starting out in real estate can be intimidating, but I'm here to show you how to build the confidence you need to succeed. From setting goals to overcoming fear, this series is the blueprint you've been looking for. I'm breaking down everything you need to know, step by step, so you can start your journey with confidence. Let's get started!"*

That's it. You see what happened there? You just turned several simple pieces of content into something people can't stop watching. That's how you become binge-worthy. And once you're binge-worthy, the game changes. You're not just another person trying to raise capital—you're the person people WANT to give their money to.

8. **Promote Across Multiple Channels:** Share your content on various platforms to reach a broader audience.

Use social media, email newsletters, and collaborations to expand your reach.

9. **Engage Authentically:** Engagement goes beyond responding to comments or messages.

It's about fostering genuine connections. Share your thoughts, ask for your audience's opinions, and create spaces for meaningful dialogue. Remember, engagement is a two-way street; it's as much about listening as it is about speaking.

10. **Encourage Sharing:** Make your content easily shareable.

This isn't just about the technical aspects, like social share buttons, but also about creating content that people want to share. This comes from the value you provide, the emotions you evoke, and the conversations you spark. Encourage your audience to share their thoughts, experiences, and how your content resonates with them.

11. **Iterate and Evolve:** Finally, understand that this is a journey of continuous learning and growth.

Use feedback, analytics, and your own reflections to iterate and evolve your content and engagement strategies. What works today might not work tomorrow, so stay adaptable, stay curious, and always be willing to pivot or deepen your approach based on what you learn.

12. **Stay Patient and Persistent:** Building a bingeable content library takes time.

Stay patient and persistent, continuously improving your content and strategies.

**Have you ever been so captivated by a pitch or a presentation that you just couldn't wait to hear more, almost like binge-watching your favorite series?**

There's a certain magic in that moment when everything clicks, and you're hanging on every word, eager to be part of the story. Now, imagine if you could harness that same magic when raising capital for your projects.

Raising capital isn't just about showcasing numbers and forecasts; it's about storytelling, creating a narrative so compelling that investors can't help but want to be a part of it.

It's about painting a picture of the future so vivid and inviting that they're practically reaching for their checkbooks before you've even finished your pitch.

# PICTURE THIS: Vanessas Story

You step into a space that feels more like home than just an apartment. A place where every detail, from the architecture to the landscaping, whispers stories of renewal, community, and a brighter future. This is more than just a building; it's the heart of a thriving neighborhood, brought back to life.

Just a few years ago, this property was nothing more than a forgotten relic, overshadowed by shiny new developments. It stood as a silent witness to better days, blending into the background of urban neglect. But we saw something different. We saw a canvas, waiting for a new story to be written.

Our journey began with a bold vision: to transform this overlooked structure into a vibrant community hub. We partnered with visionary architects and local designers who believed in our dream. Together, we imagined a place that would not only provide modern living spaces but also foster genuine connections and a sense of belonging.

Every step of our journey was fueled by a commitment to excellence and sustainability. We engaged with future residents, listening to their needs and desires. We didn't just want to build apartments; we wanted to create homes. Homes where families could grow, professionals could network, and everyone could find their place.

Today, this vision is a reality. The once-ignored complex now pulses with life and energy.

Families gather in lush green spaces, kids play safely, and professionals thrive in innovative co-working areas. It's a community that reflects our dedication to quality and our passion for creating spaces where people can truly live.

The impact has been profound. Our occupancy rates are soaring, and the project has been celebrated in local media as a transformative success.

We've not only enhanced the lives of our residents but also revitalized the entire neighborhood, driving up property values and sparking new opportunities for growth.

This is where you come in. By investing with us, you're not just supporting a real estate project; you're becoming part of a movement. A movement that values community, sustainability, and the power of transformation. You're investing in a vision that turns neglected spaces into vibrant, thriving communities.

Join us in this journey. Let's create more stories of renewal and impact, together. This is more than just a financial opportunity; it's a chance to be part of something bigger, something meaningful. We're building more than buildings; we're building futures.

But why go the extra mile to create this binge-worthy pitch content?

Well, in the world of investment, you're not just competing for funds; you're competing for attention. Investors are bombarded with opportunities, each one vying for their time and resources. So, how do you stand out? How do you make your opportunity not just seen, but irresistible?

Creating content that resonates on this level is about more than just capturing interest; it's about forging a connection. When investors feel genuinely connected to your vision, your team, and the potential impact of your project, you're no longer just another investment opportunity; you're a story they want to be part of. This connection transforms passive listeners into active, enthusiastic supporters—your vocal advocates in the world of capital.

And here's something exciting: when you create a narrative that's truly compelling, that speaks to the dreams and aspirations of your investors, it doesn't just end with the pitch. Your story begins to travel, powered by the word-of-mouth of those captivated by your vision. Suddenly, you're not the one chasing after investors; they're coming to you, drawn by the buzz and excitement generated by your content.

But let's get real for a moment. Creating this kind of content, this kind of pitch, requires more than just data. It requires passion, creativity, and a deep understanding of your audience. It's about knowing what makes them tick, what fears they need to overcome, and what dreams you can help them achieve. It's about being authentic, showing them the heart behind the numbers, and the vision behind the venture.

So, why invest the effort in creating binge-worthy content for raising capital? Because it's your opportunity to turn your pitch into an experience, one that leaves investors not just interested, but inspired. It's your chance to move beyond the transactional and into the realm of transformational, where your project isn't just a potential investment, but a cause they believe in, a story they want to help write.

So, we've been chatting about the magic of creating content that people can't get enough of, right? But let's shift gears a bit and talk about something that might seem a world apart but is actually tied in closely: raising capital.

And, while we're at it, how about we also explore finding that ideal avatar for your content, whether it's for a podcast or posts on your favorite social platforms?

When you're in the business of raising capital, the principle of creating binge-worthy content doesn't just apply—it's essential. Think about it. Investors, just like any audience, are inundated with pitches, presentations, and proposals day in and day out. So, how do you make yours stand out? How do you make it so engaging, so compelling, that they can't help but want to be a part of your story?

That's where your storytelling chops come into play. Crafting your narrative in a way that not only highlights the potential for returns but also connects on a deeper level with your investors' aspirations, values, and passions can transform your pitch from just another investment opportunity to an irresistible proposition. It's about painting a picture so vivid, so enticing, that they see not just the financial gains but the broader impact and the shared vision.

Now, let's weave in the concept of finding your perfect avatar, especially when you're branching out into podcasts or making waves on social platforms like Facebook, Instagram, and TikTok. Identifying your avatar—your ideal listener or follower—is like picking out a face in a crowded room that you know will light up the moment you start speaking.

It's about understanding not just demographics but psychographics: what drives them, what challenges them, what excites them, and what keeps them up at night.

For your podcast or social media content, this means diving deep into who your audience is and what they care about. Are they seasoned investors looking for the next big thing? Are they enthusiasts of the market you're tapping into? Or are they people passionate about the impact and story behind the investment? Each platform has its vibe, its language, and its culture. Facebook might be more about building community and engaging in deeper discussions, Instagram about captivating visuals and stories, and TikTok about quick, engaging, and often more lighthearted content.

Creating content tailored to your avatar across these platforms means speaking their language, tapping into their interests, and engaging them in a way that feels personal and direct. It's about making them feel seen and heard, whether through a podcast episode that digs into the nitty-gritty of an investment strategy or an Instagram post that showcases the human stories behind your projects.

In essence, whether you're raising capital or building your presence on social media, the key lies in creating content that resonates deeply, engages authentically, and connects personally.

By understanding your audience, crafting your narrative, and speaking directly to their interests and passions, you're not just reaching out; you're inviting them into a journey.

And it's this journey, filled with shared visions and values, that turns listeners into advocates, followers into fans, and potential investors into committed partners.

By shifting the focus towards raising capital, we maintain the essence of creating engaging, compelling content but with a clear emphasis on building narratives that resonate deeply with investors, drawing them into your story and vision.

Getting started is about taking that first step with confidence and curiosity. It's about committing to a process of discovery, creation, and connection. So, take a deep breath, find your voice, and jump into the adventure of becoming truly binge-worthy. The world is waiting to hear what you have to say.

Keep in mind, today's audiences are incredibly savvy and can easily spot content that feels insincere or manipulative. It's vital to reflect on whether your entertainment naturally aligns with your brand's essence or if it comes across as a forced stretch. Always remain authentic to your brand's core values and avoid the temptation to deceive your audience.

Share your successes, sure, but also your challenges and what you've learned. That authenticity? It's a magnet for connections. Social media isn't a billboard. It's a two-way street. Respond to comments, jump into discussions, share your thoughts.

Make every interaction a demonstration of your expertise and passion. That active engagement shows you're not just there to take; you're there to give. Share content that helps your audience – market insights, investment tips, real stories about real deals. Regularly update your audience about your projects. Share insights, challenges, and triumphs. Keep them engaged with your journey

If you're adding value, you're engaging right.

The market's crowded with investors. Stand out by being authentically you, don't hide your ambition. Flaunt it. Your authenticity lies in your relentless pursuit of growth and success. Let your content, your interactions, all scream your ambition to dominate the market.

Got a unique approach to real estate? Great. A specific niche you're passionate about? Even better. Own it, and let it shine through in everything you do.

Stay consistent in your message and your style. That consistency? It's a cornerstone of authenticity. It builds a brand people recognize and trust. Don't just scratch the surface. Dive deep into the aspects of real estate investing that interest you. Whether it's a video on market analysis or a post on investment strategies, go deep.

Show your audience the brains behind the operation. Use your platform to educate but do it with intensity. Host webinars, write in-depth articles, create content that empowers your audience – and positions you as the expert they need!

Depth in understanding leads to depth in engagement It positions you as an expert, someone worth listening to and investing with.

Build genuine relationships in the industry. Attend networking events but go there with the intent to connect on a personal level, not just for business opportunities. You want to be the name on everyone's lips in real estate. Connect with energy and purpose.

At every conference, every meeting, make your presence felt. It's not just about shaking hands; it's about leaving a mark. Be the person who connects people. Introduce investors to opportunities, bring partners together. When you're the hub, the go-to person, your network – and your net worth – skyrockets. Tell the stories behind your investments. The how's and whys, the wins and the losses. These in-depth stories? They resonate, they teach, they connect!

In the world of real estate investment, authentic engagement is about crafting connections that last. It's about trust, human connection, engagement, authenticity, and depth. Think different, think deeper, and create a brand that's as innovative as it is genuine.

That's how you change the game!

## But remember that content consumption doesn't stop at selling.

In this world where everyone's fighting for a slice of your attention, it's easy to think that the end game of content is just to sell. But here's the truth, the real deal that too many miss: the journey doesn't end at the sale. In fact, that's where it really begins. This isn't just about transactions; it's about transformations. It's about building a community, a tribe, a family that's invested not just with their wallets but with their hearts.

When we talk about raising capital for multifamily real estate, or any venture for that matter, it's easy to get caught up in the numbers game. But what if I told you that the real magic happens after the deal is done? That's right. Because every investor you bring on board, every dollar that's invested, it's not just fuel for your project; it's a vote of confidence in your vision, your mission, your story.

So, how do you keep the story going? How do you make sure that content consumption doesn't stop at selling? You make your investors, your audience, part of the narrative. You update them not just on the progress but on the impact. You show them the difference their investment is making, not just on their bank accounts but in the real world, in real communities, in real lives.

But here's where it gets even more interesting. This ongoing narrative, this continuous engagement, it does something powerful. It turns your investors into advocates, your audience into ambassadors. They start sharing your story, your content, because it's now part of their story.

And suddenly, you're not just a person or a company raising capital; you're a movement, a cause, a revolution that people want to be part of.

And in a world where people are bombarded with information, with options, with pitches, the connections you build are your most valuable asset. So, yes, use content to sell, to persuade, to convert. But don't stop there. Use it to connect, to engage, to inspire. Use it to turn transactions into relationships, investments into legacies.

Because at the end of the day, the true measure of success isn't just in the properties you acquire or the returns you generate. It's in the community you build, the lives you touch, the legacy you leave. And that, my friends, is a story worth telling, a story worth being part of.

So, remember, the content journey doesn't stop at selling. If anything, that's where the real adventure begins.

# Binge-Worthy Content Creation Challenge

### Challenge Overview

The purpose of this challenge is to help you practice creating binge-able content. You will go through the process of planning, creating, and promoting a series of content pieces designed to keep your audience engaged and wanting more. This challenge will test your understanding of the principles discussed in the guide and allow you to put them into action.

### Challenge Instructions

**Step 1:** Identify Your Audience

**Objective:** Understand who your target audience is.

**Task:** Create a detailed audience profile. Include demographics (age, gender, location), interests, pain points, and content preferences.

**Deliverable:** Write a one-page summary of your target audience profile.

**Step 2**: Develop a Compelling Storyline

**Objective:** Craft a narrative arc that will captivate your audience.

**Task**: Outline a storyline for a series of 5-10 content pieces. Ensure it has a clear beginning, middle, and end, and includes elements of tension and suspense.

**Deliverable:** Submit a detailed outline of your content series, highlighting key plot points and cliffhangers.

**Step 3:** Plan a Consistent Content Schedule

**Objective:** Establish a reliable posting schedule.

**Task:** Create a content calendar for your series, detailing when each piece will be published and promoted.

**Deliverable:** Provide a content calendar for at least one month, including dates, content titles, and promotion plans.

**Step 4:** Produce High-Quality Content

**Objective:** Ensure your content is of high quality and engaging.

**Task**: Produce the first piece of your content series. Pay attention to production quality, editing, and post-production.

**Deliverable:** Submit the first piece of content (e.g., blog post, video, podcast episode), along with a brief explanation of the production process and any tools used.

**Step 5:** Incorporate Interactive Elements

**Objective:** Make your content interactive and engaging.

**Task:** Add interactive elements to your content, such as polls, quizzes, or calls to action encouraging audience participation.

**Deliverable:** Provide screenshots or descriptions of the interactive elements you incorporated into your first content piece.

**Step 6**: Promote Your Content

**Objective:** Use social media and other platforms to drive traffic to your content.

**Task**: Create a promotional plan for your content series, including social media posts, email newsletters, and any other promotional activities.

**Deliverable:** Submit a promotional plan and examples of promotional materials (e.g., social media posts, email templates).

**Step 7**: Analyze and Improve

**Objective:** Use analytics to measure success and make improvements.

**Task:** After publishing the first three pieces of your content series, analyze their performance using key metrics such as engagement rates, watch time, and feedback.

**Deliverable:** Write a report summarizing your findings and propose at least three improvements based on your analysis.

## Submission Guidelines

- Compile all deliverables into a single document or presentation.
- Ensure each step is clearly labeled and includes all required materials.
- Submit your completed challenge via the designated submission method for review.

## Evaluation Criteria

Completeness: All steps and deliverables are completed and included.

Quality: Content is of high quality and engaging.

Creativity: Interactive elements and storylines are creative and compelling.

Analysis: Insights from analytics are well-thought-out, and proposed improvements are actionable.

## Tips for Success

- ✓ Be thorough in your audience research to create content that truly resonates with them.
- ✓ Focus on creating a strong, engaging storyline to keep your audience hooked.
- ✓ Consistency is key. Stick to your content schedule to build anticipation and reliability.

✓ Quality matters. Invest time in producing and editing your content to a high standard.

✓ Engage with your audience directly to build a sense of community and encourage participation.

✓ Use analytics to continuously improve your content and strategy.

By completing this challenge, you'll gain practical experience in creating binge-able content and be better equipped to engage and grow your audience. Good luck!

**Authenticity Challenge:**

For the next 7 days, commit to showing up authentically in every interaction. Whether it's a business meeting, a casual conversation, or networking, focus on being your true self and speaking from a place of honesty and integrity.

At the end of the week, reflect on how others responded to your authenticity. Did you feel more connected or comfortable?

Share your experiences in the community group, and let's discuss how being genuine has transformed your relationships."

**Key Takeaway**: Authenticity is the cornerstone of genuine engagement which sets the stage for continuous improvement. Growth is a never-ending journey, and being dedicated to it is key.

In Chapter 12, we'll explore the importance of continuous improvement and how dedicating yourself to growth can open up new opportunities in both business and life."

# D = Dedication to Growth:

*"Growth is the great separator between those who succeed and those who do not. When I see a person beginning to separate themselves from the pack, it's almost always due to personal growth."*

—JOHN C. MAXWELL

The final component underscores the importance of continual growth and learning in the real estate sector. So let's dive into something crucial in your journey – the 'D' in The Common T.H.R.E.A.D Method, which stands for 'Dedication to Growth.'

Let's get real: growth isn't optional. If you're not growing, you're stuck. And being stuck? That's how you lose in this game—whether it's real estate or anything else. The "D" in The Common T.H.R.E.A.D. Method is **Dedication to Growth**, and that's the fuel that separates the winners from everyone else.

Growth is messy. It's uncomfortable. You know why? Because it's supposed to be. When you're growing, you're stretching yourself, leveling up, pushing past limits. It's not just about doing more it's about **becoming** more. You're shifting your mindset, expanding your skills, and evolving every day.

Here's the kicker: Growth doesn't just happen. It's intentional. Maxwell nails it when he says, *"Change is inevitable, but growth is optional."* Things are always going to change—markets, trends, circumstances. You? You have a choice. You can ride the wave or get left behind. If you're not choosing growth every single day, you're choosing stagnation. Period.

## Growth is a Higher Frequency

Here's something people don't talk about enough: growth operates on a higher frequency. Think about it: When you're in a growth mindset, everything shifts. You feel more alive, more energized, like you're vibrating on a different level. Growth is a vibe. It's a different energy that makes everything start to click.

When you're stuck, you're operating on a low frequency. You're seeing the same things, feeling the same frustrations, and making the same mistakes.

But when you start growing, you level up, and suddenly, the game changes. You start to see opportunities you didn't even know were there. You're not stuck in old thought patterns anymore—you're free. That's what growth does. It tunes you into a higher frequency where you can see, do, and achieve more than you ever thought possible.

Maxwell says, *"Change is inevitable, but growth is optional."* But when you choose growth, you're tuning into a frequency where success, fulfillment, and bigger opportunities are all within reach. It's like moving from a cramped room into a wide-open space. There's room to breathe, explore, and grow. And when you operate at that higher frequency, things start to happen.

## Adapt or Die: Flexibility Is Key

Look, growth is not a straight line. It's more like a rollercoaster, and you'd better be ready to hang on. Things will go sideways, obstacles will pop up, and guess what? You've gotta roll with it. That's the game.

Being adaptable means staying on your toes. When things don't go as planned (and let's be honest, they rarely do), you can either whine about it or pivot and keep moving forward. The winners? They're the ones who adjust. They're the ones who see change as an opportunity, not a roadblock. Flexibility isn't just about staying in the game—it's about **winning** the game.

Maxwell gets it: Real growth happens when you're uncomfortable. You don't grow when things are easy; you grow when you're pushed, when the pressure's on, when you're forced to think and act differently. That's why adaptability is crucial. If you can't pivot when things change, you're toast.

## Courage Over Comfort

Now, let's talk about fear for a second. If you're comfortable, you're not growing. Full stop. If you want real growth, you've got to embrace the discomfort. Lean into it. Don't run from it. Maxwell says, *"Courage isn't the absence of fear; it's acting in spite of it."* That's how you grow. You've gotta take risks, make the tough calls, and face the fear head-on.

Listen, the path to success is full of uncertainty. You're not always going to have all the answers, but that's okay. What's important is that you keep moving forward, even when the road ahead isn't clear. That's where the magic happens—on the other side of your comfort zone. You push through the discomfort, and before you know it, you're not just surviving challenges—you're **thriving** through them.

## Growth is the Journey, Not the Destination

Let me break it down: Growth isn't a destination. You don't wake up one day and think, *"Cool, I've grown enough. I'm done."* Nah, it's a constant process. It's like setting sail without a map. You're going to hit rough waters, face storms, and question why you even started this journey. But that's the point.

If you only do what's comfortable, you're going to stay exactly where you are. Growth happens when you push yourself, when you dive into the unknown, when you take risks. Starting that new business, pitching that big idea, switching careers—whatever it is, these are the leaps that get you to the next level.

The road to growth is never smooth. You're going to get knocked down. You'll face setbacks. But here's the thing: Each challenge you overcome makes you stronger. It builds your resilience. Keep your eyes on the horizon, know what you're aiming for, and when the seas get rough, remember why you set sail in the first place.

Oh, and one more thing—flexibility is everything. The game changes. Market conditions shift. Your ability to adjust? That's what's going to make or break you. You've got to be quick on your feet, ready to change course if necessary.

If you're not adapting, you're falling behind. Period.

The ones who win? They're the ones who adjust, pivot, and keep moving forward no matter what gets thrown at them. Flexibility isn't just about survival—it's about coming out stronger on the other side.

## Shopify: A Masterclass in Growth

You want to see growth in action? Look at Shopify. They've got growth baked into their DNA, not just for themselves but for every entrepreneur on their platform.

Tobi Lütke, the founder, said it best: *"We want to make entrepreneurship as easy as possible so anyone, anywhere can start and scale a business."*

Shopify's entire business model is based on **helping other people grow**. They're not just sitting there collecting checks. They're constantly pushing to make their platform better, faster, and more efficient, because they know their success is tied to their merchants' success. When you succeed, they succeed. It's that simple.

That's why they're constantly innovating new features, AI-driven tools, better payment systems—you name it. Shopify's out here removing barriers so entrepreneurs can do what they do best: hustle. They're not just a tool; they're a full-on **growth engine**. And that's the mindset you need to adopt: If you're helping others grow, you'll grow too.

**Growth is also about curiosity. It's asking questions, not just to find immediate answers, but to uncover deeper truths. Why do certain things work the way they do? How can we do better, be better? This curiosity is what drives innovation, what propels us forward. It's what makes leaders stand out.**

When we talk about growth, it's essential to recognize the role of curiosity—it's like the engine that drives us to keep exploring and pushing boundaries. Curiosity isn't just about asking questions for the sake of answers. It's about being intrigued by what you don't know. It's about that itch to dig deeper and uncover layers beneath the surface.

Think of it this way: when you're curious, every question is a doorway to a new room of knowledge and insight. You might start with a simple "why does this happen?" and suddenly, you're down a rabbit hole, exploring "how" and "what if." It's this journey of questioning that broadens your understanding, not just piling up facts.

This curiosity it's not passive. It's an active, engaging force. It makes you reach out, read more, talk to people, experiment, and even make mistakes. And here's the kicker—it's those deeper truths you uncover along the way that often lead to the best ideas and solutions. They don't just appear; they're unearthed through your relentless questioning and exploration.

In conversations, this might look like not settling for the first answer you get. It's about probing further, asking follow-up questions, and being genuinely interested in understanding different perspectives. This is how you get to the heart of matters, whether you're learning a new skill, solving a problem at work, or just trying to understand someone better.

And the beauty of it? Curiosity keeps things fresh. It keeps you engaged with life, constantly learning and adapting. It's not just about accumulating knowledge—it's about expanding your perspective and continuously evolving. That's what growth is really about, isn't it? It's not a destination; it's this exciting, ongoing journey of discovery. So, let's keep asking, keep wondering, and see where this curiosity takes us.

But here's an important aspect about growth—it's not just a personal marathon; it's a relay race. It's a collective effort where we pass the baton back and forth, learning from each other, sharing insights, and soaking up different perspectives like sponges. This isn't something you do in isolation. It thrives on interaction and collaboration.

It's like being part of a mastermind group, where each member brings something unique to the table.

Think about it. When you share your experiences or listen to someone else's story, it's not just about swapping tales—it's an exchange of wisdom. You get to see through someone else's lens, challenge your assumptions, and expand your own understanding. It's like each person you interact with adds a new layer to your perspective, helping you see the world in a more nuanced way.

And it's not just about learning from people who are like you or who agree with you. The real growth often comes from engaging with those who challenge you, who think differently. It might be uncomfortable at times, sure, but that discomfort? That's where the magic happens. It's where you're pushed to reconsider, to adapt, and to grow.

Let's not forget the strength that lies in diversity. Each person brings their unique flavor to the table, creating a richer, more vibrant concoction of ideas and experiences.

It's like a potluck of perspectives, where everyone contributes something different, and together, it just works—it's better than anything you could whip up on your own.

So, embrace this journey with others. Ask questions, share your thoughts, listen deeply, and be willing to change your mind. Remember, growth isn't just about moving forward on your own; it's about moving forward together, building a community of learners and thinkers who inspire and push each other to be better. That's how we all grow—not in isolation, but in concert, with and through each other.

Now, let's talk about the dedication part. Growth doesn't happen overnight. It requires persistence, resilience, and, above all, dedication. It's like planting a seed. You water it, give it sunlight, but most importantly, you give it time. The growth of that seed – your growth – is a testament to your dedication and patience.

This isn't just a fancy term; it's the backbone of your success, especially in something as dynamic as real estate investment. Think about it. The world of real estate, particularly multifamily investments, is ever-changing. The market today is not what it was ten years ago, and it won't be the same ten years from now. Your growth should mirror this constant state of change.

Markets evolve, tenant needs shift, and investment strategies adapt. If you're not dedicated to growing – not just in your portfolio size but in your knowledge, skills, and understanding of the market – you're going to be left behind.

But here's the best part—dedication to growth? It's not boring. It's an adventure. Every day, you've got a new opportunity to get better, to sharpen your tools, and to keep pushing the limits of what's possible. Treat your real estate portfolio like a garden. Some days you're planting seeds, other days you're pulling weeds. But every single day, you're doing something to push growth forward.

And let me be clear growth isn't always linear. Some days you'll make huge leaps; other days, it'll feel like a slow grind. That's normal. But as long as you're dedicated, as long as you keep moving forward, you'll get there.

But the key is to keep moving even when you experience...

**Imposter Syndrome** that insidious feeling of self-doubt that creeps in despite your obvious successes and achievements. It doesn't discriminate – it can affect anyone, anywhere, at any stage in their journey. But guess what? You have the power to crush it! to understand it, tackle it and over Imposter Syndrome, with powerful insights, personal stories, and practical strategies!

Let's take a minute and dive into the raw, unfiltered fear I felt the first time I asked my very first investor for money. We're talking about the crippling fear of being an IMPOSTOR.

The deal I'm talking about was monumental. This was Monopoly on steroids—the deal that could change everything. The kind that shifts your trajectory if you and your partners nail it and bring it to closing. And let's not even get started on the 5-7 years of managing the property, keeping your promises to investors, and ensuring those quarterly returns are paid out just as you said they would be.

No, what I'm getting at is the imposter syndrome. That annoying little voice in your head whispering, "You haven't done a deal this size before. Who are you to ask for $50-$100 thousand dollars?" The phone on my desk felt like it weighed a ton, glaring at me, "I'm too damn heavy to pick up. The person on the other end is just going to say NO. So why not just go downstairs, grab that leftover pizza from last night, and stick it in the microwave?"

I was on a diet, trying to lose that eternal 10 pounds, but instead of giving in, I decided to lift some metaphorical weights. I went back to my desk, picked up that 2-ton phone sitting there, and as my fingers were about to press the CALL button, I hesitated again.

At that moment, I pulled up the Deal Analyzer, reviewed the returns on the deal I was about to offer as a gift to this investor, and finally, I made the decision to press that call button.

I was secretly hoping the investor wouldn't pick up so I could retreat to the kitchen and warm up that pizza. But to my utter surprise (and probably because the universe had something to do with it), the investor answered.

OMG, now what do I do? First, I quickly told myself, "I am ready, prepared, and confident. I've got this!"

I then incorporated what I teach in this book. I used The Common T.H.R.E.A.D Method. This wasn't a sales call; it was an exploratory conversation to see what we had in common. Turns out, we both had a love for travel and finding local restaurants off the beaten path with good music and wine. We both dreamed of traveling to Tuscany to find those places. But the investor had two kids going to college and wasn't sure how he could afford both based on his salary.

From our conversation, I had several questions running through my head, but the wheel in my mind stopped at, "Could you tell me about a past investment that you're particularly proud of, and what made it stand out for you?"

I asked him this question because the deal I was offering was a Unicorn—a 96-unit apartment in a prime location that not only cash flows every quarter but also provides a great equity position when we sell the property.

As we continued talking, I could feel his excitement building. He started asking all the right questions, diving deeper into the details. By the end of our conversation, not only had I secured his investment, but I had also built a solid relationship based on mutual interests and trust. That's the key takeaway here: when you're authentic, prepared, and focused on building genuine connections, you can overcome that fear and achieve incredible results.

So, next time you're staring down that giant phone, remember this story. Embrace the fear, prepare like your life depends on it, and connect on a human level. That's how you turn those intimidating calls into game-changing deals. That's how you win.

Imposter Syndrome stems from a mix of early experiences, societal pressures, and personal perfectionism. You might think your success is just luck, but it's time to change that narrative and own your achievements.

**How It Shows Up:**

**Perfectionism:** You set sky-high standards and beat yourself up over minor mistakes.

**Overworking:** You feel like you have to work twice as hard to prove your worth.

**Dismissing Praise:** You brush off compliments and downplay your successes.

## Recognizing Imposter Syndrome

Recognizing Imposter Syndrome is the first step to conquering it.

**Look out for these signs:**
- Feeling Like a Fraud: Constantly fearing that you'll be "found out."
- Attributing Success to Luck: Thinking your achievements are just a fluke.
- Overachieving: Pushing yourself to the brink to prove you're worthy.
- Fear of Failure: Avoiding new challenges because you fear you won't measure up.

- Comparing Yourself to Others: Constantly feeling inferior to those around you.

## Self-Assessment Questions

- Ask yourself these questions to see if you're dealing with Imposter Syndrome:
- Do I downplay my achievements and attribute them to luck or help from others?
- Am I afraid of being exposed as a fraud, despite evidence of my competence?
- Do I feel I must work harder than others to prove my worth?
- Am I reluctant to accept praise or recognition for my work?

## Overcoming Imposter Syndrome

### Recognize and Reframe:

Awareness is your superpower. Recognize those negative patterns and reframe them.

Challenge those irrational beliefs and replace them with empowering thoughts.

### Reprogram Your Mind:

Use Cognitive Behavioral Therapy (CBT) techniques to rewire your brain. Replace self-doubt with self-belief. Say it loud and clear: "I am capable and deserving!"

### Build a Support System:

Share your feelings with mentors, friends, or a therapist. Surround yourself with people who lift you up and remind you of your worth.

# Celebrate Your Wins:

Keep a success journal and regularly document your achievements. Celebrate every win, no matter how small. Each step forward is proof of your growth and capability.

### Powerful Strategies to Crush Imposter Syndrome

**1** **Acknowledge Your Feelings:** Recognize that imposter feelings are normal and acknowledge them without judgment.

**2** **Share Your Experience:** Open up to trusted friends, mentors, or colleagues about your feelings. Sharing can alleviate the burden and provide reassurance.

**3** **Focus on Facts:** Keep a record of your accomplishments, positive feedback, and moments of success. Reviewing these can provide a reality check against negative thoughts.

**4** **Accept Mistakes as Part of Learning:** Understand that everyone makes mistakes and that they are a natural part of the learning process.

**5** **Set Realistic Goals:** Break tasks into manageable steps and set achievable goals. This can prevent feelings of being overwhelmed and help build confidence.

# Positive Self-Talk to Silence the Doubts

**Embrace Your Power:**

**Practice Self-Compassion:** Treat yourself with the same kindness and understanding that you would offer a friend in a similar situation.

**Acknowledge Your Achievements:**

- I've earned my success through hard work and dedication!
- My achievements are a testament to my skills and effort!

**Reframe Negative Thoughts:**

- Mistakes are my steppingstones to greatness!
- Perfection isn't the goal; progress is!

**Focus on Growth:**

- I am constantly evolving and growing!
- Every challenge is an opportunity to shine!

**Practice Self-Compassion:**

- I am enough just as I am!
- I am worthy of all the success and happiness in my life!

**Challenge Irrational Beliefs:**

- Feeling like an imposter is a common experience, but it doesn't define me!
- I have the skills, talent, and drive to succeed!

### Celebrate Successes:

- I am proud of all I've achieved!
- My hard work is paying off, and I deserve to celebrate!

### Focus on Strengths:

- I bring unique strengths and perspectives to everything I do!
- My contributions make a difference!

### Before a Presentation:

- I am ready, prepared, and confident. I've got this!
- Nervousness is just excitement in disguise!

### After Receiving Praise:

- I accept this compliment with gratitude. I earned it!
- Positive feedback is a reflection of my hard work and talent!

### When Facing a New Challenge:

- This is my chance to grow and excel!
- I am capable and ready to conquer this challenge!

### Daily Affirmations:

- Start your day with powerful affirmations. Repeat them and feel the energy surge through you: "I am strong, I am capable, I am unstoppable."

### Mindfulness and Meditation:

- Stay grounded with mindfulness and meditation.
- Breathe deeply and remind yourself of your power and worth.

### Visual Reminders:

- Surround yourself with positive quotes and affirmations.
- Let them be constant reminders of your greatness.

### Seek Support:

- Build a circle of champions who uplift and support you. Together, you are unstoppable!

Imposter Syndrome may try to hold you back, but you have the power to break free. By recognizing its roots, challenging its hold, and embracing your true potential, you can conquer self-doubt and rise to new heights. Remember, the journey to self-acceptance and confidence is ongoing, but with determination and support, you can achieve greatness.

So, here's my challenge to you: How will you dedicate yourself to growth today? Maybe it's learning a new aspect of the real estate market, or perhaps it's mentoring someone eager to get into the field. Whatever it is, make that commitment. The path to success is a constant climb, and your dedication to growth is your surest step forward. Your future self – and your investment portfolio – will thank you.

Remember, in the world of real estate, and in life, the only way to truly excel is to keep growing. Stay hungry, stay foolish, and let's crush it together.

As we continue on our respective journeys, let's make a commitment to ourselves – to remain dedicated to our growth, to be lifelong learners. Let's embrace the challenges, celebrate the victories (no matter how small), and most importantly, let's support each other in this journey.

So, what's one step you can take today towards your growth? Remember, it doesn't have to be big. Sometimes, the smallest step can lead to the greatest journey. Let's take that step together.

Alright, let's talk about raising capital for multi-family deals because this is where the rubber meets the road. You want to get into real estate? You want to scale big? It's not just about finding properties; it's about securing the bag—getting that capital to make your moves.

First off, understand this: raising capital is a grind. It's like planting a seed. You don't just plant that seed and expect it to grow overnight. No way. You gotta water it, nurture it, give it sunlight. In the world of real estate, that means networking, building relationships, and proving your worth every single day.

You think investors are going to just throw money at you because you've got a hot tip on a property? Think again. You need to show them dedication. You need to show them you're not just another guy with a dream but someone who's all in, someone who's done their homework, knows their market, and has a solid plan to turn their investment into a profit.

And here's the key: be relentless. When it comes to raising capital, it's about persistence. You get a no? You go again. You refine your pitch, you come back stronger. You learn what resonates with investors—what makes them tick, what scares them, what gets them excited. Then you use that knowledge. Tailor your approach, hit them with the facts, the figures, the strategy that shows why your multi-family deal is the one to back.

Remember, every interaction, every meeting, every pitch is a chance to learn and adapt. Just like watering that seed, you're nurturing these relationships.

This isn't a one-off; it's about building trust over time. Show your investors that their money isn't just a transaction to you—it's a partnership. You're in it for the long haul, and you're just as committed to their success as you are to your own.

### Key Point 1: Growth as a Frequency

**Expansion**: Growth isn't just a goal—it's a frequency you need to *tune into*. It's not something you check off a list; it's an energy, a way of living that you consciously engage with every day. When you're locked into the frequency of growth, you're aligned with progress and forward momentum. Think of it like this: just as you'd adjust a radio dial to get the clearest signal, growth requires constant tuning. You've got to stay adaptable, keep learning, and embrace change if you want to stay in sync with that frequency.

**John C. Maxwell's Input**: Maxwell emphasizes that **growth is intentional**. He once said, *"You'll never change your life until you change something you do daily. The secret of your success is found in your daily routine."* Growth, then, isn't some magical event—it's about making intentional decisions every single day that move you closer to who you want to be. It's about living in that frequency of learning, even when it's uncomfortable.

**Your Perspective**: When you commit to the frequency of growth, you're not coasting—you're actively seeking out ways to level up. It's not about being perfect; it's about showing up consistently, learning from your experiences, and pushing yourself to evolve. Tuning into growth means accepting that it's going to be uncomfortable sometimes, but it's also the only path that leads to real transformation.

### Key Point 2: Maxwell's Perspective on Growth

John C. Maxwell doesn't just talk about growth—he lives it. He says, *"Growth inside fuels growth outside."* That means growth isn't just something that happens in your career or bank account—it starts inside you. It's mental. It's emotional. It's personal. If you're not growing on the inside, you're not going to see it on the outside. That's why it's crucial to develop self-awareness, focus on your mindset, and work on your inner game if you want to experience real, lasting growth.

This resonates so deeply because it's easy to get caught up in external results—money, status, success. But real growth? That comes from the work you do internally. It's about building resilience, expanding your capacity to handle challenges, and staying grounded in who you are. When you invest in yourself, the results naturally show up in your life and business. Growth isn't just about numbers going up—it's about *you* going up.

## Key Point 3: Personal and Professional Parallels

Growth doesn't just happen in your career or your personal life—it happens everywhere. It's like a ripple effect. The habits you develop in one area spill over into others. If you're dedicated to growth in your business, that mindset is going to bleed into your relationships, your health, your finances—everything. There's no such thing as compartmentalizing growth. Once you're tuned into that frequency, it touches every part of your life.

Maxwell talks a lot about how **growth compounds over time**. He's said, *"Small disciplines repeated with consistency every day lead to great achievements gained slowly over time."* This is critical to understand because real growth doesn't happen in leaps—it happens in layers. Every time you push a little harder, every time you learn a new skill or adapt to a challenge, you're adding to that foundation. And before you know it, the ripple effect has taken over your entire life.

This is why growth feels exponential. You might not notice the impact immediately, but when you look back after a few months or years, you see how far you've come. That's the power of staying committed to the frequency of growth—it doesn't just help you level up in one area; it lifts *everything* up.

## Key Point 4: Adaptability and Change

Here's the truth: If you want to grow, you've got to be willing to *adapt*. Growth means constantly navigating new territories—new challenges, new information, new setbacks. It's not a straight path; it's more like surfing.

You've got to learn how to ride the wave, pivot when needed, and stay balanced through the ups and downs. That's what growth demands: flexibility, openness, and the willingness to keep adjusting.

Maxwell says, *"Change is inevitable. Growth is optional."* What he's getting at is this: change is going to happen whether you like it or not. The question is, are you going to grow through it? Most people resist change because it's uncomfortable, but those who thrive are the ones who embrace it as part of the growth process. They see it as an opportunity to evolve, not as a setback.

Look, change isn't always pretty. It's messy. It's unpredictable. But if you can adapt, if you can lean into that discomfort, you'll come out the other side stronger, smarter, and more resilient. That's the frequency of growth—it's not about avoiding challenges, it's about learning how to navigate them like a pro. Flexibility is your secret weapon in a world that's constantly shifting.

## Key Point 5: Dedication to Helping Others Grow

One of the most powerful aspects of the frequency of growth is that it's contagious. When you grow, the people around you start to grow too. Whether it's your team, your family, or your network, your dedication to your own growth inspires others to rise to the occasion. That's the real win: creating an environment where everyone is leveling up together.

Maxwell has always been a huge advocate for lifting others up as you grow.

He says, *"A leader is one who knows the way, goes the way, and shows the way."*

Growth isn't just about your personal success—it's about paving the path for others. The more you grow, the more you can guide and mentor the people around you, creating a ripple effect of growth in your community.

This is why growth is about more than just self-improvement—it's about creating a movement. When you're dedicated to growth, you're not just focused on your own journey. You're focused on how you can help others rise too. Whether it's sharing your insights, supporting your team, or mentoring someone who's a few steps behind, you're playing the long game. And in that game, everyone wins.

**Growth Mindset Challenge:**

For the next 7 days, dedicate yourself to learning something new that will contribute to your personal or professional growth. This could be reading a book, attending a webinar, or practicing a new skill.

At the end of the week, reflect on what you've learned and how it can be applied to your journey. Share your biggest learning moment in the group and discuss how this new knowledge has inspired your growth.

**Key Takeaway**: Keep grinding, keep learning, and stay dedicated. Raising capital for multi-family deals isn't for the faint-hearted. It takes guts, it takes grit, and above all, it takes dedication. Are you ready to put in the work? Are you ready to make those deals happen? Let's get it done. Be the hustler I know you can be, and turn those real estate dreams into solid, profitable realities.

With growth comes the ability to spot opportunities. In Chapter 13, we'll look at how to identify common *T.H.R.E.A.D.s* in conversations and create opportunities through shared interests and passions

Now that we've dug into the relentless dedication it takes to grow—whether that's in real estate or any aspect of your life—let's shift gears. Growth isn't just about external success; it's about mastering your internal game. Because no matter how much you hustle, if you can't control your emotions, your state, and how you show up every day, you're playing a losing hand.

In the next chapter, Désirée Ferrari Agüero explores how to harness the power of your emotional state to create instant shifts that can change the outcome of any situation. This is the next level—the difference between grinding and thriving. Ready to unlock it? Let's go.

# CHAPTER 13

# Subconscious Influence:
## *The Secret Power Behind Your Results*

*"You are like a captain navigating a ship. You must give the right orders, thoughts and images to your subconscious which controls and governs all your experiences."*

—Joseph Murphy

## Your State: The 30-Second Shift That Changes Everything

**Want to be able to create an instant shift in your mood and the direction of your day?** Whether you're heading into an important meeting, preparing for a negotiation, or just trying to push through a tough day, you've already been tapping into this power—sometimes without even realizing it. But once you learn to feel it consciously, especially in those high-stakes moments, you'll become unstoppable in both your career and life.

Did you know that your body language and posture send powerful signals to your brain about how you're feeling? The way you hold yourself—how you breathe, your gestures, even the expressions on your face—triggers powerful changes in your mental and emotional state. Your mental and emotional state, shaped by how you carry your body, actually determines the emotions you feel—not the other way around. Once you understand this, you unlock the power to shift your emotions whenever you choose.

Everything starts with how you show up—how you feel in your body and mind influences how you connect with others and with yourself. When your state is aligned, you radiate trust and confidence, two critical pillars of building success-ful relationships, like we talked about in earlier chapters. It's about stepping into your power so you can weave those deeper, more authentic connections—both in your personal and professional life.

We often think we slump, sigh, or tense up because of how we feel. But here's the game-changer: it's actually the opposite. Your brain senses your mood based on how you're holding your body. So, when you want to change your mood, the fastest, most effective way is to change your body first. This simple shift in your physiology is the key to mastering any emotional state on demand.

Many of us fall into mental and emotional patterns that trap us in the same emotional loops—whether it's stress, doubt, or frustration. These emotions show up repeatedly, even when we're desperate to break free from them. And those patterns aren't just mental—they're also ingrained in how we physically carry ourselves, often becoming habitual postures that reinforce our emotional states.

Tony Robbins is a master at teaching instant state changes. You can liter-ally *feel* your emotional state change by shifting your physiology—and it can happen in as little as 30 seconds. Once your body shifts, you'll sense your energy, mood, and focus shift with it. It's that fast!

Mastering your state gives you control over your energy and presence, allow-ing you to show up in a way that builds trust and rapport—two core elements of the T.H.R.E.A.D. framework. When you're in control of how you feel, you're better equipped to connect with others, respond with emotional intelligence, and create meaningful interactions.

Think about the last time you felt really anxious or overwhelmed. Your breathing was probably shallow, and your body tense, right? Now, imagine the sensation of deliberately slowing your breath and taking deep, intentional breaths. Sense the calm that washes over you. You've likely noticed how that instantly calms your mind. That's because your *body* is sending your *brain* a message: "We're safe. We can relax now."

It works the same way with shifting your emotional state. When you adjust your posture, even something as subtle as lifting your head or relaxing your shoulders, you're creating a feeling in your body that sends a new signal to your brain: "We're confident. We've got this." Your brain responds by shifting your focus to match your new posture. And before long, your internal language—the way you talk to yourself—begins to change. Instead of telling yourself, "I'm stressed," or "I can't handle this," you'll start feeling thoughts like, "I'm in control," or "I've got this."

This ability to manage your state is critical to The T.H.R.E.A.D. Method. By consciously choosing how you show up, you set the stage for authentic communication and deeper connections.

Once you master this technique, you can feel whatever emotions you want, whenever you want. You'll be able to stop feeling the emotions that drag you down or prevent you from handling situations the way you really want to.

I'll never forget the first time I experienced this firsthand. At one of Tony Robbins' live events, I learned how to change my state in an instant. It was incredible. I went from feeling completely overwhelmed to calm and confident in just a few seconds. Before then, I had no idea something so simple could have such a massive impact on my life. Then I could see how easily I had been creating my own moods, whether good or bad. It's like flipping a switch that changes everything—how you feel, how you think, and how you show up.

In the workbook, I'll teach you the exact steps to change your state in 30 seconds, so you can experience the power of this technique for yourself. Now that you know how this works, just imagine the possibilities! You can use it to your advantage in a high-stakes meeting, negotiation, or any moment of stress. Master the ability to consciously shift your state in an instant...and *watch the magic happen!*

# How the Words We Choose Control Us or Empower Us

**What if I told you that the words you choose—whether spoken out loud or in your own mind—are shaping the reality of your life every single day?** When you say the words out loud, their effect multiplies exponentially. The words you speak (or even just *think*) stir up emotions within you, and those emotions direct your focus.

Think of The T.H.R.E.A.D. Method and language as two sides of the same coin. The T.H.R.E.A.D. Method equips you with the insight to understand the deeper dynamics of a situation, giving you the awareness needed to recognize patterns, emotions, and underlying beliefs. Language then becomes your tool to shape and steer those dynamics. Together, they empower you to influence both your internal state and how others respond, helping you navigate conversations and situations with greater intention and confidence.

Imagine you're in a negotiation and sense hesitation from the other party. By applying The T.H.R.E.A.D. Method, you gain clarity on the emotions at play, and with the right language—words of reassurance, collaboration, and clarity—you guide the conversation toward a positive outcome. Just as you use the method to read the deeper dynamics of a situation, your language allows you to direct those dynamics toward success.

When you use words that excite or inspire you, those positive emotions build and, suddenly, you're creating a euphoric experience. On the other hand, the same process can lead to negative outcomes if the words you choose trigger frustration, fear, or doubt. Before long, you're zeroing in on more things that justify and intensify those emotions, creating a perfect storm for a downward spiral, or even an emotional outburst. You might notice this when you replay negative conversations in your mind or repeat certain phrases that keep you stuck in a particular feeling.

Most of the words you use are from habit, programmed into your subconscious mind. It knows the words you use the most, so you continue to use them without realizing that you're repeating patterns that either empower or control you—every single day.

When you say the words out loud—especially to others—their effects are intensified. The trajectory of a situation shifts quickly and powerfully in the direction of your thoughts and feelings, whether they lead to an uplifting, empowering path or a downward spiral of frustration. Your words now impact the people around you, shifting their energy and emotions, and together, your collective thoughts and feelings intensify. You're creating the exact scenario you're thinking about, whether it's something you want or something you don't want.

This brings us to a simple truth: **What you think about, you bring about.** If you anticipate that a situation will not go well, your actions and decisions will reflect that belief. Your belief will influence what you think is possible, and you will choose your words and actions based on that limited perspective. These choices, in turn, have a profound impact on the outcome. And when it doesn't go well, you may think, "I knew it," without realizing that *your* focus and language played a key role in creating that result.

But here's the powerful truth: **You can drastically shift your focus and influence the outcome.** By changing your language, you can shift from fear-based thinking to empowering actions. Do you want to navigate life from a place of fear, or make choices and take actions from a place of empowerment?

Words don't need to be spoken aloud to influence you. When you think a thought, it creates a neural pathway in your brain. The more you think that thought, the stronger the neural pathway becomes, solidifying a pattern or habit in your way of thinking. When you tie strong emotion to a thought, it rapidly accelerates the strengthening of that pathway. Now, imagine how quickly these pathways become strong when you repeatedly think the same thoughts *and* they're tied to intense emotions! As these neural pathways strengthen, the thoughts become automatic—you don't even have to think about it. Your brain already knows the direction to take, reinforcing the same patterns over and over again.

But here's the exciting part: **You can change these pathways!** Just as easily as your brain has reinforced negative or limiting beliefs, you can start building new, empowering pathways with intentional language and thought patterns. With repetition, positive self-talk can reshape your brain, opening up new emotional responses and possibilities. **You** are in charge of this process—it's literally a matter of rewiring your mind to create the outcomes you desire.

Here's my invitation to you: **Look around at your life and notice the patterns that keep repeating but don't serve you.** Think of a situation that consistently stirs negative emotions in you. What are the thoughts you tend to think about that situation, about the people involved, or about how things are likely to go? What are the words you tend to use regarding this situation? How do you feel when you use those words? Are you aware of your power to change the situation? What words could you choose instead that would shift the emotion?

What could you say to yourself that feels less emotionally charged and allows you to see the situation from a more neutral or open perspective? When you change your internal dialogue, you change the pattern of your situation. Change just one mechanism in a machine, and the whole system functions differently. The same is true in life—when you shift how you show up, the entire situation transforms.

**You are literally the creator of your life, and it begins with the language you use.**

Let's explore how different words can dramatically alter perception. Tony Robbins illustrates this beautifully when he describes how using words like furious, enraged, or pissed off immediately intensifies negative emotions—and that just fuels the fire. Notice how your body reacts just by thinking these words: furious, enraged, pissed off.

**Here is your true power.** I began practicing this in my own life during moments where I would normally react with intense emotion. Instead of diving into frustration or anger, I started using neutral or even disarming phrases like, "That's interesting!" or "Isn't that fascinating!" Almost immediately, I noticed how the tension melted away, and I became *genuinely curious* about what was really happening. By stepping back, I gave myself space to observe the situation objectively, rather than letting my emotions take over.

When you approach situations with curiosity instead of judgment, it opens up new possibilities. You start to notice things you hadn't seen before. So ask yourself: "When I step back and observe, what do I notice? What might be going on with the other person that I haven't considered yet?" Coming into any situation with this perspective will completely shift your experience, and the outcome.

You may not be able to control the situation, and you definitely can't control others. But you *can* control how you respond. As Tony Robbins says, **"Master your emotions, master your life."**

Here's how this looks in real life. Let's say you're a real estate investor who usually thinks, "This deal is going to be tough," or "I'm not sure I'll get the terms I want." That mindset brings anxiety or doubt, which impacts how you show up in negotiating the deal. The other side picks up on that energy, and suddenly the deal feels tense or harder than it needs to be...for everyone.

Now let's replay the same scenario, this time shifting to a different mindset. Before the negotiation, you consciously shift your thoughts to, "I'm confident and ready," or "I'm excited to show how this deal will benefit both sides." You walk into the meeting calm, focused, and sure of yourself. Instead of saying, "I hope we can agree," you now say, "Here's how these terms are a win for both of us." This subtle shift changes the entire vibe. It turns the negotiation into a collaborative effort rather than a battle, opening up space for new possibilities.

By changing your internal language, you shifted your state, which changed both your energy and the words you used. (More on energy and state later!) And all this together changed how people responded to you. Now you're building trust, showing confidence, and creating more successful outcomes.

From today forward, start paying close attention to how you feel in your body as you think different thoughts or use different words, whether in your own mind or out loud. Do you feel any heaviness, tightness, or discomfort? If so, pause and notice the specific thoughts or words that tend to trigger those sensations. How do you feel when you think those thoughts or use those words? More importantly, how would you *like* to feel instead?

Remember, when you control yourself, that will change the outcome.

Consider this: What thoughts could you shift to that would support the feelings you want to experience? Even if they don't feel realistic or likely in this moment, are you open to exploring them as possibilities? After all, something only becomes impossible when *you* decide that it is. As long as you remain open to the possibility, it stays within reach.

The same goes for the words you use. What words could you *choose* that support how you'd like things to go or how you'd feel if everything worked out exactly as you want?

This isn't about forcing positivity; it's about becoming aware of the language that holds you back and intentionally choosing words and thoughts that move you toward the outcomes you want. **This is where your power lies**—not in control or force, but in the real power of choosing the words and thoughts that will shape your experience. Practice catching the words that stir up the feelings you don't want, and consciously replace them with words that align with what you do want.

Now that you have a deeper understanding of the powerful impact of your words, it's time to put this knowledge into action! I'm thrilled for you to jump into the workbook, where practical exercises and transformative tools will bring this work to life. This is where the real magic unfolds—where you turn your new insights into real results...in your life! Your journey to mastering your language begins here, and the workbook is your bridge to creating those powerful shifts you've been learning about. LET'S GOOOO!!!

# Your Life is a Mirror of Your Beliefs

What if everything you believed about money, love, success, and yourself was shaping your entire life, right now? Imagine waking up tomorrow and realizing everything in your life is a direct reflection *of what you believe*. Your brain filters out the noise, constantly seeking evidence to prove your beliefs right, even if those beliefs are outdated or untrue. So the question is, are your beliefs empowering you to live your best life, or are they silently holding you back?

Think about the last time you walked into a situation, whether it was a business deal or a difficult conversation, and you *expected* it to be tough. As soon as something didn't go smoothly, your brain jumped to conclusions: "I knew it. This was going to be difficult." From that point on, your mind locked on, reinforcing the belief that things were hard, and you found yourself reacting as though the situation was impossible.

On the other hand, imagine walking into the same situation believing everything would go well. Even when bumps arose, your brain stayed focused on finding solutions. Your *belief* in a positive outcome guided your responses, allowing you to navigate challenges effortlessly.

This is the power of belief. Your brain will always find evidence to match what you believe, whether your belief supports you or shackles you.

Beliefs don't just influence your internal state—they shape how you relate to others. One of the core principles of The T.H.R.E.A.D. Method is recognizing how your beliefs affect the connections you make and the way you show up in the world. When your beliefs empower you, they strengthen your relationships and allow you to build deeper trust with yourself and others.

Whatever you believe, from your daily interactions to your major life decisions, it's *your beliefs that create your life experience*. This is why changing your beliefs is the secret to transforming the life you're living into the life you truly crave. Henry Ford once said, "Whether you think you can or think you can't, you're right." This perfectly illustrates how powerful our beliefs are in shaping our actions and outcomes.

What beliefs are currently creating your experiences? Are they aligned with the reality you want to create?

If you believe making money requires endless effort and hustle, you'll constantly see people burning themselves out just to make ends meet, reinforcing that narrative in your mind. But shift your belief to one where money flows easily, and suddenly you start noticing those incredibly successful people who barely work a few days a week yet keep raking in millions. The world hasn't magically transformed—*your belief* has, and now your brain is working overtime to filter reality to align with that new perspective.

Beliefs are so powerful that they can distort reality in surprising ways. Consider the case of the man who believed he was a corpse. No matter how much people tried to convince him otherwise, he held firmly to his belief that his body was not alive. When a clinician asked him if corpses could bleed, the man said no. The clinician asked the man if he'd be willing to submit to a finger prick and the man agreed. After the clinician pricked his finger and it began to bleed, the man stared in disbelief for a few moments then finally said, "Well, I'll be damned—corpses *do* bleed!"

As you can see, your brain will distort what's true to match your belief. In this man's case, he simply adjusted his belief that corpses don't bleed *to match his stronger belief* that he himself was a corpse.

This is why it's so easy to stay stuck in patterns, even when they don't serve you. Once you've formed a belief, whether it's about yourself, your career, or your relationships, your brain will filter out any information that contradicts that belief and will highlight anything that reinforces it.

Your brain will lock onto evidence, twisting reality to match what you believe— whether it's real or not. And you'll feel it—deep in your gut—as frustration or relief, depending on whether that belief is limiting you or setting you free. That's how powerful your beliefs are—they shape not only your emotions but also your reality.

Take Sir Roger Bannister, for example. He was the first person to *shatter the belief* that a mile couldn't be run in under four minutes. Before he did it in 1954, people thought it was physically impossible. People thought the human body could not withstand the strain of running a mile in under four minutes—they believed your heart would give out, your lungs would collapse.

**No one believed it could be done.**

It was impossible!

*You were crazy to even attempt it.*

The experts believed that, *if it were possible*, the four-minute mile would only be broken under perfect conditions: 68-degree weather, no wind, and on a hard, dry clay track. But then Bannister defied their expectations, running on a cold, wet day, proving that *what the mind believes is far more powerful* than any conditions. Imagine him, pushing through the cold, damp air as it stung his skin, breaking through barriers no one thought possible. His *belief* in the possibility of breaking the four-minute barrier overrode those limitations and he finished the mile in 3 minutes and 59.4 seconds. His belief in what *could* be done made the impossible *real*. Then, within just two months, the world watched in awe as two more runners followed Bannister's lead, smashing through the once unbreakable barrier. Since Bannister accomplished this feat, over 1750 runners have followed suit. *The belief had shifted, and suddenly, the impossible became possible.*

The circumstances of your life, whether it's your career, your relationships, or your financial situation, are all reflections of what you believe to be true about yourself and the world. I remember when I first realized this. I'd been stuck in patterns for years, not realizing my beliefs were dictating every outcome of my financial life. The shift wasn't easy at first, but once I started rewiring my thinking, everything in my life changed.

I remember the constant weight of fear hanging over me, even as I was earning over $100,000 a year. It didn't matter how much money I made, I felt like I was always on the verge of going broke. It was exhausting, both mentally and emotionally. My credit card debt stayed high, and I went back and forth between patterns of spending freely and then panicking, wondering how I was going to pay for everything now, and being filled with anxiety every time I spent money. My deep belief was that no matter how much I earned, I was always just a step away from a life of poverty.

Fast forward a couple of years, to when I was making less money, yet *my beliefs had shifted.* I began to believe that there was always plenty of money to support me. I no longer worried about how much I spent or thought that I couldn't pay my bills, because I believed that money would continue to flow into my life with ease. And it did! My financial *reality shifted to match my new beliefs.* Even though my rent was 50% *higher,* even when unexpected expenses came up, I always had more than enough money to cover everything and to still pay all of my bills easily.

What are the beliefs you're holding that are limiting you? Look at the areas of your life where you feel stuck. What do you believe about yourself, your abilities, or how the world works that's holding you back?

Imagine how freeing it will be to rewrite those limiting beliefs! In the workbook, we'll dive deeper into the steps to identify and shift limiting beliefs so you can start creating your dream reality. Now that you understand how your life mirrors your beliefs back to you, take time to reflect on your current circumstances and challenge any beliefs that no longer serve you.

Once you identify those limiting beliefs, start looking for evidence that contradicts them. For example, if you believe that success only comes through struggle, begin noticing people who succeed with ease. If you believe that love is hard to find, look for couples who have effortlessly found each other. Remember, your reality will always match your beliefs.

Feel the weight lift off your shoulders as you release old beliefs that have been keeping you stuck, and feel the rush of excitement as you embrace the new ones that will sculpt your future!

Right now, in this moment, you have the power to shift your beliefs and open doors to possibilities you've never even considered. Imagine what could change when you start seeing the world through a new, empowered lens!

Here's something important to remember: There's a well-known saying, "What I fear, I create." This is the essence of a self-fulfilling prophecy. Whatever you focus on and believe will happen is exactly what you will create in your life, whether you want it or not. The best part? *You get to choose* what you focus on and what you believe. Your beliefs can either lock you into fear and limitation or open doors to possibility and abundance.

Now that you know your life is a mirror of your beliefs, what will you choose to believe today? What beliefs are holding you back from the life you truly want, and how can you begin to challenge them?

Your beliefs are the single most powerful determinant of your success, determining every aspect of your life, whether you're aware of it or not. By shifting your beliefs, you can begin to filter the world through a new lens that empowers you rather than limits you.

Your life won't just change—it will *transform* in ways you've never imagined. Every belief you rewrite is a step toward a future you didn't even know was possible.

Now it's your turn. The next belief you choose to rewrite could be the key to unlocking the life you've always dreamed of. So, what's stopping you? Let's dig into the workbook now and start transforming your reality—one belief at a time. Your future is waiting.

With every belief you rewrite, you open the door to a future filled with endless possibilities. Transformation is a journey, one step at a time, and the next belief you choose to challenge could be the very key to unlocking the life you've always envisioned. Now, let's take that same energy of transformation and apply it to something bigger—the art of storytelling in raising capital.

In many ways, raising capital is more than just securing funds—it's about weaving stories together, creating connections, and building something that resonates deeply with others. It's not just your story that matters; it's how your story aligns with the dreams and values of your investors. This is where detective work comes in: spotting the sparks, the common threads, and shared visions that lead to a collective journey of growth and success.

# CHAPTER 14

# Detective Work for Common T.H.R.E.A.D's: *Spotting the Sparks*

*"Forget talent. If you have it, fine. Use it. If you don't have it, it doesn't matter. As habit is more dependable than inspiration, continued learning is more dependable than talent."*

—OCTAVIA BUTLER,

Blood Child: and Other Stories

Raising capital is storytelling at its finest. It's an invitation to write a communal story where each contribution, each investment, creates a shared chapter of success, challenges, and growth.

Keep this in mind and watch how the story unfolds. It's not just about raising funds; it's about raising aspirations, dreams, and possibilities. Now go out there and start writing some epic stories!

Think of raising capital not as a financial transaction but as a journey where each investor you meet is a character in your story. What makes this story great? It's the connections, the shared interests, the common T.H.R.E.A.Ds. Your Story, their Story...Here's the thing – it's not just about your story; it's about finding the overlap with your investors' stories.

You can be like a detective and stumble across them over coffee, at community events, even in the comment section of a LinkedIn post. Every interaction is a chance to discover a new T.H.R.E.A.D, to add another layer to your story. Every story creates a **Ripple Effect**, and here's the cool part – each connection you make, each common T.H.R.E.A.D you find, can lead to more.

People talk share, and before you know it, your story is spreading, creating ripples that bring even more opportunities your way.

## So, Here's How I Play Detective all the time!

Whenever I'm out there – be it at some networking event, a casual meet-up, or even scrolling through online forums – I've got my detective hat on. But I'm not looking for clues to solve a mystery; I'm searching for sparks. You know, those little signs that someone might just be part of what I call my 'tribe.' It's about picking up on those little hints in conversations, the kind of stuff that's easy to miss if you're not paying attention.

When I'm in a conversation, my ears perk up at certain keywords. Like if someone mentions 'community impact' or 'tech innovation' – that's music to my ears. It's like a little signal that we might be on the same wavelength.

You can learn a lot by watching how people react to certain topics. Someone gets really animated talking about renewable energy? That's a cue. They lean in when discussing startup culture? Another cue. These reactions are like little signposts pointing to what they value.

Once you catch these cues, the next step is to dive deeper. 'Oh, you're interested in renewable energy? Me too. What projects caught your eye recently?'

Now we're not just making small talk; we're connecting on stuff that matters to us. And it's not just about listening; it's about sharing, too. If we're talking about sustainable living, I'll throw in a story about how I tried composting at home. It's these personal tidbits that turn a chat into a real connection.

This is where the magic happens – finding that common T.H.R.E.A.D. Maybe we both have a thing for old-school jazz or a passion for community gardening.

It's those shared interests and values that weave the stronger T.H.R.E.A.D's in our relationship tapestry, and it's these connections that last. They're built on genuine shared interests, not just on the convenience of business or social obligations.

Say I'm at a conference, and I overhear someone talking passionately about sustainable living – a topic close to my heart. That's a spark right there. I'll chime in, and before you know it, we're deep in conversation about eco-friendly projects.

It's like finding a kindred spirit.

Sometimes, it's about finding solidarity in our challenges. At a local business meet-up, I hear someone lamenting how it's nearly impossible to find good real estate deals in today's market. I give them a reassuring smile and say, "I hear you, but trust me, the gems are out there waiting to be discovered. It's like a treasure hunt – sometimes you just need the right map." And just like that, our shared frustration turns into an optimistic dialogue about strategies and persistence, opening the door to not just a deeper conversation but a potential partnership in this adventurous quest for real estate treasures.

Online, I keep an eye out for comments or posts that resonate with my way of thinking. Like someone who values transparency in business dealings. When I spot that, I reach out.

It's these shared perspectives that often lead to meaningful connections. When you spot a spark, don't just stand there. Strike up a conversation. 'Heard you mention you're into sustainable tech. That's my jam. Working on any cool projects?' Just like that, you're no longer strangers. And remember, it's not just about that one-time interaction. Follow up with an email, a LinkedIn connect, or even a coffee invite. Keep fanning those sparks into flames.

## Practical Application: Finding Common Ground

1. **Research Connections**: Before meeting someone new, do a little detective work. Find out about their interests, background, or recent projects. Use this information to connect.

2. **Ask Open-Ended Questions**: During conversations, ask questions that invite the other person to share more about themselves. "What's been inspiring you lately?" is a good start.

3. **Follow Up with Value**: After identifying a common interest, share a relevant article, event, or introduction. Show that you're genuinely invested in the connection.

Once you've identified common threads, it's important to maintain the rhythm of conversation. In the next chapter, we'll cover techniques for keeping conversations engaging and flowing naturally.

# CHAPTER 15

# Understanding the Rhythm of Conversation

**T**hink of a conversation like jamming out with your friends in a band. Each person's got their own instrument (or in this case, their voice), and together, you're trying to make this beautiful piece of music, aka a smooth chat. We're going to dive deep into what makes a conversation really tick – think of it as getting the band to groove together perfectly.

We'll look into how important it is to hit your cues at the right time, keep the tempo going just right, and really connect with the emotion of the piece. By breaking down these parts, I want to help you become a master conversationalist, whether you're chatting it up at a coffee shop or sealing the deal in a boardroom. It's all about making those interactions count, making them memorable, and most importantly, making them feel good for everyone involved.

In any business, especially one as interactive as real estate, mastering this rhythm can be the difference between closing a deal or walking away empty-handed. It's not just about what you say; it's how and when you say it.

First things first: listening. As I have talked about in other chapters is the most underrated skill in conversation. When you're dealing with clients, investors, or even learning from a mentor, listening helps you catch the beat of the conversation. What are their needs? Their fears? Their aspirations? When you listen, really listen, you start to dance in sync with them.

Now, let's talk about timing. In a conversation, timing is everything. Knowing when to pitch your idea, when to ask a question, and when to just listen, can make all the difference.

It's like finding the right moment in a song to jump in. Good questions are your secret weapon. They're like the spotlight in a dark room, focusing the attention where you want it.

And not just any questions – open-ended ones that make people think and open up. Instead of asking a client, "Do you like this property?" try, "What excites you about this property?" See the difference? One is a dead-end, the other opens up a highway.

Now, let's add a layer–active listening. This is where you not only hear what's being said but also what's left unsaid. It's about reading between the lines, catching those subtle cues in tone, body language, and even what's not being said. In real estate, this can be the difference between understanding a client's true needs versus just hearing their surface-level requests.

But here's where it gets interesting – the art of mirroring. This doesn't mean you mimic the other person. It's about matching their energy, their pace of speaking, and their level of enthusiasm. It's like dancing – you move in sync. If they're excited, match that energy. If they're more reserved, tone it down. It's all about creating that comfortable rapport where real connections happen.

Finally, humor – Let's be honest, who doesn't like a good laugh? Used strategically. Humor breaks down barriers and lightens the mood, making complex or stressful topics like real estate investing more palatable.

When we talk about the rhythm of conversation, remember, it's not a military march. It's more like a salsa dance – unpredictable, fun, and sometimes you step on a few toes. Oops!

So, how do you add humor to your conversation without turning it into a stand-up comedy show? Well, first, know your audience. Dropping a joke about cap rates might get you some chuckles in a room full of real estate pros, but might earn you blank stares at a kindergarten show-and-tell.

Timing is your best friend here, just like in any good joke. It's the pause before the punchline, the suspense before the surprise. And in business conversations, it's knowing when to lighten the mood or when to keep it serious. You don't want to crack a joke when discussing a sensitive topic. Trust me, it's like laughing at a funeral – not cool.

Let's talk about relatability. The best humor is the kind people can relate to. In real estate, it's those shared experiences – like the thrill of closing a deal or the frustration when things don't go as planned. Sharing a light-hearted comment about common struggles can build rapport faster than you can say "property management headache."

But here's the key – self-deprecation. Laughing at yourself shows you're human and not just a real estate robot. It's like saying, "Hey, I make mistakes too, but I'm cool with it." Just don't overdo it. You don't want to come off as the clown of the real estate circus.

Remember, the goal here is to make your conversations engaging and memorable, not to audition for a comedy club. A little humor goes a long way in making complex topics like real estate investing more approachable and enjoyable.

So, keep practicing that rhythm, throw in a joke or two, and watch how your conversations not only become more effective but a whole lot more fun. After all, who says real estate has to be all suits and seriousness? Let's shake things up a bit!

So, as you move forward, think about how you're engaging in conversations. Are you listening to the beat? Are you moving in time with the rhythm? This isn't just a skill; it's an art. And like all arts, it takes practice. So, go out there, start conversing, start listening, and find your rhythm.

Understanding the rhythm of conversation is akin to understanding the flow and beat of a musical piece, where each participant in the dialogue plays an instrument, contributing to the overall harmony of interaction.

This chapter will delve into the nuanced dynamics of conversational rhythm, exploring how timing, pacing, and emotional resonance contribute to effective communication. By dissecting these elements, we aim to provide readers with the insights needed to navigate and engage in conversations more effectively, enhancing both personal and professional interactions.

# The Essence of Conversational Rhythm

Conversational rhythm is the invisible beat that guides the flow of dialogue. It involves the tempo at which information is exchanged, the pauses that allow for reflection and response, and the intensity or softness of the spoken words. Just like in music, where rhythm provides structure and coherence, in conversation, it facilitates understanding and connection.

## Timing and Pacing

Timing in conversation refers to the opportune moments for interjection, response, and transition between topics. It's about knowing when to speak, when to listen, and when to change the course of the dialogue. Effective timing can enhance the clarity and effectiveness of communication, preventing misunderstandings and fostering a more dynamic exchange of ideas.

Pacing, on the other hand, involves the speed and rhythm of the conversation. It's about matching the energy and flow of your dialogue partner, creating a synchronized exchange that feels natural and engaging. Pacing can vary significantly depending on the context, subject matter, and the relationship between the participants.

## Emotional Resonance

Emotional resonance is the harmony of feelings and empathetic connection established during a conversation. It means truly understanding and sharing the emotions of the person you're speaking with. This involves paying close attention to their words, tone of voice, and body language to pick up on their feelings. By doing this, you allow participants to feel heard, understood, and connected.

**Simplified Explanation:** Emotional resonance is about really tuning into what someone else is feeling and responding in a way that shows you get it. It's like being on the same emotional wavelength as the other person.

**Example:** Imagine you're talking to an investor who seems worried about the risk involved in a new project. They mention they've had a bad experience in the past. You notice their voice quivers slightly and their posture becomes tense. Instead of just pushing your project, you acknowledge their feelings by saying, "It sounds like that previous investment was really tough for you. I can understand why you'd be cautious. Let's talk about how this opportunity is different and how we can mitigate those risks."

By acknowledging their past experience and showing empathy, you create a connection that goes beyond the business discussion. This emotional resonance builds trust and shows that you care about their concerns, not just the deal.

# Practical Strategies for Mastering Conversational Rhythm

1. **Active Listening:** This involves fully concentrating on what is being said rather than passively hearing the message of the speaker. Active listening allows for better timing and pacing, as it provides the listener with a deeper understanding of the speaker's emotions and intentions.

2. **Mindful Pausing:** Taking intentional pauses can give both the speaker and the listener time to process the information, reflect, and formulate responses. This can prevent hasty interjections and ensure that the conversation flows smoothly, without unnecessary interruptions.

3. **Adapting to Context:** Understanding the context and adjusting the rhythm of the conversation accordingly is crucial. Conversations in a professional setting may require a different pace and emotional tone compared to a casual chat with a friend.

4. **Observation and Mimicry:** Observing the conversational style of others and mimicking aspects of their rhythm can improve one's own conversational skills. This doesn't mean losing authenticity but rather adapting your natural style to complement the flow of the current dialogue.

5. **Feedback and Adjustment:** Soliciting feedback on your conversational style and being open to adjustment can lead to improvements in timing, pacing, and emotional resonance. Constructive feedback can provide insights into how others perceive your conversational rhythm and areas where you can improve.

## Practical Application: Mastering Conversational Flow

1. **Practice Pausing**: During your next conversation, make a conscious effort to pause and let the other person speak. Use pauses to create a natural rhythm.

2. **Non-Verbal Cues**: Pay attention to body language, facial expressions, and tone of voice. These cues can tell you a lot about how the other person is feeling and what they're thinking.

3. **Keep It Engaging**: Use stories, examples, and analogies to keep conversations interesting. Avoid monologues—make it a dialogue.

**Key Takeaway**: By understanding and mastering the rhythm of conversation, individuals can enhance their ability to communicate effectively, build stronger relationships, and navigate social interactions with greater ease and confidence. This chapter aims to equip readers with the knowledge and skills necessary to engage in conversations that are not only informative and productive but also emotionally resonant and harmoniously paced.

# CHAPTER 16

# "The Art of the Un-Pitch"

*"Sell the problem you solve, not the product."*

—**Unknown**

L et's talk about something that I think is super important for anyone looking to raise capital or get people to invest in their ventures.

This concept that might seem a bit unconventional at first -

I like to call it **"THE ART OF UN-PITCH."**

You know how everyone hates the stereotypical used car salesman, right? The guy who's all about the hard sell, pushing you to make a decision right now, all while giving off this sleazy vibe. Nobody likes that. And guess what? Investors don't either. If you come off too pushy or desperate, you'll be seen just like that used car salesman, and that's a surefire way to scare people off.

In the world of endless pitches and sales tactics, we're often taught that to succeed, we must pitch, sell, and convince.

So Andy, how do you avoid that? How do you "un-pitch"?

It's all about flipping the script. Instead of trying to sell someone on your idea, you want to engage them in a conversation. Show them your passion, but also show them that you're not desperate for their money. It's about being authentic, being real. Think about it like dating. You wouldn't propose marriage on the first date, right? You get to know the person, let them get to know you, and see if there's a mutual interest.

This is what I envision as the "Art of the Un-Pitch" – it's not about selling; it's about inspiring... It's about giving your investors something they didn't even know they needed.

The Un-Pitch. It's not about selling; it's about connecting, understanding, and solving. It's about being so in tune with your investors and the market that the deal almost seals itself.

The Un-Pitch is where you're not pitching at all. Sounds crazy, right? But stick with me. It's about having a conversation, a real one. It's about listening more than you talk. It's about understanding what keeps your investors up at night, what dreams they're chasing, and what fears they're trying to outrun. And then, it's about showing them how your opportunity aligns with their goals, not as a sales pitch, but as a natural part of the conversation.

Imagine sitting down for coffee with a potential investor, and instead of launching into a rehearsed spiel, you start by asking them about their first big win in investing. You get them talking about what they've learned, what they're looking for now, and why. You share a bit of your own journey, the highs and the lows. And through this exchange, you find common ground.

Now, when you start talking about your current project, it's not a pitch. It's a continuation of your conversation. You're not trying to convince them of anything.

You're simply sharing an opportunity that you genuinely believe aligns with what they've told you they're looking for. You talk about the risks because you respect their intelligence and you know trust is built on transparency. You outline the potential because you're excited about it and you think they should be too.

This is the art of the Un-Pitch. It's about making every interaction feel like a collaboration, not a transaction. It's about building relationships where your investors don't just feel like they're part of something; they are part of something.

They're not just investing in a property; they're investing in a vision, a shared goal, and most importantly, they're investing in you.

So, how do you master the Un-Pitch? It starts with authenticity. Be real, be you. It's about empathy, putting yourself in their shoes and understanding their perspective. And it's about knowledge, knowing your stuff so well that you can talk about it naturally, without needing a PowerPoint to back you up.

Remember, people can smell a sales pitch a mile away, and nobody likes the smell. But when you come at it from a place of genuine connection and shared interest, that's when the magic happens. That's when the Un-Pitch becomes your most powerful tool in raising capital.

Now that we've got the foundation of the Un-Pitch, let's take it a step further. The real magic happens when you start living the Un-Pitch. It's not just a technique; it's a mindset. It's about being so genuinely invested in your relationships and your projects that the line between your life and your pitch disappears. You're not pitching; you're just being. And in being, you're naturally attracting people to your cause.

Here's the thing: the world of real estate investment is crowded, noisy, and full of people trying to make a quick buck. But you? You're different. You're not in it just for the money. You're in it for the game, the community, the chance to create something lasting. And this passion, this authenticity, it's contagious. It's what sets you apart in a sea of sameness.

And that authenticity? It's not just about how you show up in real estate, it's about how you approach every connection you make. Just like in real estate, it's the genuine relationships that stand the test of time.

Take a page from Basecamp's playbook.

They don't push their products with over-the-top sales pitches or fancy marketing campaigns. Instead, they focus on **un-pitching**—allowing their product to speak for itself and build genuine connections with their customers. **Jason Fried** and **David Heinemeier Hansson**, the founders of Basecamp, believe that the best way to win people over is by being **honest, simple**, and **transparent**.

**Fried once said:**

*"We think it's better to have real conversations with real people, not try to manipulate or persuade them with hype."*

This quote perfectly captures the **power of un-pitching**. Basecamp doesn't rely on flashy marketing to convince people to buy their software. They believe in building a **great product** that solves real problems for their customers—and letting that be the reason people stick around.

Think about it. Basecamp is all about **keeping things simple**. They don't over-promise or try to be everything to everyone. Instead, they focus on doing one thing really well: **project management**. And they're transparent about what they can and can't do. They don't pitch features that don't exist or hype up future promises. Instead, they focus on **delivering value now**.

Here's the thing: In a world full of noise, Basecamp's **quiet confidence** stands out. They don't need to push sales because they've created a product that solves problems and **makes people's lives easier**. And that's the secret. When you have a product that genuinely improves people's workflows, they talk about it for you. They become your best advocates. That's the power of **un-pitching**—letting your customers do the talking.

Basecamp's approach is all about **trust**. They trust their customers to recognize the value in what they're offering without being sold to. And in return, their customers trust them to be honest, reliable, and straightforward. It's a long-term strategy that focuses on building relationships instead of making a quick sale.

Here's the deal: **Un-pitching** is about being **real**. It's about knowing that the product you're offering is good enough to stand on its own. You don't need the gimmicks, the hype, or the hard-sell tactics. And when you approach business this way, you create **loyal** customers who aren't just buying a product—they're buying into a **philosophy**.

That's how Basecamp wins. They don't pitch. They don't push. They just **deliver**.

**So, what does this mean for you? Just like Basecamp, you can win by focusing on real connections instead of flashy pitches.** So, how do you live the Un-Pitch? It starts with your why. Why are you doing this? What drives you? What's the story behind your hustle? This is what people connect with. Not the numbers, not the projections, but the human story behind the investment...

Share this story everywhere – on social media, in your blog posts, during your meetings. Let it be the heartbeat of your brand.

Next, focus on giving more than you take. This might sound counterintuitive in a world that's all about ROI, but trust me, it's the key to long-term success. Share your knowledge freely. Help others without expecting anything in return. Be the person who's always adding value, whether it's through insightful posts, helpful advice, or just being a sounding board for someone else's ideas. When you give more than you take, you build a community of people who trust you, believe in you, and want to support you.

But Andy what if they don't show interest?

That's okay! Not everyone will be interested, and that's perfectly fine. The goal isn't to get everyone to invest; it's to find the right people who are genuinely excited about your vision.

By un-pitching, you're building relationships and trust, which is way more valuable in the long run than a quick yes.

Building real, meaningful relationships takes time. But when you do it right, those relationships will be much more fruitful and sustainable. People invest in people they trust and believe in, not just ideas. So, focus on being authentic, building trust, and creating connections. That's the art of the un-pitch.

You're not looking for a quick win; you're building a legacy. This means being patient, staying consistent, and always playing the long game. It means nurturing your relationships, even when there's no immediate deal on the table. It means staying true to your values, even when the market is tempting you to cut corners.

Finally, be relentless in your pursuit of excellence. In everything you do, strive to be the best. Not just in your deals, but in your relationships, your content, your presence. Excellence attracts excellence. When you're known for your unwavering commitment to quality, people will be drawn to you. They'll want to be part of what you're building, not just because of the potential financial return, but because they respect and admire who you are and how you operate.

Living the Un-Pitch is about embodying the values, the passion, and the authenticity that make people want to invest in you. It's about being so genuinely yourself that people can't help but want to be part of your journey. So, forget the pitch. Focus on being real, adding value, and building relationships that last.

### That's how you raise capital. That's how you build a legacy.

In the realm of real estate, your ability to positively influence others is key. The Un-Pitch is an opportunity to impact and inspire your investors. It's about showing them possibilities and empowering them to see the potential. It's an opportunity to connect on a deeper level. Understand their goals, fears, and dreams. This isn't just about finding them a property; it's about understanding their journey and how this investment fits into their larger life picture. Be open, be genuine, be you. When you meet with potential investors, try setting aside the glossy presentations and rehearsed speeches. Instead, invite them into a dialogue, a real, human conversation about what matters most.

For instance, when discussing a multifamily investment opportunity, don't just talk about the financials. Start with the vision, the purpose behind the project.

Maybe it's about creating a sustainable living space that fosters community and connection. Share stories of the people who will live there, the lives that will be touched and enriched by the investment.

And then, listen! Listen to what your investors are truly seeking. Are they looking for financial returns, or are they also seeking to make a positive impact, to be part of something meaningful? The art of the Un-Pitch is as much about hearing as it is about speaking. It's about finding that common ground where your vision aligns with their values.

When you engage in an Un-Pitch, you're not just presenting an opportunity; you're inviting your investors to be part of a journey. You're opening a space for collaboration, for a shared mission. This approach builds trust, not just in the investment but in you as a person, as a leader with a vision that goes beyond profits.

Remember, people invest in people. They invest in stories, in dreams, in the possibility of creating something together that's larger than themselves. So, the next time you find yourself in a room with potential investors, resist the urge to pitch. Instead, engage in an Un-Pitch. Share, listen, and connect. And watch as this genuine approach transforms your interactions, your relationships, and ultimately, your success in the world of investment.

Let's throw out the Old Sales Script and Build TRUST!!

When approaching high-net-worth individuals who may back your real estate venture, research should be priority number one.

Peruse their social media presence to piece together details that reveal patterns about how they spend their time, what causes they support, places they frequent, and personality quirks that come across.

Maybe it's a shared passion for Sports, Music, Cars, Fashion, Travel, or a mutual fascination with cutting-edge building technology these common T.H.R.E.A.D's make your story resonate with theirs and build TRUST.

In the Un-Pitch, authenticity is your most valuable asset. It allows for connections that are based on trust and mutual respect. Engage in conversations that matter. It's not just about the technicalities of the deal but about the human experience behind it. What does owning this property mean for them? How does it align with their life's journey?

TRUST is built through empathy and understanding. Show that you care about their needs and desires. This authentic concern for their well-being will set you apart in the real estate world

Imagine you're discussing market challenges with a colleague. Instead of just commiserating, you shift the conversation to brainstorm creative solutions. What if we tackled this from a completely different angle?

This leads to a collaborative discussion where you both share and develop innovative ideas. It's no longer a gripe session but a creative think-tank session. You're building rapport not just through shared difficulties but through shared creativity and problem-solving.

Or when you're in a meeting with a potential investor, instead of launching into a presentation, you start with a question, something like, 'What inspires you about real estate investment?' This opens a dialogue, a chance for the investor to share their story, their motivations.

As they speak, you discover that they're not just driven by returns; they're passionate about community impact. This is your cue to shift the conversation from a conventional pitch to an Un-Pitch. You might say, 'It's interesting that you mention community. Our latest project isn't just about building apartments; it's about creating a space where people can connect, grow, and thrive together. Let me tell you about the first family who will move in once it's completed.'

And then, you share a story. Not statistics or projections, but a narrative about a young family, about their search for a safe, nurturing environment, and how your project is designed to meet those very needs. It's a story that aligns with the investor's passion, making the conversation not just about financial investment but emotional investment as well.

As the conversation unfolds, you weave in the financials, not as the headline, but as supporting details.

You discuss how sustainable design not only benefits the community but also leads to long-term cost savings. You talk about the value of creating a space that people are proud to call home and how it translates into lower turnover and stable returns. Throughout this Un-Pitch, your focus remains on the human element, on building a connection that transcends numbers. You're inviting the investor to be part of a story, a mission, a community. And in doing so, you're not just seeking an investment; you're forging a partnership based on shared values and vision.

### Example 1: Un-Pitch for a Historical Renovation Project

Let's say your conversation leads into discussing a historical renovation project, instead of focusing on the cost and potential ROI, you start the conversation with a story. You might say, 'You know, this building isn't just brick and mortar; it's a piece of history, a story in every stone. Do you remember the old cinema downtown that brought so much joy in the '60s? That's our next project.'

You watch the investor's eyes light up as they recall their own memories of the place. You've connected on a personal level, and now the numbers you discuss aren't just figures; they're part of a story to resurrect a beloved landmark. The conversation shifts from investment to legacy, from profit to preservation and pride.

### Example 2: Un-Pitch for a Sustainable Living Complex

Or perhaps you're pitching a sustainable living complex. Instead of leading with eco-friendly features and energy efficiency stats, you invite the investor into the vision. 'Imagine a community that lives in harmony with nature,' you might say. 'A place where every home is a testament to our commitment to the environment. That's what we're building.'

You share anecdotes of future residents who are passionate about sustainability, drawing a picture of a community that's not just about green technology but about a shared lifestyle and values. The investor isn't just funding a construction; they're investing in a movement, a collective aspiration for a better, more sustainable future.

### Example 3: Un-Pitch for a Multi-Generational Housing Complex

Lastly, consider you're presenting a multi-generational housing complex. Instead of detailing the amenities and investment benefits, you share a vision of community and connection. 'This project is about bringing generations together,' you might suggest. 'It's about creating spaces where grandparents, parents, and children can share their lives, where wisdom and youth meet.'

You narrate stories of families longing for such a community, of the joy and support such living arrangements bring. The conversation isn't just about financial investment; it's about investing in family, in community, in a way of living that brings people closer.

Think of each real estate interaction as an adventure. It's not just about the property or the investment; it's about the experience you create around it. How does this property inspire a sense of adventure or opportunity in your client's life.

In the Un-Pitch, trust the "T" in the T.H.R.E.A.D Method is your foundation. This trust comes from genuine interactions, consistent value, and an unwavering commitment to their best interest. Shift the focus from what you're offering to what it means for them. How does this investment align with their values and goals? Engaging in this kind of dialogue creates a partnership, not just a client relationship A COMMON T.H.R.E.A.D.

Be authentically you. In the Un-Pitch, there's no room for pretense. Your genuine passion for real estate, your belief in what you're offering, should shine through. Authenticity builds connection and trust like nothing else. Educate your clients.

Empower them with the knowledge they need to make informed decisions. When you focus on empowering rather than selling, you create a relationship based on respect and mutual growth.

In every interaction, ask yourself – how can I provide immense value here? Whether it's through insightful market analysis, tailored advice, or sharing your expertise, make sure each interaction leaves them better off.

Every great product, every innovation, tells a story. Think about how Apple products aren't just gadgets; they're part of a lifestyle, a dream. Your Un-Pitch should do the same. It's not about features; it's about the story, the why behind the product. Your Un-Pitch should be straightforward, clean, and focused. It's not about overwhelming with data and jargon; it's about getting to the heart of what makes your product or idea revolutionary.

The goal of the Un-Pitch is to create a moment of wonder, an 'aha' experience. It's about showing a glimpse of a better future made possible by what you're offering. It's not a transaction; it's a transformation. Connect with your investors on a human level. Show them how your property fits into their aspirations, their story.

Think of the classic Apple product reveals. They weren't just announcements; they were unveilings of a future we wanted to be part of.

Your Un-Pitch should have that same feel – a reveal of something exciting, something game-changing. Be passionate. If you don't believe in what you're saying, no one else will. Your authenticity is what makes the Un-Pitch compelling. It's not just about persuading; it's about believing.

The first step in the Un-Pitch is leveraging personal connections to secure funding is identifying shared passions, experiences, or interests between yourself and potential investors. These similarities form the foundation for developing authentic relationships that lead to winning over investors.

Now the fun begins!

Schedule an introductory 30-minute coffee meeting. Come armed with a few open-ended questions about things you uncovered online to break the ice. If golf seemed prominent, say "I noticed from your Instagram you spend time on the golf course. What is it about the sport that you enjoy so much?"

Based on their eyes lighting up when discussing certain subjects, double down on those T.H.R.E.A.Ds. Find ways to ask follow-up questions, pivot the conversation to relate to your own experiences, or express your own passion for those interests if authentic.

The goal is identifying at least one significant commonality during this first meet-up. Whether it's golf, philanthropy towards a specific cause, small business investing, or affinity for contemporary art–simply establish shared ground.

If you only talk business and investment potential without exposing common T.H.R.E.A.D's, you'll lose out on the relationship component critical for securing capital down the road.

Leave the meeting having explicitly noted out loud at least one parallel interest between the two of you. Then suggest keeping in touch to explore it further. Now your relationship can blossom beyond this surface-level connection as you nurture authentic bonds rooted in mutual interests over time.

**Let's explore what this would look like:**

### Example 1: The Story of Transformation

I would likely highlight the transformative power of real estate.

"This project didn't just offer returns; it created a community center that brought people together.'" Then ask, 'How do you see your investments transforming spaces and lives?'

It's about aligning their investment with a bigger, more meaningful picture.

### Example 2: Creating a Legacy

When discussing long-term investment opportunities, emphasize the aspect of legacy.

"Imagine creating spaces that will benefit communities for generations.

What legacy would you like your investments to leave?'

This conversation elevates the discussion from mere financial gain to creating enduring value and legacy through real estate.

### Example 3: Customer-Centric Investment Approach

In a conversation with potential investors, center on customer needs. Understand what the investor is really looking for.

"What's your ideal investment scenario? Let's explore how we can tailor opportunities to match your long-term goals."

It's about aligning investments with the investor's personal aspirations and market trends.

## Example 4: A Mock Conversation

Setting: The inviting hum of a cozy café, the aroma of freshly brewed coffee mingling with quiet conversations. Sarah, exuding warmth with a bright smile and a cup of coffee, takes a seat across from Ben, a discerning investor whose eyes hint at a measured skepticism.

Sarah: Morning, Ben! Today, we're trading the bland boardrooms and predictable presentations for something more genuine. "The Mill House" comes to life not in slides, but over coffee—my treat. Let's dive into a real conversation.

Ben: (with a curious smirk) Straight from the heart, is it? I'm accustomed to a barrage of numbers and tactical plans. What makes your approach stand out, Sarah?

Sarah: (her eyes twinkling with excitement) Picture this, Ben: the soft warmth of the morning sun, a gentle city breeze in your hair. Imagine welcoming the day with rooftop yoga, the city's skyline as your backdrop, enveloped by the scent of fresh herbs from our urban garden. "The Mill House" offers more than living space; it's about crafting a lifestyle.

Ben: (leaning back, curiosity piqued) Lifestyle, you say? This 'experiential living' trend is intriguing. Rooftop yoga is quite a concept. But my world revolves around concrete figures, Sarah. I need substantial data, not just visions of yoga poses.

Sarah: (confidently) The numbers speak for themselves, Ben! Think energy-efficient homes, a strategic location, and rental projections that surpass expectations.

But "The Mill House" is not just about returns; it's about creating a vibrant heart, a place where life thrives, yoga sessions included or not.

Ben: (a subtle smile forming) A poetic pitch, Sarah. But investors need solid strategies, not just eloquence. How about the practical aspects? Making sure that rooftop space is ready for all weathers and ensuring all legal boxes are checked.

Sarah: (flipping open a notebook full of meticulous plans and illustrations) I've got it all covered, Ben! From storm-resistant barriers to versatile shading systems, and even an indoor yoga studio with skylights for overcast days. "The Mill House" is fully equipped to welcome both the sun worshippers and the yoga enthusiasts.

Ben: (finishes his coffee) You've offered more than a proposal, Sarah; you've painted a picture, blending tangible numbers with an inspiring vision. But such a sanctuary requires a thriving community. How do you plan to attract people to "The Mill House"?

Sarah: (her eyes gleaming with a hint of mischief) About building that community... I believe you know someone who's quite adept at nurturing connections, perhaps through yoga? Someone very close to you... your wife, perhaps?

Ben: (taken aback) My wife? How did you...?

Sarah: (smiling playfully) Let's just say I have a knack for uncovering shared passions, whether it's for serene dawns or yoga sessions. When I learned about your wife's renowned yoga studio, it seemed like destiny was pointing us to this very rooftop.

Ben: (a genuine smile emerges) You're full of surprises, Sarah. But I'm intrigued. Show me the detailed plans, the community engagement strategies, and let's see if "The Mill House" can truly become a vibrant urban community, perhaps with a unique link to your yoga enthusiast friend.

Sarah: (earnestly) Ben, I believe that together, we can turn this vision into a living, breathing reality. "The Mill House" represents a new chapter in urban living, one that we can author together. Perhaps over our next cup of coffee, we can delve into the details and explore the possibilities of this partnership. How does that sound?

Amidst the gentle clatter of the café and the easy camaraderie around them, a conversation becomes a pathway from vision to reality. The lesson?

In the world of investment, sincerity, a touch of creativity, and a well-crafted plan can transform a simple coffee chat into a partnership, intertwining shared dreams, rooftop yoga aspirations, and perhaps, a personal connection through an investor's spouse's passion for yoga.

### Practical Application: Using Stories to Connect

1. **Craft Your Signature Story**: Think of a story that represents who you are and what you stand for. Practice telling it in a way that's engaging and relatable.
2. **Collect Stories**: Make a habit of collecting stories—your own and others'. Use them to illustrate points and connect with different audiences.
3. **Adapt Your Story**: Tailor your stories to your audience. What parts of your story will resonate most with them? Adjust your delivery accordingly.

**Key Takeaway**: The art of the un-pitch is about building genuine connections and understanding others' needs. Practical examples are great, but they don't hit you in the gut like a good story does. Stories are everything—they're how you really connect with people.

So, let's break down how you can use storytelling to embed the THREAD method into every single one of your interactions.

In Chapter 15, we'll explore the power of storytelling and how crafting a narrative can help you build trust and engagement in any conversation. Trust me, this is where the real magic happens.

# CHAPTER 17

# The Power of Story Telling

CREATIVE  BRAND  CONTENT  MARKETING

*"I'm writing my story so that others might see fragments of themselves."*

—LENA WAITHE,

Screenwriter for Bones and Master of None

The essence of the Common T.H.R.E.A.D Method in storytelling, especially within the context of real estate and beyond, is about tapping into the universal narratives that connect us all because you know what's more powerful than numbers, graphs, and data when you're raising capital?...

## A STORY!

And I don't mean some fluffy narrative about your company. I mean a story that **transports** people—a story so immersive, it makes them forget they're sitting in a meeting and gets them emotionally invested in your vision.

For me, this passion for storytelling goes way back. While other kids were outside playing, I was inside, completely lost in the pages of a book. I wasn't just reading I was being **transported** to other worlds, living those stories right alongside the characters. Whether it was Jack London's *The Call of the Wild* or J.R.R. Tolkien's *The Hobbit*, I wasn't just an observer...

I was part of those worlds.

I felt Bilbo Baggins' hesitancy as he left the Shire, Jack's wildness in the Yukon, and even Scout Finch's fierce sense of justice in *To Kill a Mockingbird*.

I was obsessed with stories that took ordinary people and transformed them into something greater.

## That's The Common Thread that links every story I love—

It's why Luke Skywalker's rise from farm boy to Jedi Master resonates just as much as King Arthur pulling the sword from the stone or Katniss Everdeen defying the odds in *The Hunger Games*. It's why Ripley fighting for survival in *Alien* is as inspiring as Jo March breaking the mold in *Little Women*. Each of these characters starts small, but their journey is **huge**.

That's why these stories work—they reflect the common threads of life. We see ourselves in them, because we all want to rise above where we started.

But here's the thing—I never really had the words to express how all those experiences of being immersed in stories were shaping me until I started doing research for this book.

It wasn't until I came across an article by Sean Malone about the **Three Basic Tenets of Transportation Theory** that it all clicked.

Like Sean, I spent my entire life trying to understand the nature and purpose of storytelling. It's been a driving force behind everything I do. But until I started writing this chapter, I didn't consciously realize how those countless hours spent devouring stories as a kid would eventually help me raise capital.

And that's where the **Common T.H.R.E.A.D. Method** comes in. The essence of the Common T.H.R.E.A.D. Method in storytelling, especially within the context of real estate and beyond, is about **tapping into the universal narratives that connect us all**. This method goes beyond the surface, finding the deeper connections that bind us together, regardless of our diverse backgrounds or experiences.

By exploring why stories work using this method, we can uncover the **fundamental reasons** stories resonate so powerfully and how they can be harnessed to forge even deeper connections. Stories allow us to strip away the differences and find that shared human experience. And when you can do that—when you find those common threads—you're not just telling a story.

You're creating an emotional bond, a **shared journey** that brings people together.

## 1. Narrative Transportation: How Avatar Built Pandora—and Why You Need to Build Your Own World for Investors

When you watched *Avatar*, you weren't just seeing a movie—you were living on Pandora. The world was so real, so vivid, that for two hours, you weren't thinking about your phone, your to-do list, or anything else. You were transported into a world where you cared about the Na'vi, their environment, and their struggle.

That's exactly what you need to do when you're pitching to investors. You need to **transport** them into the world of your business. Make them feel it, live it, breathe it. If they can't imagine themselves in the future you're building, they're not going to invest. You've got to paint a picture so compelling that they forget about their current portfolios and start thinking, "I need to be part of this."

The key is to immerse them so deeply that your business feels real—like they're already living in that vision with you. Just like *Avatar* made us believe in Pandora, you need to make investors believe in your company's future.

## This isn't just a pitch—it's an experience.

So, **build your Pandora**. Tell the story that makes investors forget they're in a meeting—one that transports them out of the boardroom and into the future you're building. Make them feel like they're not just backing a company but becoming part of something much bigger, something that **matters**. When you do that—when you craft a story that taps into the common threads that connect us all—**that's when the magic happens**.

## 2. Cognitive and Emotional Engagement: The Balance of Head and Heart, Just Like *Avatar*

*Avatar* didn't just hook you with its visual effects. Sure, Pandora looked amazing, but what really got people was the **emotional** connection. The story of the Na'vi fighting for their survival, the love story between Jake and Neytiri, the ethical dilemmas of exploiting a planet for resources—this was all about getting your heart involved, not just your brain.

When you're raising capital, you've got to hit both the **head and the heart**. Your financials, your business model—those are for the head. Investors need to know they're putting their money into something that's smart, scalable, and profitable.

But here's the thing: numbers alone don't move people to action. People invest in people, in missions, in visions. That's where the heart comes in.

Tell them **why** you started this company. What problem are you solving that really matters? How is your business making a real difference in the world? Investors aren't just writing a check—they're buying into your passion, your mission, and your story.

Just like *Avatar* made you care about an alien world, you need to make investors care about your business. Hit them with the facts, but don't forget to hit them in the gut, too. That's what sticks.

## 3. Changing Worldview: How *Avatar* Shifted Perspectives and How Your Story Should Do the Same

When people walked out of *Avatar*, they didn't just leave thinking "cool movie." They left thinking about the environment, about the way we treat our planet, about how we exploit resources.

The movie **shifted perspectives**. It made people rethink their values.

That's the magic of a great story—it can change the way people see the world. And guess what? That's exactly what you need to do when you're raising capital.

Your goal isn't just to get a check—it's to **shift** the way investors think about your business, your industry, and the future.

You want them walking away from your pitch thinking, "I can't unsee this." Your story should challenge their assumptions, make them question the status quo, and get them excited about where the world is going—and how your company is leading the charge. Just like *Avatar* got people to care about an alien planet, your pitch should make investors care deeply about the future you're building.

The **Common Thread Method** is all about this. It's not just about data points; it's about crafting a narrative that pulls people in and **changes** them. Investors aren't just putting money into your business—they're investing in a new way of thinking, a new way of seeing the world.

Look, at the end of the day, raising capital isn't just about having the best numbers. It's about having the best story. And the best stories transport people, engage their emotions and intellect, and leave them seeing the world in a different light.

If you want to raise serious capital, stop thinking about your pitch as a PowerPoint presentation and start thinking about it like James Cameron thought about *Avatar*. You're not just telling investors what you're doing—you're taking them on a journey into the future.

So, **build your Pandora**. Tell the story that makes investors forget they're in a meeting—one that transports them out of the boardroom and into the future you're building. Make them feel like they're not just backing a company but becoming part of something much bigger, something that **matters**.

When you do that—when you craft a story that taps into the common threads that connect us all—**that's when the magic happens**.

Because when you find those common threads, you're not just pitching a business; you're creating a narrative that resonates with something deep inside people.

You're speaking to their values, their ambitions, their desire to be part of a journey that leads to change. Investors don't just want to hear about growth potential—they want to feel connected to the mission, the vision, and the impact. That's what makes them lean in.

When your story aligns with those universal human experiences—whether it's the underdog's rise, the hero's journey, or the fight against the odds—you're not just asking for capital. You're inviting them to **believe** in the story, to become part of that transformation.

That's when your pitch stops being about dollars and cents and starts being about purpose and potential.

And when you can do that? That's when the deal happens. That's when you get the buy-in, not just on paper, but in the hearts and minds of the people who can help make your vision a reality.

The essence of the Common T.H.R.E.A.D Method in storytelling, especially within the context of real estate and beyond, is about tapping into the universal narratives that connect us all. This method goes beyond the surface, finding the deeper connections that bind us together, regardless of our diverse backgrounds or experiences.

By exploring why stories work using this method, we can uncover the fundamental reasons stories resonate so powerfully and how they can be harnessed to forge even deeper connections.

## The Universality of Stories

Stories have a unique ability to transcend the specifics of their setting, characters, and plot to touch on universal themes of struggle, triumph, loss, and love. These themes are the "Common T.H.R.E.A.D's" that everyone can relate to on some level. When a real estate story talks about transforming a neglected neighborhood into a thriving community, it's not just a tale of investment and return; it's a narrative about renewal, hope, and the collective aspiration for a better life. This connection resonates because, at its core, it mirrors the universal human experience of seeking improvement and belonging.

# Emotional Resonance

The Common T.H.R.E.A.D Method leverages the emotional resonance of stories to create a powerful connection. Stories that tap into our shared emotions—be it joy, fear, anticipation, or relief—engage us more deeply than any array of facts and figures could. This emotional engagement is crucial in real estate and other contexts because it transforms passive listeners into active participants who feel personally invested in the narrative's outcome. By identifying and weaving these emotional T.H.R.E.A.D's into a story, a storyteller can create a compelling narrative that feels relevant and personal to a wide audience.

# Bridging Differences

In our increasingly fragmented world, finding and emphasizing common T.H.R.E.A.D's helps bridge differences among people. Stories that highlight shared values, challenges, and dreams have the power to unite diverse groups by focusing on what we have in common rather than what divides us. In real estate, for instance, focusing on the universal desire for a safe, welcoming community can bring together stakeholders with varied interests, from investors to residents to local government officials.

# Memory and Recall

The Common T.H.R.E.A.D Method also enhances memory and recall. We're more likely to remember stories that connect with us on a personal level, especially when they evoke strong emotions or resonate with our own experiences. This memorability is invaluable, whether you're pitching to investors, marketing a property, or advocating for community development. A well-told story that finds and pulls on these common T.H.R.E.A.D's can linger in the audience's mind long after the facts have faded, motivating action and fostering a lasting connection.

# Inspiring Action

Ultimately, the power of the Common T.H.R.E.A.D Method lies in its ability to inspire action. By revealing the universal themes and emotions that underpin our individual experiences, this approach can motivate people to come together and work towards a common goal. In real estate, compelling narratives that speak to our shared humanity can inspire investors to commit, communities to rally around a project, and individuals to engage with and support their local neighborhoods.

The magic of storytelling, particularly when applied through the Common T.H.R.E.A.D Method, lies in its capacity to find and highlight these invisible bonds that connect us all. Whether in real estate or any other domain, stories built on this foundation can have a profound impact, moving beyond mere transactions to create meaningful, lasting relationships and changes.

Imagine we're not just observers of the transformation but part of the story itself. As we delve into the tales of revitalized communities and lives uplifted by strategic investments in multifamily real estate, we're also tracing the common T.H.R.E.A.D's that connect us all—our shared dreams, challenges, and aspirations for better living spaces and stronger communities.

The Common T.H.R.E.A.D Method isn't just a storytelling technique; it's a way of finding and highlighting those universal experiences and emotions that resonate deeply with both investors and tenants alike. As I share the journey of a property from overlooked to cherished, I'm weaving a tapestry of common T.H.R.E.A.D's—hope, renewal, and community—that ties the story directly to the hearts of those listening.

Now, let's talk about crafting these stories with the Common T.H.R.E.A.D Method in mind. When I describe the transformation of a dilapidated building into a vibrant community hub, I'm not just recounting an investment success; I'm inviting my audience to see themselves as part of this narrative.

They're not just passive investors; they're co-creators of a future where every person has a safe, welcoming place to call home. This approach deepens the connection, making the pitch more persuasive and memorable because it aligns with the core values and visions of the audience.

By identifying and articulating these common T.H.R.E.A.D's, we make our stories more than just tales of financial gains; we transform them into narratives of collective achievement and shared human experiences. This connection is what turns a pitch into a conversation, a transaction into a partnership. It's about showing how every investment in multifamily real estate is an investment in the fabric of our communities, weaving together stories of individual triumphs into a larger narrative of communal success.

And when we master the art of storytelling through the Common T.H.R.E.A.D Method, we're not just selling or persuading; we're engaging in a dialogue that transcends the typical investor pitch. We're sharing visions of what can be achieved when we pull on those T.H.R.E.A.D's that bind us, envisioning a future crafted through shared goals and mutual understanding. This method elevates our narratives, ensuring they're not only heard but felt, remembered, and acted upon.

Through this lens, storytelling becomes a powerful tool for connecting, influencing, and inspiring action. The Common T.H.R.E.A.D Method enriches this tool, making every narrative not just a story of investment but a shared journey towards building better communities and forging stronger connections. It's these common T.H.R.E.A.D's that truly resonate, drawing us closer to the heart of what makes storytelling such an invaluable asset in the world of multifamily real estate investment.

Alright, let's delve into the world of raising capital and explore why stories play a crucial role in this domain. So, picture this: You're an entrepreneur with a brilliant idea, seeking funding to turn your vision into reality. In the realm of raising capital, numbers and figures certainly matter, but the real magic lies in crafting a compelling story that captivates investors and makes them feel emotionally invested in your venture.

Stories play a crucial role in sales and investor pitching because they effectively communicate the essence, potential, and value of a project or idea. Here are the key insights from the research:

1. **Engagement and Memorability:** Stories engage the audience more deeply than mere facts, making your pitch more memorable. Storytelling transforms a sales pitch from a mere transaction into a compelling narrative that resonates on a personal level with buyers and investors. It encapsulates complex ideas into relatable narratives, making them easier to remember and advocate for

2. **Building Trust and Connection:** Through storytelling, salespeople and entrepreneurs can create a connection with their audience. This connection is crucial in building trust, an essential component when convincing buyers and investors of the value of a product or venture. Stories convey not just the value of the product or idea but also the passion and commitment of the people behind it, fostering a deeper sense of trust and investment

3. **Enhancing Persuasiveness:** The structure and content of stories, when aligned with strategic entrepreneurial storytelling (SES), enhance the persuasiveness of pitches. A well-crafted story not only illustrates the problem and its solution but also highlights the uniqueness and value proposition of the product or idea, making it more persuasive to investors and customers alike

4. **Conveying Company Values and Vision:** Stories allow companies to share their values and vision in a way that's engaging and compelling. This not only helps in selling a product or service but also in attracting investment by aligning the investors' values with those of the company, thereby creating a stronger motivation for investment

5. **Facilitating Understanding and Relatability:** By using narratives, entrepreneurs can explain complex ideas in a way that's accessible and relatable to their audience. Stories help break down technical jargon and abstract concepts into digestible and engaging content, facilitating a better understanding and relatability of the pitch

6. **Making Your Project Relatable:** Imagine telling a story that brings your real estate project to life. It's about painting a vivid picture that makes potential investors feel connected and excited. You're not just sharing numbers and projections; you're sharing a vision, a future where they can see the growth and opportunities. This kind of storytelling can really make your project stand out in a sea of investment opportunities

7. **Exploring Different Ways to Get Funded:** Real estate's got a whole toolbox of ways to raise funds. It's not just about selling a property and leasing it back; there are all kinds of models and deals you can explore. By weaving these options into your narrative, you can really show potential investors how innovative and thoughtful you are in maximizing the value of their investment

8. **Talking Strategy on Money Matters**: Deciding on how you're going to structure your capital is a big deal. It's like putting together a puzzle where every piece is crucial. Through storytelling, you can break down these decisions in a way that's easy to grasp, showing your investors that you're making smart choices to protect their investment and give them the best returns possible

9. **Building Your Story:** At the end of the day, your project is more than just bricks and mortar; it's a story waiting to be told. A compelling narrative can capture the imagination of your investors, making them feel like they're part of something special. It's about creating a connection that goes beyond the financials, one that can really rally people behind your vision and drive your project forward

In short, nailing your storytelling can be your secret weapon in attracting investors and getting the funds you need for your real estate projects. It's about making them see what you see and feel what you feel. And remember, every investor loves a good story, especially one where they see themselves winning.

Let's start by creating a narrative framework in our conversations. This isn't just about telling stories; it's about crafting a journey for our listeners, where every word and gesture guides them through a landscape of understanding and connection. Think of it this way: when you're telling a story, you're not just sharing information; you're inviting someone into a world you've created.

Now, how do we make this world not just informative but also immersive and relatable?

# That's where the Narrative Common T.H.R.E.A.D Framework comes in.

By exploring these themes, I invite you to delve into complex emotional landscapes, reflecting on your own experiences and how these universal themes have shaped your journey. Each theme offers a pathway for deep connection, storytelling, and understanding, essential for engaging with others, including potential investors or partners, on a profound level.

## ASSIGNMENT:

Pick one of these Universal Themes and write a narrative from your own experience that you can use to weave into a conversation.

1. **Loss of a Job:**
   - Navigating the emotional turmoil of job loss.
   - The journey to self-reinvention and finding new purpose.
   - Lessons learned in resilience and adaptability.

_____

_____

_____

_____

_____

_____

_____

2. **Transitioning to a New Career Path:**
   - The challenges of leaving a familiar field for unknown territory.
   - The process of acquiring new skills and knowledge.
   - Embracing change and finding fulfillment in a new career.

_____

_____

_____

_____

_____

_____

_____

3. **Friendship and Loyalty:**
   - Stories of enduring friendships that have impacted personal growth and success.
   - The importance of loyalty and trust in building and sustaining relationships.
   - Navigating challenges and conflicts within friendships.

_____

_____

_____

_____

_____

_____

By exploring these themes, your workbook invites readers to delve into complex emotional landscapes, reflecting on their own experiences and how these universal themes have shaped their journey.

Each theme offers a pathway for deep connection, storytelling, and understanding, essential for engaging with others, including potential investors or partners, on a profound level.

## Crossroads of the Hero's Journey: Stories as Catalysts for Connection

During a routine follow-up on Zoom with a remarkable individual I had briefly encountered at a Capital Raising conference, we found ourselves navigating the initial awkwardness typical of post-conference connections. These events, brimming with potential yet constrained by time, often leave deeper conversations for the digital corridors of scheduled calls. And so, amidst the dance of introductory small talk—a ballet of "How are you?" and "What have you been up to?"—we tiptoed around the edges of a more substantive exchange.

The conversation stumbled initially, much like hesitant steps into an unfamiliar dance. The fear of a misstep, of presenting an uninteresting facade, loomed. My attempt to delve into her upcoming TED talk met with a polite but firm deflection. "No, I'm good... I want to know more about you," she demurred, signaling a still-present barrier of unfamiliarity.

In response, I unfurled the tapestry of my own story, a narrative steeped in personal struggle and the poignant theme of LOSS. I shared the promise made to my mother, a dream of a journey along the Pacific Coast Highway in a gleaming Corvette, a dream unfulfilled as time, traded hour for hour against the demands of life, slipped inexorably away. My mother's battle with dementia, a slow retreat from the world, underscored the heartache of promises unkept. This tale, a distillation of my why, laid bare the impetus behind my drive to redefine the value of time in the realms of personal and professional wealth.

As my story unfolded, I noticed a shift. The distraction that had her glancing at her phone vanished, replaced by a reflective attentiveness. My narrative, it seemed, had bridged the gap between us, turning a professional exchange into a moment of shared vulnerability.

With the floor now hers, she reciprocated with a story of her own—a journey marked not by material lack but by emotional upheaval. The loss of her father to cancer, a devastating breakup, and the revelation of a previously unknown sibling painted a portrait of a life suddenly unmoored. Her narrative culminated in an admission: these were the T.H.R.E.A.D's of the TED talk she had been reluctant to share.

In that moment, our common ground emerged from the fog of initial awkwardness. **LOSS**, a theme as universal as it is deeply personal, had woven its way through our stories, binding them. This revelation underscored a foundational truth I had touched on in earlier chapters: the power of storytelling and shared experience in forging connections, in life and in the business of raising capital.

As the call drew to a close, the impact of our shared stories lingered in the silence that followed. It was a profound reminder that beneath the veneers of professionalism and achievement lies a mosaic of human experience, rich with triumph and tragedy. Our conversation, once hemmed in by the formalities of a professional follow-up, had evolved into a testament to the transformative power of vulnerability and connection.

This experience reinforced a crucial lesson: in the world of investor relations and beyond, it's not just the strength of your proposition that matters, but the depth of your human connection.

Our shared narratives of loss had not only unveiled a common T.H.R.E.A.D but had also illuminated the path to genuine engagement and trust.

The true power of the T.H.R.E.A.D methodology, I realized, lies not merely in its ability to uncover commonalities but in its capacity to forge bonds that transcend the transactional. As we said our goodbyes, I reflected on the unexpected journey we had taken. From tentative introductions to a profound exchange of personal truths, we had traversed a landscape of emotion and insight, emerging not just as professional acquaintances but as individuals deeply connected by the shared fabric of our experiences.

In the end, the key to unlocking the doors to meaningful relationships and successful capital raising isn't found in the meticulous crafting of pitches or the strategic navigation of networks. It resides in the simple, yet profound act of sharing our stories, of embracing vulnerability as a bridge to understanding and trust. This, I realized, is the cornerstone of not just investor relations, but of all human relation—a truth as enduring as the stories we share.

# Part 2: Crafting the Narrative

**Now Let's shape these into a coherent narrative:**

1. **Identify the Core Message**

   What is the main message or theme you want to convey through your story? How does this reflect on your character, values, or vision?

   _____

   _____

   _____

2. **Relate to the Investment**

   Think about how your journey parallels the potential investment. What aspects of your story can reassure or excite an investor about your capability to navigate this new venture?

   _____

   _____

   _____

   _____

**Practical Application: Identifying and Engaging Investors**

1. **Define Your Ideal Investor**: Write down the key traits of your ideal investor. What are their goals, values, and concerns? Use this profile to guide your networking efforts.

2. **Targeted Networking**: Identify events, groups, or online platforms where your ideal investors hang out. Focus your networking efforts there.

3. **Personalize Your Pitch**: Customize your pitch to speak directly to the interests and needs of your ideal investor. Make it about them, not you.

With storytelling as a tool, let's focus on how to apply these principles in a specific context: networking with investors. In Chapter 17, we'll cover how to identify the perfect investor profile and engage them effectively.

# CHAPTER 18

# Networking Know-How:
## *Spotting the Perfect Investor Avatar*

L et's get real about matching your deal with the right investor. It's like putting together a puzzle; instead of forcing pieces together, you're looking for that perfect fit.

For example, if you're working on a sustainable housing project, you might target investors who have previously funded eco-friendly initiatives and have shown interest in green technologies.

First things first, you got to know your own deal inside out. What's its heartbeat? Is it about flipping homes, building communities, or creating sustainable living spaces? Get clear on that, because clarity is king.

Now, here's where it gets interesting. You got to find your investor avatar, that person who doesn't just bring the cash but brings the vibe, the vision, the values that match your project. But how? It's not guesswork; it's about doing your homework.

You start by painting a picture of your ideal investor. What's important to them? Is it innovation, community development, environmental impact? This isn't about making assumptions; it's about research, real talk, and listening. You dive into the networks where these investors hang out. You listen more than you talk. You engage, ask questions, understand what makes them tick.

But here's the key – you got to be genuine. If you're all about sustainable living and your potential investor is all about maximum profit at the expense of everything else, it's not a match. Don't force it. The right investor will align with your values, and when they do, it's not just a deal; it's a partnership.

And when you find that match, it's like magic. Because now, you're not just pitching; you're collaborating. You're not just building; you're creating. You're not just in it for the money; you're in it for the shared mission, the mutual goals, the collective vision.

Remember, in the world of real estate investing, it's not just about finding an investor; it's about finding the right investor. It's about knowing your deal, knowing your audience, and when you find that sweet spot, where your deal's heartbeat matches the investor's pulse, that's when you go all in. That's how you build not just a project, but a legacy.

Let's break it down. Say you've got an investor, let's call him Mark. Mark's not just a walking wallet. Maybe he's into tech, or he's passionate about sustainability, or he's all about giving back to his community.

Whatever it is, you need to know that, because that's the key to really engaging with him. When you talk to Mark, or any investor, it's not a pitch; it's a conversation. You're not selling; you're storytelling.

You're telling Mark how your project isn't just a good investment; it aligns with who he is. If he's into tech, talk about the innovative aspects of your project. If he's into sustainability, highlight the eco-friendly elements.

And it's not just about the first conversation. You've got to be consistent. Keep the dialogue going. Share updates that resonate with Mark's interests. Make him feel like he's not just investing his money; he's investing in something that's a part of who he is.

But here's the thing, and it's crucial – you've got to be authentic. People can smell BS a mile away, especially investors. You can't fake this. If you're not genuinely aligned with Mark's values, he'll know.

And that's not just bad for one deal; it's bad for your reputation long-term.

So, you do the homework. You put in the work to really understand your investors. And when you find that alignment, you go all in. You nurture that relationship. You provide value, consistently and authentically. And over time, that's how you build not just a deal, but a partnership, a relationship that can grow and evolve over years.

**Alright, so you think you've found a potential investor who might fit the bill. But how do you know for sure? You vet them. And I mean really vet them. It's not just about if they've got the money. It's about if they've got the mindset, the heart, the vision that aligns with yours. Here's how you dig deep:**

1. **Ask About Their Past Investments:** 'Tell me about some of the projects you've invested in.' This isn't just chit-chat. It's your way of understanding their track record, their appetite for risk, and the types of ventures they're drawn to. Are they all about rapid returns, or are they in it for the long haul? Do they invest in cookie-cutter projects, or do they go for the ones that make a difference?

2. **Understand Their Motivations:** 'What drives you to invest in real estate?' This is where you get a peek into their world. Is it just about the money, or is there something more? Maybe they're passionate about revitalizing neighborhoods or creating sustainable living spaces. You're looking for that spark, that thing that gets them out of bed in the morning.

3. **Gauge Their Risk Tolerance:** 'Can you tell me about a time an investment didn't go as planned? How did you handle it?' Real estate's not always sunshine and rainbows. You need to know how they deal with the storms. Do they panic and bail at the first sign of trouble, or do they stick it out, adapt, and learn?

4. **Align on Values and Vision:** 'Where do you see your investment portfolio in 5 years? 10 years?' This isn't just future talk. It's about seeing if their long-term vision aligns with your project's trajectory. Are they in it for quick flips, or are they looking to build and grow with projects that have a lasting impact?

5. **Check for Commitment**: 'How hands-on do you like to be in your investments?' Some investors want to be in the trenches with you, while others prefer to stay on the sidelines. Neither's right or wrong, but you got to know what you're signing up for. Make sure their involvement level matches what your project needs.

Remember, every question you ask is a piece of the puzzle. You're not just looking for an investor; you're looking for a partner, someone who's riding the same wave as you. So take your time, ask the tough questions, and listen. Really listen.

Because when you find that investor who truly aligns with your avatar, that's when the real magic happens. That's when 1 plus 1 doesn't equal 2; it equals 10.

Let's imagine we've just crafted this detailed, vibrant investor avatar, a true masterpiece that captures the essence of your ideal investor.

Now, how do we bring this masterpiece to life in your marketing, communication, and presentation? This is where the magic of the Common T.H.R.E.A.D Method comes into play, weaving a tapestry that connects your strategy, your message, and your investor avatar in perfect harmony.

**Here are some tips to guide you:**

1. **Marketing with Precision and Passion:**

View your marketing materials through the lens of your investor avatar. Every ad, every post, every brochure should feel like it's speaking directly to them. Highlight aspects of your investment opportunities that align with their values, interests, and lifestyle as outlined in the avatar.

But don't stop there. Weave in the Common T.H.R.E.A.D – those shared values and goals that resonate with your broader investor community. This approach not only personalizes your marketing but also taps into the collective ethos, creating a sense of belonging and connection among your investors.

2. **Communication that Resonates and Relates:**

When you communicate, whether in writing or in person, imagine you're having a conversation with your investor avatar. Use language that reflects their level of expertise and interests. Address their fears, speak to their aspirations, and most importantly, listen. Active listening helps you refine your understanding and adapt your message, ensuring that it's not just heard, but felt.

Again, let the Common T.H.R.E.A.D be your guide. Your communication should not only cater to individual preferences but also echo the shared narrative, reinforcing the sense of community and collective purpose.

### 3. Presentations that Engage and Enthrall:

Think of your presentations as a story where your investor avatar is the protagonist. Each slide, each statistic, each projection should be a chapter that moves their story forward, bringing them closer to their goals. Be it financial security, legacy building, or impact investing, your presentation should be a journey that they are compelled to embark upon.

And as you narrate this story, let the Common T.H.R.E.A.D be the underlying current that ties everything together. Highlight how each investment opportunity is not just a personal win but a collective triumph, a testament to the shared vision and values of your investor community.

### 4. Feedback as the Brushstroke of Refinement:

Finally, view feedback not as criticism but as a brushstroke that adds depth and detail to your masterpiece. Encourage your investors to share their thoughts, their reactions, and their insights. This feedback is invaluable, helping you refine your avatar, your strategy, and your communication, ensuring that each is a true reflection of your investor's world.

In the end, utilizing your investor avatar in marketing, communication, and presentation is about creating harmony – a harmony between your message, your strategy, and the dreams and aspirations of your investors. It's about making each interaction not just a transaction, but a part of a larger, more beautiful story – a story of shared goals, collective success, and mutual growth.

So, are you ready to make this harmony your reality?

### 5. Rolling into Referrals: It's All About Timing and Trust

So, you've connected with your Avatar, and things are going great. Now, let's talk about something a bit trickier – asking for referrals. It might seem daunting, but trust me, it's all about how you approach it. And yep, you guessed it, the Common T.H.R.E.A.D method is our ace in the hole here.

## When to Pop the Referral Question

Timing is everything, right? Especially when you're talking about referrals. It's like trying to catch a wave. Too early, and you're paddling like mad going nowhere. Too late, and you've missed it entirely. The trick is to catch it just at the right moment, where everything aligns and the momentum carries you forward.

So, when's the perfect time to ask for that referral? It's not a calendar date; it's a feeling, an event, a culmination of experiences that lead to that golden moment. It's after your investor has seen firsthand the value you bring, experienced a win, felt the thrill of a successful investment. That's when they're riding the high, basking in the glow of a smart decision.

That's your moment!

Let's say you've just closed on a deal, and it's gone better than expected. Your investor is thrilled; they're seeing the tangible results of their trust in you. That's when you say, 'I'm so glad to see you're happy with the outcome. It's been a fantastic journey, and I'm looking forward to more just like it.

I was wondering, do you know anyone in your network who might be interested in being a part of similar opportunities? I've got some exciting projects on the horizon, and I'd love to extend the invitation to like-minded individuals you trust.'

See, it's not just about asking for a referral; it's about inviting them to spread the joy, the success they've just experienced. But you've got to be genuine. If the deal didn't go as planned, if the timing feels off, hold back. This is about riding the wave, not creating a splash.

And here's the kicker – once you've asked, regardless of the outcome, you show gratitude. Maybe it's a thank you note, maybe it's a shout-out in your next investor meeting, maybe it's a small token of appreciation. Whatever it is, it shows you value them, not just their wallet.

Think about it. Every investor in your circle is a gateway to dozens, if not hundreds, of potential new relationships.

But how do you tap into that goldmine without coming off as just another person looking for a handout? It's about flipping the script. It's not about what you want; it's about what you can give, and how everyone involved comes out winning. Start by looking at your offer through the eyes of your investor. What's in it for them to share this opportunity with their network?

Maybe it's exclusive access to your projects, maybe it's a first look at your investment opportunities, or maybe it's something as simple but powerful as recognition among peers.

But don't stop there. Think about what their network gets out of this. They're getting an introduction to an opportunity they might never have found on their own. They're getting the chance to invest in something vetted by someone they trust – your investor. That's not just value; that's gold.

Here's how you might frame it: 'I appreciate the trust you've placed in me, and I'm committed to not just meeting but exceeding your expectations. I believe what we're creating here is truly special, and I'd love to extend this opportunity to a select few in your network who you think would align with our vision and values. I've put together an exclusive package just for them, as a token of my appreciation for your support and trust.'

But here's the crucial part – your offer has to match your words. It can't be a generic, one-size-fits-all deal. It has to feel personal, exclusive, like a VIP ticket to an invite-only event.

And once the introductions are made, that's where you double down on delivering value. You make sure every interaction, every touchpoint, is top-notch. From the first meeting to the final handshake on a deal, every moment should reinforce their decision to trust you, to invest with you, to introduce you to their network.

Remember, this isn't about quick wins. It's about building a fortress of relationships, brick by brick. It's about becoming so valuable, so indispensable that your investors see you as a partner, an ally, a key player in their own success stories.

Let's say you've got an investor, we'll call him Dave, who's all about growth and sees every investment as a step towards bigger, bolder ventures. You've just had a breakthrough on a project that's right up Dave's alley. That's when you make your move.

You might say something like, 'Dave, your insights were crucial in making this project a success. It's investors like you who drive the kind of growth we're seeing. I believe there are more people like you, growth-minded and forward-thinking. Who in your circle do you think would be excited about joining us on this journey and experiencing the kind of success we've seen here?'

It's about acknowledging his growth mindset and subtly suggesting that he can help others join this upward trajectory. It's not just a referral; it's an expansion of his influence and a testament to his foresight.

Consider an investor like Sarah, who invests with her heart as much as her head, focusing on projects that make a real difference. After a project that aligns perfectly with her values knocks it out of the park, that's your cue.

You might approach her with, 'Sarah, your commitment to impactful investing has not only driven this project's success but has also set a standard for what we can achieve.

I'm wondering, do you know others who share your passion for meaningful investments? I'd be honored to discuss how they, too, can become part of this positive change we're creating together.'

It's about reinforcing her commitment to impact and suggesting that her referral can amplify the positive change she's passionate about."

Then there's someone like Michael, who prefers the steady, reliable route. After a particularly stable quarter or a solid return on a low-risk investment, you strike.

Try, 'Michael, your approach to investing has always been about stability and foresight, and it's paid off once again. I'm curious, do you have peers who also value a stable, calculated approach to investment? I'd love the opportunity to present them with options that meet the high standards of security and predictability that you and I value so much.'

This taps into his desire for security and positions the referral as an extension of his prudent, risk-averse strategy."

In each of these scenarios, focus on making the request for a referral feel like a natural extension of the investor's own goals and values.

It's about making the investor feel that by offering a referral, they're not just doing you a favor; they're offering a service to their contacts by introducing them to valuable opportunities. Customize your approach based on the unique characteristics and motivations of each investor avatar in your network.

So when you leverage your investor's network, make it about more than just numbers on a spreadsheet. Make it about building a community of like-minded individuals who are all invested, not just in your project, but in each other. Create a circle of success where every member, every investor, every referral is a vital part of something bigger, something extraordinary. That's how you turn connections into a movement, a movement that grows, evolves, and thrives, with you at the helm.

But what if you just got rejected by an investor your deal shot down faster than a leaky houseboat in a hurricane. It happens to the best of us right... But hold on, this ain't the end of the story, this is the chapter where you turn rejection into rocket fuel!

Remember, your real estate empire ain't built on handshakes and sugar, it's built on cunning, leverage, and the tenacity to turn lemons into cash cow daiquiris.

Let's cut to the chase. Rejection sucks. There's no sugarcoating it. You get your first 'NO,' and it feels like a punch in the gut. You've got these referrals, these warm leads, and suddenly, you hit a wall.

It stings. But here's the thing – that 'NO' is not the end; it's just a part of the game. It's a part of the process that every single successful person goes through. So, how do you deal with it? How do you turn that 'NO' into a not yet, or even a future 'YES'?

First, understand this: 'NO' doesn't mean 'never.' It means 'not now,' or 'not this way.' Every 'NO' holds a lesson, a clue to what you can do better next time. Maybe it's your pitch, maybe it's the timing, maybe it's just that the person on the other side can't see the vision yet. That's okay. Your job is to learn, adapt, and come back stronger.

In that 'NO,' there's a hidden T.H.R.E.A.D that connects us all – our common interests, our shared goals, our collective aspirations.

This is where the Common T.H.R.E.A.D Method really shines.

You're in that conversation, and it's clear this deal isn't the right fit for them. That's alright. But instead of just walking away, you dig a little deeper. You say, 'I understand this might not be the right opportunity for you, but our conversation has shown me that we share a common passion for [insert common T.H.R.E.A.D – e.g., sustainable development, community impact, technological innovation]. With that in mind, do you know someone in your network who aligns with our shared vision and might be interested in the opportunities we're creating?'

What you've done there is powerful. You've not only acknowledged the shared connection, the common T.H.R.E.A.D that binds you, but you've also transformed the rejection into a constructive conversation. You're not just seeking any referral; you're seeking a referral that's aligned with the values and interests that both you and your investor share. It's precise, it's strategic, and it resonates on a deeper level.

And here's the crucial part – it shows you've listened, you've understood, and you value the relationship beyond the transaction. You're not just after their contacts; you're after building a network that's tightly knit with these common T.H.R.E.A.D's, a network where every member is there for a reason, connected by shared values and visions.

So, when you face that 'NO,' remember the Common T.H.R.E.A.D Method. Look for that shared interest, that mutual goal, that common value. Use it to bridge the gap between a simple 'NO' and a potential 'YES' down the line. It's about turning every interaction into an opportunity to strengthen that fabric of connections, to weave a network that's not just wide, but also deeply interconnected.

But what about that nagging voice in your head? The one that starts whispering doubts every time you face rejection. Here's how you deal with it: You talk back.

You remind yourself of the wins, the successes, the progress you've made. For every 'NO,' there's a 'YES' that you worked hard for. Focus on that. Let your wins be louder than your rejections.

And then, you get strategic. You analyze that 'NO.' Was there a common T.H.R.E.A.D in the rejections? Is there feedback you can act on? Use that 'NO' as a roadmap to your next 'YES.' Maybe you need to tweak your offer, sharpen your pitch, or maybe you just need to target a different avatar, someone who resonates more with what you're offering.

Remember, resilience isn't about not getting knocked down; it's about how quickly you get back up. It's about looking rejection in the eye and seeing it for what it really is – not a stop sign, but a detour, pointing you towards a new path, a better approach, a clearer vision.

So, when that first 'NO' hits, take it in stride. Take a breath, take a lesson, and then take action. Your next 'YES' is waiting just around the corner, and it's got your name on it. It's not about avoiding rejection; it's about building the grit to push through it, learn from it, and come out on the other side stronger, —

**Let's talk about the art of the pivot. You've just faced rejection, and while most people see a closed door, you're looking for the window that just cracked open. It's about flipping the script, turning a 'NO' into a 'not this, maybe that.' Here's the play:**

You've presented your project, and it's a no-go. That's fine. But before you wrap up the conversation, you lean in, not with disappointment, but with curiosity and confidence. You say something like, 'I appreciate your honesty, and while this opportunity might not be the right fit for you, I wonder if you might know someone who would align perfectly with what we're trying to achieve.'

Boom. You're not just accepting the rejection; you're leveraging it. It's a power move, one that shows you're not deterred by a single 'NO.' You're here to play the long game.

But here's the thing – it's not just about asking for a referral. It's about making it worth their while. Maybe they're not the right fit for this project, but they could be for the next. Or maybe they know someone who is. By asking for a referral, you're not just keeping the door open; you're inviting them to be a part of your network, a part of your journey, even if this specific deal didn't pan out.

And let's not forget – the way you handle this conversation is crucial. You're not desperate; you're strategic. You're not pushy; you're professional. It's about maintaining that rapport, that respect, and that relationship, because today's 'NO' could be tomorrow's golden introduction.

Remember, every interaction in this business is currency. How you handle rejection, how you pivot, how you maintain relationships – it's all part of your capital. And when you flip the script like this, you're not just salvaging a meeting; you're investing in your future, one conversation, one relationship, one strategic move at a time.

### Practical Application: Aligning Money and Values

1. **Money Mindset Check**: Write down your beliefs about money. How do these beliefs align with your values and goals? Identify any limiting beliefs that may be holding you back.

2. **Value-Based Investing**: Consider how your investments align with your values. Are you supporting causes and projects you believe in? Make adjustments if necessary.

3. **Wealth Goals**: Set clear financial goals that align with your purpose. Break them down into actionable steps and track your progress.

**Key Takeaway**: Effective networking involves identifying and engaging with the right investors. By understanding your ideal investor and tailoring your approach, you can build stronger, more successful partnerships.

So, next time you face a 'NO,' don't just accept it; use it. Flip the script, ask for a referral, and keep building that network. Because in this game, the right connection is just as valuable as the right deal, and your ability to pivot, to adapt, and to leverage every interaction is what sets you apart.

Now that you know how to engage investors, it's time to explore the energy of money and how to align your personal and financial goals. In Chapter 17, we'll look at the frequency of money and how it connects to the *T.H.R.E.A.D. Method*.

# The Frequency of Money and Our Common T.H.R.E.A.D's

*"Wealth is not just about having money; it's about aligning yourself with the flow of abundance."*

—UNKNOWN

## Introduction: Understanding the Dance of Energy

Think of money as a guest at a party. Like any guest, it is drawn to a certain kind of music, a particular atmosphere. This guest—money—carries a unique story, a journey filled with experiences, dreams, and aspirations.

If the environment feels welcoming, the guest stays. If the vibe is off, the guest leaves.

Money, too, has its own energy, a frequency that it is naturally attracted to. Understanding this, we see that attracting money is not about chasing it but about creating the right environment—the right frequency.

But how do we tune into this frequency?

It begins with the connections we forge, the common T.H.R.E.A.D's that link us to others. These connections are like the music that draws our guest of honor—money—into the room.

So, let's shift our perspective: money is not just a piece of paper or a number in a bank account. It is a dynamic presence, one that responds to the atmosphere we create. Our task is to set the right mood, to play the right tune, and in doing so, we can invite money to stay and thrive in our lives.

# Common T.H.R.E.A.D's: The Fabric of Life

We are all like T.H.R.E.A.D's in a grand tapestry, each with our unique color and texture, yet all connected to form a beautiful pattern. These common T.H.R.E.A.D's are what bring us together. They are the shared experiences, values, and aspirations that connect our hearts. When we find these T.H.R.E.A.D's in our conversations, we create connections that are genuine and meaningful. And in these genuine connections, we find the frequency of money. Because money, my friends, flows where there is harmony, trust, and connection.

# Aligning with the Frequency of Money

## Creating Resonance

Let's think of ourselves as musical instruments. When two instruments are in tune, they create a beautiful harmony. Similarly, when we find common T.H.R.E.A.D's with others, we create a resonance. This resonance is like the sweet music that attracts money. It's about being in sync, in tune with the people we interact with.

When we align our frequency with theirs, we create a space where opportunities and resources naturally flow.

## Weaving a Life of Abundance

Life is like a beautiful tapestry, where each T.H.R.E.A.D adds to the overall design. When we focus on the common T.H.R.E.A.D's that connect us, we create a tapestry of relationships, opportunities, and abundance. The frequency of money is not something we chase; it is something we attract by being in harmony with ourselves and others. By nurturing these common T.H.R.E.A.D's, we create a life that is not just rich in wealth, but in meaning, purpose, and joy.

Think about it. When you spend money on something, you're essentially saying, 'This is important to me.' Whether it's investing in your education, supporting a cause you care about, or buying that new piece of tech that helps you work more efficiently, each transaction is a line in the story of your life. But here's where it gets interesting. Money doesn't like to sit idle. It wants to move; it wants to work; it wants to grow. The problem is, many of us haven't been taught how to put our money to work effectively.

We're stuck in old narratives that tell us to work hard, save, and maybe, just maybe, we'll have enough to retire on. But that's an outdated story, and frankly, it's not the one I want my money to tell.

So, how do we rewrite this narrative? How do we get our money to start working for us?

Imagine money as a living, breathing character in our lives, one that's often misunderstood. Most of us think of money merely as a tool, a means to an end—buying, selling, saving, investing. But let's pause and think about it from a different angle. Money, in its essence, wants to be active; it's like a restless spirit that thrives on movement and growth. It's not meant to sit idly in a jar or a bank account, gathering dust. Instead, it's designed to flow, to work, to create more opportunities not just for wealth, but for experiences, learning, and connections.

Now, think about the universal truth of circulation—how everything in our world, from the water cycle to the flow of energy, is in constant motion. Money operates on the same principle. It's most valuable when it's moving, circulating through economies, communities, and lives, enabling growth, innovation, and the fulfillment of dreams and needs.

But here's where it gets even more interesting—the untold part of the story. Money's desire to work isn't just about multiplying itself; it's about what it can enable in the process. It's about the startups that turn into companies, providing solutions and jobs. It's about the donations and investments in community projects that uplift entire neighborhoods. It's about the personal satisfaction of saving for that dream holiday or helping a loved one in need. Money, in its quest to work, ties closely to our own desires for purpose, achievement, and contribution.

So, when we think about managing our finances, investing, or making purchasing decisions, it's worth considering this perspective.

By aligning our financial decisions with our values and goals, we're not just directing where our money goes; we're engaging with it, understanding its nature, and harnessing its desire to work in ways that enrich not just our bank accounts but our lives and the world around us.

This conversation isn't about encouraging reckless spending or undervalued saving. Rather, it's an invitation to see money as a dynamically in our quest for a fulfilled life. It's about recognizing that every dollar has potential energy—a capacity to contribute to something greater than itself. And by being mindful stewards of this resource, we're not just managing money; we're weaving it into the larger tapestry of our lives, allowing it to work in harmony with our deepest aspirations and collective well-being.

## The Story We Tell Ourselves About Money

The story we tell ourselves about money has a profound impact on how we use it. If we see money merely as a means to accumulate more things, we miss out on its true potential. But if we view money as a tool for crafting a richer life story—a story not just of personal success but of contribution and connection—we start to use it in ways that reflect our deepest values and shared dreams.

So, let's start telling ourselves a new story about money. Let's see it as an ally in our quest to build a better world, as a resource that, when used wisely, can help us weave stronger connections and create lasting value. This is the untold story of money, and it's one that we all have a part in writing.

Through the Common T.H.R.E.A.D Method, we discover that our financial narratives are intertwined, revealing a collective journey towards understanding and leveraging money in a way that enriches not just our lives but the lives of others. It's a powerful realization, one that can transform our relationship with money and with each other.

In this light, the untold story of money and its desire to work is ultimately a reflection of our own stories—how we choose to engage with the world, the legacy we want to leave, and the unseen T.H.R.E.A.D's that connect our financial decisions to our broader human experience.

First, understand that investing is key. And I'm not just talking about the stock market. Investing in yourself, your skills, your health, and your relationships is just as important. These investments pay dividends in ways that money alone never could. They enrich your life and, yes, often lead to more financial opportunities. Next, let's talk about the power of passive income. This is your money working the night shift for you. Whether it's through real estate, a side business, or dividend stocks, creating sources of income that don't require your daily input is how you free yourself from the time-for-money exchange.

And here's a crucial part of the story—risk. Yes, putting your money to work involves risk. But staying in your comfort zone is, in many ways, riskier.

The world is changing rapidly. The jobs and industries we take for granted today might not exist tomorrow. So, embracing risk, learning from failures, and pivoting when necessary are all part of the journey. Now, I know talking about money, investing, and risk can be overwhelming.

But here's the thing—starting small is better than not starting at all. You don't need to be a millionaire to invest. There are tools, resources, and communities out there ready to help you take that first step.

Remember, the story money tells about our lives is not just about accumulation; it's about contribution. It's about using our resources to create a positive impact in our own lives and the lives of others. It's about leaving a legacy that goes beyond the balance in our bank accounts.

So, let's start thinking of money as an active character in our story, one that has the potential to help us achieve our dreams, support the people and causes we care about, and create a narrative that we can be proud of. Let's put our money to work and watch as the story unfolds into something truly remarkable.

# The Story Behind the Money

Let's dive into a cozy chat about something that, on the surface, might seem as dry as toast but is actually as rich and layered as your favorite cake: the story money tells. Picture us sitting down in your favorite coffee shop, cups in hand, leaning in over a worn wooden table, ready to unravel this together.

You know, money speaks volumes, not with words but with actions. It's like the most discreet storyteller in our lives, weaving narratives through our daily interactions, dreams, and decisions. When you start to listen, really listen, to what money is saying, you uncover stories of ambition, need, generosity, fear, and hope.

## Money's Tale of Ambition and Dreams

First up, ambition and dreams. Money whispers of late nights spent working over a laptop, of saving penny by penny to start that dream business, or of scrimping and saving for that once-in-a-lifetime trip. It's in these moments that money tells a tale of determination and aspiration, a reminder that with each dollar saved or spent, we're writing chapters of our own future.

## The Narrative of Need and Survival

Then, there's the raw, unvarnished story of need and survival. Money here speaks in the language of groceries, rent, and utility bills—essentials that keep the boat afloat. It's a humbling narrative reminding us of the basic needs that bind us, a common T.H.R.E.A.D in the human experience, showing that, at the end of the day, we're all in this together.

## Generosity's Warm Glow

But oh, the stories of generosity money can tell—of donations big and small of time sponsored, of dreams funded. Money, in these instances, sings in a chorus of giving, echoing in the joy of helping others.

It tells tales of scholarships given, of art supported, of communities built and rebuilt. This is money's warm, glowing narrative, showing us the impact of opening our hands and hearts.

## The Shadows of Fear and Anxiety

Yet, money also whispers tales of fear and anxiety. It's in the checking of accounts, the juggling of bills, the uncertainty of the future. Here, money's story is a cautionary tale, urging us to plan, to save, to be wise. But also, in these shadows, there's a story of resilience and strength, of finding a way through the tough times.

## And Hope, Always Hope

Finally, in every coin and note, there's a story of hope. Money tells us of investments in the future, of seeds planted today that will bloom tomorrow. It's in the saving for education, the planning for retirement, the dream of a home. Money, in these narratives, is an optimist, always looking forward, always believing in the possibility of what's to come.

In our conversation about money, we realize it's not just currency. It's a storyteller, rich with tales of human endeavor, struggle, kindness, fear, and hope. By listening to what money tells us, we learn not just about finances but about life itself, about our shared journey on this spinning globe. And as we finish our coffees and push back from the table, we know this: the story money tells is ultimately the story we choose to write with it. So, let's make it a good one, shall we?

Imagine we're unwinding after a long day, just you and me, discussing the fascinating world of raising capital for real estate, and how the Common T.H.R.E.A.D Method beautifully intertwines with the narrative that money tells in this journey.

Think of every investment in your real estate venture not just as capital but as a shared belief in a common vision. It's about people coming together, drawn by a mutual T.H.R.E.A.D—a belief in not only the financial returns but the impact and transformation your project promises to bring to a community. This is where the heart of the Common T.H.R.E.A.D Method beats the strongest, in finding and nurturing these shared beliefs and values.

Now, as we dive deeper into this conversation, consider how every dollar raised is a story in itself.

It's a story of trust, of shared dreams, and of a collective leap towards creating something meaningful. Each investor, by contributing their part, weaves their T.H.R.E.A.D into the fabric of your project, strengthening the tapestry of your shared vision.

But here's the thing about using the Common T.H.R.E.A.D Method in raising capital: it's not just about the money. It's about building a community of investors who are connected not just by financial stakes but by a shared purpose. It's about recognizing that at the core of this financial endeavor lies a universal desire to create, to belong, and to make a difference.

And as you share your vision, as you articulate not just the returns but the broader impact of your project, you're inviting others to join you in this narrative.

You're asking them to see beyond the bricks and mortar, to the stories of families who will find homes, of communities that will thrive, and of spaces that will transform. This is where the real power of your venture lies—not in the money alone but in the collective energy, passion, and vision it represents.

So, in the grand tapestry of raising capital, remember that you're not just weaving a financial story. You're crafting a narrative rich with connection, shared dreams, and mutual goals. By applying the Common T.H.R.E.A.D Method, you're not just seeking investors; you're building a community of believers, dreamers, and doers who see beyond the numbers to the true value and potential of your project.

As we end our conversation, think about how this approach transforms the act of raising capital from a transaction to a journey of shared purpose and vision.

It's a powerful reminder that at the heart of every financial endeavor lies the opportunity to connect, to create, and to change the world together.

That's the real story money tells when you're raising capital for real estate, illuminated by the Common T.H.R.E.A.D Method.

So, we've talked about money as a storyteller in our personal lives, right?

Now, let's shift gears and chat about how this plays out in the world of raising capital.

This is where the plot thickens, and the story gets even more interesting.

When you're raising capital, whether it's for a startup, a real estate project, or any venture, you're not just asking for funds. You're inviting people to become a part of a story. Each dollar raised is like a vote of confidence in the narrative you're creating.

Think of it like this – money in this context is a unifying T.H.R.E.A.D. It ties together different characters – the investors, the entrepreneurs, the dreamers – into a single storyline.

And what's this story about? It's about belief, trust, and the shared vision of creating something remarkable.

But here's the thing, and it's super important – the story you're telling with your capital raise needs to resonate. It's not just about the numbers or the business plan. It's about the 'why.' Why does this matter? Why should someone believe in it as much as you do? That's the heart of the story.

So, when you're out there, pitching to potential investors or discussing funding, remember you're not just talking about money.

You're sharing a vision, a dream, a narrative that goes way beyond the financials. You're saying, 'Join me on this journey. Be a part of this story we're writing together.'

And for my fellow investors, when you're deciding where to put your money, think about what stories you want to be a part of. What narratives do you believe in? What futures are you excited to help write?

## Resilience Challenge:

Over the next 5 days, practice resilience by facing one challenge head-on each day, whether it's in your personal life, business, or mindset. Focus on seeing each hurdle as an opportunity for growth rather than an obstacle.

At the end of the week, share in the community group how your mindset has shifted. What was the most difficult hurdle to overcome, and how did resilience help you move past it?

**Key Takeaway**: Money has its own vibe, and so does a killer story. If you want to crush it, you've got to align your cash goals with what really matters to you. Here's the deal: Raising capital? It's all about storytelling. You're not just looking for dollars—you're building a narrative where every investor is a co-author in this epic journey.

This is more than just raising money; it's about raising the bar on what's possible.

So go out there, hustle, and write the kind of story that people want to be a part of.

Let's make some magic happen!

In the next chapter, we'll focus on overcoming hurdles with resilience and a positive attitude, turning setbacks into opportunities.

# CHAPTER 20

# Riding the Rollercoaster:
## *Overcoming Hurdles with a Smile*

L et's Flip the Script on Challenges!

Let's look at them through a different lens, a fresh perspective that's going to get you not just dealing with challenges but actually thriving because of them.

First up, let's get one thing straight – the best opportunities often hide behind what we call 'challenges.' That difficult client, the market downturn, the deal that's going south?

They're not just problems; they're puzzles waiting to be solved. And when you solve them, you're not just fixing an issue; you're unlocking new opportunities.

Every challenge you face in business, believe it or not, has a common T.H.R.E.A.D with something else. That tough client? They might share a common T.H.R.E.A.D with a past success story.

Find that T.H.R.E.A.D, pull it, and see how you can apply past wins to current situations.

Think about the last time you nailed a challenge. What worked? Now, here's the kicker – how can you apply that winning strategy to your current hurdle? That's the Common T.H.R.E.A.D method in action. It's about pattern recognition and remixing your past victories into new ones.

Here's something we often overlook: how can technology or the latest trends turn this challenge into an advantage? Got a market that's tanking? Maybe it's the perfect time to leverage new virtual real estate tools or dive into a market segment everyone else is ignoring.

Markets are shifting? Don't just react – look for the common T.H.R.E.A.D. How did you adapt to changes in the past? What can those experiences teach you about today's market? This method isn't just about solving problems; it's about learning from them

Let's talk about work-life balance as a challenge. We glorify the hustle, but what about the hustle in taking care of your mind and body? Sometimes, the biggest challenge is to step back, recharge, and hit it harder the next day.

Ever thought about what a challenge in another industry can teach you about your own? That's right – sometimes, the solution to your problem lies in how someone in a completely different field solved theirs. Cross-industry learning is a goldmine.

Here's a fun take – use your challenges as a way to build community.

Challenges aren't just personal; they're universal. Share your journey, the ups and downs, and how you're connecting the dots with the Common T.H.R.E.A.D method. You'll be surprised how this transparency can attract others, building a community of like-minded hustlers, especially on social media, in your blog, or at networking events.

Let's talk about the fun side of challenges. Yes, you heard me right – fun! Because let's face it, if we can't laugh at our misadventures in real estate (or life), we're missing out on some great stories.

Embrace the Chaos

Challenges in real estate? As common as finding a Starbucks on your street corner.

But here's the twist: each challenge is like a plot twist in your favorite sitcom. Unexpected, sometimes ridiculous, but always a chance for a good laugh and a lesson learned.

Working on a project that's going sideways? Use it as a bonding experience. Everyone loves a good fail story – especially when there's a killer comeback attached. Got a deal that fell through spectacularly? Share it group grumbling sessions can be surprisingly therapeutic spin it into a tale of learning and resilience. Just remember, it's us against the problem, not us against each other.

Plus, who doesn't love a good 'I messed up, but look at me now' story?

Stuck in a tough spot? Ask yourself, 'What sitcom character does this situation remind me of?' Trust me, finding the humor in adversity can be a game changer. It's about focusing on the silver, or let's say, the comedic lining of every cloud."

In the face of challenges, keep your sense of humor front and center. Laugh at the absurdities, and brainstorm solutions while you're at it. Sometimes the best ideas come when you're not taking everything so seriously.

Remember: life's a rollercoaster, and so is real estate investing. The highs are thrilling, the lows are... well, educational (and sometimes funny). Embrace each twist and turn with a smile, and watch as those challenges strengthen your connections, one laugh at a time.

**Personality Connection Challenge:**

For the next 7 days, focus on adapting your communication style to better connect with different personality types. Each day, engage with someone who has a different approach, communication style, or personality than your own.

Reflect on how adjusting your approach helped bridge the gap and create a stronger connection. Share in the group which personality type was the easiest and which was the hardest to connect with, and what you learned from the process.

Building resilience is important, but understanding personality types is key to connecting with everyone. In Chapter 19, we'll explore how to leverage *T.H.R.E.A.D.s* across different personality types to build stronger relationships.

# Leveraging Common T.H.R.E.A.D's Across Personality Types

INTROVERTS AND THE POWER OF
COMMON T.H.R.E.A.Ds

Introverts often prefer deep, meaningful conversations over small talk, which can be an advantage in finding and nurturing common T.H.R.E.A.D's. They tend to listen more and speak less, but with greater thoughtfulness. Introverts are typically good observers, allowing them to pick up on subtle cues and interests that can form the basis of a common T.H.R.E.A.D.

Introverts usually excel in one-on-one settings or small groups. Capital raising conversations can be structured in such environments where introverts feel more comfortable and in control. Introverts can also use written communication, such as emails or messages, to initiate conversations and follow up, using their strength in written expression to establish and explore common T.H.R.E.A.D's.

Introverts can focus on building deeper connections based on a few, well-selected common T.H.R.E.A.D's. This depth can lead to stronger, more meaningful business relationships. Introverts are often more comfortable in and suited for long-term relationship building, which is beneficial for sustained business and investment partnerships.

Instead of trying to connect with everyone, introverts can focus on a few key individuals with whom they share strong common T.H.R.E.A.D's. This approach can be more manageable and effective. Introverts can prepare for interactions by researching potential common T.H.R.E.A.D's beforehand. This preparation can increase confidence and the ability to steer conversations.

Platforms like LinkedIn can be advantageous for introverts, allowing them to connect with others over shared professional interests and experiences in a less overwhelming setting. Introverts can share their knowledge and insights through blogs, articles, or social media posts, attracting like-minded individuals and potential investors. Introverts often value authenticity, which can be a powerful trait in building trust.

Genuine interest in shared T.H.R.E.A.D's can lead to more authentic and fruitful investment conversations.

The thoughtful and considered communication style of introverts can be very effective in explaining investment opportunities and persuading potential investors. Introverts can use their natural tendencies towards depth, observation, and authenticity to leverage common T.H.R.E.A.D's in raising capital. By creating comfortable environments for interaction, focusing on quality connections, and utilizing technology, introverts can effectively engage in capital raising activities, in real estate and beyond.

Their approach, while different from more extroverted strategies, can be equally, if not more, effective in forming lasting and fruitful business relationships.

This section addresses the unique ways in which introverts can navigate the world of business and investment, using their inherent strengths to find and utilize common T.H.R.E.A.D's for capital raising. It's a valuable addition that acknowledges and empowers diverse personality types in the business world.

Discussing how extroverts can leverage their natural tendencies and common T.H.R.E.A.D's for raising capital provides a balanced perspective, complementing the discussion on introverts. Extroverts often bring a different set of strengths to networking and relationship-building, which can be highly effective in business contexts, including capital raising for various ventures, not just in real estate.

## The Extroverted Approach to Common T.H.R.E.A.D's

Extroverts generally find it easy to engage in social settings. Their comfort with interactions can be an asset in networking events, where establishing multiple connections quickly is often beneficial.

The natural energy and enthusiasm of extroverts can be contagious, making them effective at engaging others and generating excitement about business opportunities.

Extroverts often have a broad network, which they can tap into for identifying potential investors or partners. Their ability to maintain a wide array of contacts can open up diverse opportunities for capital raising. Extroverts can effectively use group settings, such as conferences or social gatherings, to introduce and discuss business ideas, utilizing their ability to communicate with groups confidently.

Extroverts are typically comfortable initiating conversations, which is a significant advantage in identifying and exploring common T.H.R.E.A.D's.

Their ability to quickly build rapport can help in rapidly establishing connections and exploring mutual interests that can lead to business discussions.

Extroverts are often skilled storytellers. They can use this skill to weave compelling narratives about their business ventures, engaging potential investors emotionally and intellectually. Extroverts' persuasive and often charismatic communication style can be advantageous in pitching investment opportunities and convincing potential investors of their value.

While extroverts are naturally inclined to speak, balancing this with active listening is crucial. Showing genuine interest in others' ideas and feedback can enhance their ability to form meaningful business connections. Being responsive to others' cues and adapting the conversation accordingly can help extroverts in maintaining effective and mutually beneficial dialogues.

Extroverts can use their spontaneous nature to adapt to different networking situations and people, making the most of unexpected opportunities.

Their flexibility allows them to comfortably engage with a wide range of personalities and backgrounds, broadening their potential investor base.

This section focuses on how extroverts can use their outgoing nature, ease of communication, and broad networks to leverage common T.H.R.E.A.D's in business and investment contexts. By harnessing their natural strengths in building wide-reaching connections and effectively communicating their ideas, extroverts can successfully engage in capital raising activities.

Balancing their enthusiasm with active listening and adaptability further enhances their ability to form lasting and productive business relationships.

This section provides a comprehensive look at how extroverts can use their inherent traits for successful networking and capital raising. It highlights the importance of their natural sociability, communication skills, and ability to connect with diverse groups, which are crucial in building a wide and effective business network.

## Harnessing the Best of Both Worlds / Understanding Ambiversion:

Ambiverts strike a balance between the reflective, deep-thinking qualities of introverts and the outgoing, social tendencies of extroverts. This balance can be a significant advantage in understanding and relating to a wide range of personalities. One of the key strengths of ambiverts is their adaptability to different social contexts. They can adjust their approach based on the situation and the people they are interacting with.

Ambiverts can comfortably engage in both deep, one-on-one conversations and more dynamic, group interactions. This versatility allows them to navigate various networking scenarios effectively. Their ability to read social cues and adjust their approach makes them adept at finding and engaging with common T.H.R.E.A.D's in diverse settings. Ambiverts have the unique ability to form deep connections through thoughtful conversations while also maintaining a broad network of contacts.

They can engage in meaningful discussions about detailed, complex subjects and also partake in lighter, more general conversations, making them versatile communicators.

Ambiverts can tailor their conversational style to suit the individual they are speaking with, whether it requires a more introspective approach or a dynamic, enthusiastic one.

They can balance active listening with articulate speaking, ensuring a two-way exchange that fosters mutual understanding and rapport Ambiverts can adapt their approach to align with different types of investors—whether they need detailed analytical information or a more vision-oriented pitch.

Their ability to employ both logical and emotional persuasion techniques allows them to connect with a wider array of potential investors.

Ambiverts naturally blend empathy with their analytical thinking, making them effective at understanding and addressing investors' concerns and motivations. They are often good at regulating their emotions and responses, which can be crucial in maintaining professionalism and poise in various business situations.

This section highlights how ambiverts, with their unique combination of introverted and extroverted qualities, can effectively utilize common T.H.R.E.A.D's in capital raising. Their balanced approach, adaptability, and versatility in communication and networking enable them to connect with a diverse range of individuals and navigate different social and business scenarios effectively. By leveraging these strengths, ambiverts can build robust networks and successfully engage in capital raising activities across various contexts.

Incorporating the ambivert perspective broadens the understanding of how different personality types can use common T.H.R.E.A.D's to their advantage in business. Ambiverts' ability to adapt and balance various communication and networking styles makes them particularly adept at building and maintaining diverse and effective business relationships, crucial for successful capital raising endeavors.

### Practical Application: Engaging Different Investor Types

1. **Identify Investor Types**: Think about your past investor meetings. Can you identify the different personality types you've encountered? Write down their traits.

2. **Tailor Your Approach**: Develop specific strategies for each investor type. How can you connect with a data-driven investor? What about a relationship-focused one?

3. **Un-pitch Practice**: Focus on relationship-building rather than pitching. Ask questions, listen, and understand their needs. Make it about them, not about closing the deal.

**Key Takeaway**: With an understanding of personality types, let's take a deeper dive into investor psychology. In the next chapter, we'll explore the nine investor personality types and how to engage them without pitching.

# CHAPTER 22

# The 5 Investor Personality Types — And How to Un-Pitch Them

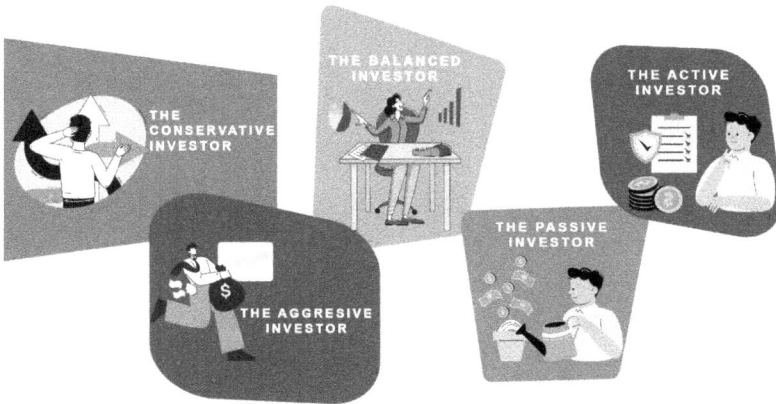

You've got this killer business idea that you're convinced could totally shake things up. Now, all you need is to find someone with cash who believes in your vision as much as you do.

Chatting with potential backers is a bit like a dance. Everyone's got their own rhythm and method to figure out if they're going to take a chance on your dream or pass it by, worried it might just crash and burn.

Having kicked off a few startups myself, I've been on both sides of the table. I've pitched, I've listened, and let me tell you, I've met all sorts of investors. From all those meetups, I've noticed they kinda fall into five main categories.

Once you get a read on the type of investor you're pitching to, you can tailor your story to hit just the right notes. This way, you're not just throwing info at them; you're connecting, showing them why your venture is the next big thing.

So, here's a quick rundown of the **five investor personalities** you're likely to bump into and what they're looking for in your pitch.

**#1. Meet the "Property Portfolio Analyst"** – this investor is all about diving deep into the numbers of your real estate deal. They're less caught up in the grand vision of transforming neighborhoods or the architectural beauty of your projects. What really gets them going is your deal's financials, the projected returns, and solid evidence of cash flow. From the get-go, they're sizing up your investment's growth potential.

You can tell you're dealing with a Property Portfolio Analyst when they start showing off their mastery of real estate analytics or when their communication is peppered with terms like NOI (Net Operating Income), Cap Rate, or Cash-on-Cash Return. They'll probe into why your projections only span three years instead of five, question the absence of cash flow analysis for dividends, and how you plan to allocate investment capital.

### How to pitch to the spreadsheet scrutinizer

When it's time to pitch to the Property Portfolio Analyst, brace yourself for a deep dive. You're dealing with a real estate number cruncher, so make sure your financials are bulletproof. Have your projections, market analysis, and financial assumptions polished and ready to withstand scrutiny.

**Go To: commonthreadmethod.org for a free pitch deck**

### #2. The Visionary Developer

This investor is all about the big picture and the potential impact of your real estate project. They're drawn to innovative, transformative developments that promise to redefine neighborhoods or offer new living experiences. They're less concerned with the immediate numbers and more interested in the long-term vision and sustainability of the project.

**Spotting them:** They're the ones who get excited about the architectural design, community benefits, and environmental sustainability aspects of your project.

They'll ask about your vision for the property, the legacy you aim to create, and how the development fits into the broader urban landscape.

**Pitching to them:** Focus on the transformative aspects of your project. Highlight how it aligns with future trends in real estate, its potential to attract a new demographic, and its contribution to the community or environment.

### #3. The Fix-and-Flip Analyst

This type of investor is interested in the short-term potential of real estate investments. They look for properties that can be quickly renovated and sold for a profit. Their main concerns are the cost of repairs, the speed of the turnaround, and the market's appetite for flipped properties.

**Spotting them:** They'll zero in on the purchase price, renovation budget, and after-repair value (ARV) of your project. They're likely to ask detailed questions about your contractor team, timelines for renovation, and your strategy for marketing the property post-flip.

**Pitching to them:** Your pitch should be focused on the numbers: acquisition cost, renovation budget, projected ARV, and timeline. Emphasize your track record (if applicable), your team's efficiency, and your marketing strategy for the flipped property.

### #4. The Cash Flow Connoisseur

This investor type is all about the steady, ongoing income that real estate can provide. They're drawn to properties with strong rental potential that promise reliable cash flow. Their main focus is on occupancy rates, rental yields, and the management of the property.

**Spotting them:** They ask about your tenant acquisition strategy, property management plans, and the stability of rental income. They're interested in vacancy rates, maintenance costs, and any factors that could affect the property's ability to generate consistent cash flow.

**Pitching to them:** Highlight the demand for rentals in your property's area, your management strategy, and any data or trends that support stable or growing rental income. Provide details on occupancy rates, average rental yields, and how you plan to minimize vacancy and maintenance costs.

### #5. The Equity Growth Seeker

This investor is focused on the long-term appreciation potential of real estate. They're interested in markets or properties that are likely to see significant growth in value over time, whether due to economic development, demographic shifts, or scarcity of land.

**Spotting them:** They're curious about market analysis, growth forecasts, and factors driving demand in your project's area. They might ask about historical appreciation rates, future development plans for the area, and how your property is positioned to benefit from these trends.

**Pitching to them:** Focus on the growth potential of the area your property is in, backed by data and analysis. Discuss how your project is uniquely positioned to capitalize on future appreciation and outline any strategies you have for enhancing the property's value over time.

**Certainly! If we're expanding the investor types for a section in a book on real estate investment, here are a few more nuanced profiles that could add depth and variety to your narrative:**

### #6. The Community Impact Investor

This investor is driven by the desire to make a positive impact on communities through real estate investments. They look for projects that not only promise financial returns but also contribute to social good, such as affordable housing, community centers, or eco-friendly developments.

**Spotting them:** They're interested in the social impact metrics of your project, such as how many affordable housing units you're adding or the environmental sustainability features of your development. They might ask about partnerships with local organizations or community feedback on your project.

**Pitching to them**: Emphasize the social and environmental benefits of your project, detailing how it addresses specific community needs or challenges. Highlight any partnerships with local organizations, community engagement efforts, and the long-term positive impacts on the area.

### #7. The Historical Preservationist

This type of investor has a passion for preserving historical properties and integrating them into modern real estate portfolios. They value the unique character and potential of older buildings and are interested in projects that restore and repurpose them for contemporary use.

**Spotting them:** They ask detailed questions about the historical significance of the property, restoration plans, and how you intend to maintain the integrity of the original architecture while updating it for modern use.

**Pitching to them:** Focus on the historical value of the property, your restoration approach, and how the project will blend historical preservation with modern functionality. Highlight any tax incentives or grants for historical preservation that might enhance the financials of the project.

### #8. The Luxury Market Maven

This investor specializes in high-end real estate in premium markets. They're interested in properties that offer luxury amenities, exclusivity, and high potential for appreciation. Their focus is on attracting high-net-worth individuals and offering unique, upscale living experiences.

**Spotting them:** They're keen on understanding the luxury features of your property, the profile of the target market, and how you plan to market and brand the property to attract affluent buyers or tenants.

**Pitching to them:** Showcase the luxury aspects of your project, from high-end amenities and finishes to exclusive services and branding. Discuss your marketing strategy for reaching the luxury segment and any partnerships with luxury brands or services.

### #9. The Diversified Portfolio Builder

This investor looks to diversify their investment portfolio across different types of real estate, including residential, commercial, industrial, and retail. They're interested in the risk management and potential for balanced returns that come from a diversified real estate portfolio.

**Spotting them:** They ask about how your project fits into a diversified investment strategy, the risk profile compared to other real estate segments, and potential synergies with other types of properties.

**Pitching to them:** Highlight the role your project can play in a diversified real estate portfolio, discussing its risk-reward balance, market resilience, and how it complements other real estate investments in terms of cash flow, appreciation potential, and market cycles.

Each of these investor types brings a different perspective to the table, and understanding their priorities can help you tailor your pitch to meet their specific interests and concerns in the realm of real estate investing.

### Practical Application: Weaving It All Together

1. **Review Your T.H.R.E.A.D**: Reflect on how you've applied the T.H.R.E.A.D principles. Where have you seen success? Where can you improve?
2. **Celebrate Connections**: Identify the top five relationships you've built this year. Send them a message of appreciation or set up a meeting to reconnect.

**Commit to Growth**: Set one personal and one professional goal for the next six months. Use the T.H.R.E.A.D method to guide your actions and achieve these goals.

Having navigated through the various facets of the *T.H.R.E.A.D. Method*, you're now equipped to build and sustain meaningful relationships that drive success.

In the conclusion, we'll recap the key principles and offer final words of encouragement as you embark on your journey to master the art of connection.

# CHAPTER 23

# Weaving Your Own Success Story

Y ou've made it to the end, but really, this is just the beginning.

As we conclude, remember that the *T.H.R.E.A.D. Method* is not just a strategy; it's a holistic approach to building meaningful relationships that foster growth and success.

You've learned to Weave Trust, Human Connection, Rapport, Emotional intelligence, Authenticity, and Dedication to Growth into the fabric of your interactions.

These principles are your toolkit for transforming how you connect with others and how you approach your business. Your journey to success is just beginning, and with the *T.H.R.E.A.D. Method* as your guide, you're well-equipped to navigate the complexities of raising capital and building lasting partnerships.

Remember, every conversation is an opportunity to apply these principles, turning potential investors into lifelong partners and partners into raving fans.

Your journey to success starts now!

It's time to put all this into action!

**Here's the truth: No one's going to do it for you.** It's up to you to take these tools and make them work. You've got the roadmap. You've got the strategies. But none of it matters if you don't start weaving your own success story right now. This isn't about waiting for the perfect moment or the perfect opportunity—those don't exist. It's about making things happen with what you've got, where you are, right now.

## Trust the Process

You've heard it before: trust the process. But it's more than just a saying—it's a mindset. Trust is the glue that holds everything together. When you show up consistently, when you keep your word, and when you lead with integrity, people notice.

Trust doesn't happen overnight, but once you've got it, it's your most valuable asset. Guard it, nurture it, and it will pay off more than anything else.

## Make Real Connections

Stop treating people like transactions. Stop looking at what you can get and start thinking about what you can give. Real, human connections are where the magic happens. Talk to people. Listen to their stories. Share yours. Find those common threads that bind us all together. When you build genuine relationships, you build a network that's got your back, and that's priceless.

## Be Authentically You

Forget the scripts. Forget the "right" way to do things. Forget trying to be someone else because you think it's what others want. The only person you need to be is you. Authenticity is your superpower. When you show up as your true self, you attract the right people, the right opportunities, and the right energy.

People can smell fake from a mile away, and they'll walk the other way. But show up real, and they'll be drawn to you like a magnet.

# Tell Your Story

You've got a story that no one else has. Your experiences, your challenges, your wins—they're all part of what makes you unique. Don't hide them. Don't downplay them. Use them. Share them. Storytelling isn't just a way to connect—it's a way to inspire, to lead, and to change the game. When you tell your story, you give others the courage to tell theirs. And that's how movements start.

# Take Action

Knowledge is useless without action. You've got all the tools you need. Now, it's time to use them. Take what you've learned and start applying it—today. Build trust, make connections, be authentic, tell your story, and most importantly, keep moving forward. There will be bumps in the road, and that's okay. Embrace them. Learn from them. And keep going.

**This is your life, your story, your legacy. You've got the power to make it something incredible. So go out there and make it happen. The world is waiting to see what you're going to do.**

Let's go make some noise!

# *Acknowledgments*

**W**riting this book has been a journey, and I am deeply grateful to everyone who has supported me along the way. Without your guidance, encouragement, and inspiration, this book would not have been possible.

First and foremost, I want to thank my family. To my grandfather, whose wisdom and kindness have always been a guiding light. And to my daughter, who brings me joy and motivation every single day and reminds me why I strive to be better.

I'm immensely grateful to my mentors, whose insights, feedback, and expertise have been invaluable. To Jen and Stacy Conkey, who saw something in me that I knew was there but never had anyone believe in quite like they did. They empowered me to find my own strength, encouraging me to step onto their Warriors of Wealth stage and share my story. Being asked to MC their events is an honor I'll always hold dear.

To Alok Appadurai, who stood by me in my darkest hours, when hope felt out of reach. He gave me the nudge I needed to get back on the path, restoring my faith in myself and my dreams.

To Brad Hart, for pushing me to see the bigger picture, and to Keely Hubbard, for your guidance and constant inspiration.

To my friends, who have been my sounding boards, cheerleaders, and confidants, thank you for your unwavering support. Your encouragement kept me going through the long nights and challenging moments.

I also want to acknowledge the many people I've met and worked with throughout my career. Every interaction, whether brief or lasting, has contributed to my understanding of the principles in this book. Thank you for sharing your experiences, wisdom, and perspectives with me.

A heartfelt thank you to my editor, [Editor's Name], for your patience, dedication, and meticulous attention to detail. Your commitment to bringing out the best in this manuscript has been a crucial part of this book's success.

To my publisher, [Publisher's Name], thank you for believing in this project and for your support in bringing this book to the world. Your enthusiasm and professionalism have made this process a pleasure.

I also want to express my gratitude to the mentors I have yet to meet. I'm eager to learn from your insights and experiences and look forward to the knowledge and guidance you will share. The journey of growth and learning never ends, and I'm excited about the future paths our interactions will take.

Lastly, to the readers—thank you for choosing this book. I hope the principles of the *T.H.R.E.A.D method* resonate with you and help you build meaningful, lasting relationships in your personal and professional lives. Your journey is just as important as mine, and I am honored to be a part of it.

With deep gratitude, Andy

# *Appendices*

## A Quick Reference Guide to the T.H.R.E.A.D Principles

### T–Trust: The Invisible Force

#### Key Points:

- Trust is the foundation of all meaningful relationships.
- It is built through consistency, reliability, and integrity.
- Trust requires honesty and transparency.

#### Actionable Steps:

1. **Be Consistent**: Always follow through on your promises and commitments. This shows that you are reliable.

2. **Communicate Openly**: Share your intentions, plans, and any challenges you may face. Honesty builds trust.

3. **Show Integrity**: Make ethical choices and be true to your word. Let your actions reflect your values.

### H–Human Connection: Bridging Hearts and Minds

#### Key Points:

- Genuine human connections go beyond business transactions.
- Understanding and empathy are crucial for deep connections.
- Building relationships is about finding common ground.

**Actionable Steps:**

1. **Listen Actively**: Pay full attention to what others are saying. Show that you value their thoughts and feelings.
2. **Find Common Interests**: Engage in conversations about hobbies, interests, or experiences you share.
3. **Show Empathy**: Understand and appreciate the emotions and perspectives of others.

## R–Rapport Development: Cultivating Connections Naturally

**Key Points:**

- Rapport is built through mutual respect and understanding.
- It is essential for establishing trust and creating strong relationships.
- Finding common ground and shared interests fosters rapport.

**Actionable Steps:**

1. **Start with a Compliment**: Acknowledge something positive about the person you're interacting with.
2. **Mirror and Match**: Subtly mirror the body language and tone of the person you're speaking with to create a connection.
3. **Ask Open-Ended Questions**: Encourage the other person to share more about themselves and their experiences.

## E–Emotional Intelligence in Conversations

**Key Points:**

- Emotional intelligence involves being aware of and managing your emotions and those of others.
- It helps in navigating difficult conversations and building deeper relationships.
- Empathy and self-awareness are key components.

**Actionable Steps:**

1. **Observe Emotions**: Pay attention to both verbal and non-verbal cues. Understand the emotional tone of the conversation.

2. **Stay Calm and Composed**: Even in tense situations, maintain your composure. This helps keep the conversation productive.

3. **Use Empathetic Responses**: Acknowledge and validate the feelings of others. Show that you understand their perspective.

## A–Authenticity: The Key to Genuine Engagement

**Key Points:**

- Authenticity means being genuine and true to yourself.
- It builds trust and respect in relationships.
- People value honesty and transparency.

**Actionable Steps:**

1. **Be Yourself**: Don't try to be someone you're not. Authenticity resonates more than perfection.

2. **Share Your Vision**: Be open about your goals, values, and what drives you. This helps others connect with you.

3. **Admit Mistakes**: If you make a mistake, own it. Apologize and learn from it. Honesty strengthens trust.

## D–Dedication to Growth: Continuous Improvement

**Key Points:**

- Growth is a continuous journey, both personally and professionally.
- Dedication to growth ensures long-term success and fulfillment.
- Embrace change and be open to new learning experiences.

**Actionable Steps:**

1. **Set Personal Development Goals**: Identify areas where you want to improve and set achievable goals.
2. **Seek Feedback**: Regularly ask for feedback from peers, mentors, and colleagues. Use it to grow and improve.
3. **Invest in Learning**: Attend workshops, read books, and stay updated on industry trends. Commit to lifelong learning.

## How to Use This Guide

- **Keep It Handy**: Refer to this guide whenever you need a quick reminder of the T.H.R.E.A.D principles.
- **Apply It Daily**: Use these principles in your everyday interactions, whether you're meeting with investors, clients, or team members.
- **Reflect and Adjust**: After each interaction, reflect on how well you applied these principles. Adjust your approach as needed to build stronger relationships.

## Recommended Reading and Resources

### Books on Building Trust and Relationships

1. **"The Speed of Trust: The One Thing That Changes Everything"** by Stephen M.R. Covey
   - This book delves into the importance of trust in relationships and provides practical strategies for building and maintaining trust in both personal and professional settings.
2. **"Dare to Lead: Brave Work. Tough Conversations. Whole Hearts."** by Brené Brown
   - Brené Brown explores how vulnerability, empathy, and trust are crucial for effective leadership. Her insights are invaluable for anyone looking to foster strong, authentic relationships.

3. **"How to Win Friends and Influence People"** by Dale Carnegie

   - A classic book on the art of communication and building relationships. Carnegie's principles are timeless and align well with the T.H.R.E.A.D method.

4. **"Never Eat Alone: And Other Secrets to Success, One Relationship at a Time"** by Keith Ferrazzi

   - This book focuses on the importance of networking and building meaningful connections. Ferrazzi shares strategies for creating a broad and supportive network.

## Books on Emotional Intelligence and Personal Growth

1. **"Emotional Intelligence: Why It Can Matter More Than IQ"** by Daniel Goleman

   - Daniel Goleman's groundbreaking work explains the role of emotional intelligence in success and how it can be developed and applied in various areas of life.

2. **"Mindset: The New Psychology of Success"** by Carol S. Dweck

   - This book explores the concept of mindset and how adopting a growth mindset can lead to personal and professional success.

3. **"Atomic Habits: An Easy & Proven Way to Build Good Habits & Break Bad Ones"** by James Clear

   - Clear's book provides practical advice on how to create and maintain habits that lead to continuous improvement and success.

4. **"The Power of Now: A Guide to Spiritual Enlightenment"** by Eckhart Tolle

   - Tolle's insights on mindfulness and presence are invaluable for anyone looking to improve their self-awareness and emotional intelligence.

## Books on Authenticity and Leadership

1. **"Radical Candor: Be a Kick-Ass Boss Without Losing Your Humanity"** by Kim Scott

   - Kim Scott's book offers guidance on how to be a strong, effective leader while maintaining authenticity and empathy.

2. **"Start with Why: How Great Leaders Inspire Everyone to Take Action"** by Simon Sinek

   - This book explores the importance of purpose and authenticity in leadership, providing a framework for building trust and inspiring others.

3. **"The Gifts of Imperfection: Let Go of Who You Think You're Supposed to Be and Embrace Who You Are"** by Brené Brown

   - Brown encourages readers to embrace vulnerability and authenticity as the keys to living a fulfilling life.

## Websites and Online Resources

1. **TED Talks**

   - Website: www.ted.com
   - TED Talks offer a wide range of presentations on topics related to trust, leadership, emotional intelligence, and personal growth. Some recommended talks include Brené Brown's "The Power of Vulnerability" and Simon Sinek's "How Great Leaders Inspire Action."

2. **Harvard Business Review (HBR)**

   - Website: www.hbr.org
   - HBR provides articles and resources on leadership, emotional intelligence, and building strong relationships in business.

### 3. Mind Tools

- Website: www.mindtools.com
- Mind Tools offers practical tools and resources for personal and professional development, including topics like communication, leadership, and emotional intelligence.

## Podcasts

### 1. **"The Tim Ferriss Show"** by Tim Ferriss

- Tim Ferriss interviews top performers from various fields, exploring their habits, routines, and insights. Many episodes focus on building relationships, personal growth, and success strategies.

### 2. **"The Tony Robbins Podcast"** by Tony Robbins

- Tony Robbins covers a wide range of topics related to personal development, business success, and building meaningful relationships.

### 3. **"WorkLife with Adam Grant"** by Adam Grant

- Adam Grant explores the world of work, including how to build trust, foster strong relationships, and lead with empathy and authenticity.

## Online Courses

### 1. Coursera: Emotional Intelligence Specialization

- Website: www.coursera.org
- This specialization covers the fundamentals of emotional intelligence and how to apply it in various professional settings.

### 2. LinkedIn Learning: Building Trust

- Website: www.linkedin.com/learning
- A course focused on understanding trust and strategies for building trust in personal and professional relationships.

### 3. Harvard Online: Leadership Principles

- Website: <u>online-learning.harvard.edu</u>
- This course offers insights into effective leadership, focusing on trust, empathy, and authentic engagement.

## How to Use These Resources

- **Expand Your Knowledge**: Use these books, websites, and courses to deepen your understanding of the principles discussed in this book.
- **Apply What You Learn**: Take actionable steps from these resources to apply in your daily life and business interactions.
- **Stay Updated**: The world is constantly changing, and so are the dynamics of relationships. Continue to learn and adapt by exploring new resources and insights.
- T.H.R.E.A.D Worksheets and Templates

I'm honored to include a special contribution from Desiree' Ferrari Aguero who has written Chapter 13. Subconscious Influence: The Secret Power Behind Your Results

With a wealth of experience in her field, Desiree' brings a unique and invaluable perspective on Subconscious Influence: Désirée is a transformational life coach and conscious parenting coach who believes that a dream life isn't just meant to be fantasized about—it's meant to be lived, right here and now! Blissfully married to her husband, Eli, she cherishes their beautifully blended family of amazing young humans. Each of the 4 kids, with their distinct quirks and personalities, has been a teacher in disguise, helping her heal, learn, and grow both as a parent and as a human being.

Désirée dedicates her time to each of her businesses, helping others transform their lives. With a fiery passion, she guides individuals to shift their mindsets and manifest the lives they've been craving. As a conscious parenting coach, she specializes in healing the often-complicated relationships between parents and their children—even those enigmatic teenagers! Her goal is to help parents become the trusted allies their kids lean on for guidance, love, and support.

Adding another layer to her multifaceted life, Désirée dives into the world of real estate investing, focusing on multi-family properties that not only build wealth but also communities. In her venture as a contributing author, she delves into the realms of subconscious influence and beliefs, exploring how our language and physiology impact our focus and emotional state. Her writing inspires readers to turn these insights into actionable steps to unlock new levels of personal growth and fulfillment.

If you're ready to stop dreaming and start living, to heal relationships and truly enjoy the journey of parenting, Désirée is here to help you make that powerful shift. With her unique blend of passion, experience, and insight, she'll help you craft the life you've always craved so you can start living it right now! Take the leap—because your transformation starts the moment you decide it does.

www.ingramcontent.com/pod-product-compliance
Lightning Source LLC
Chambersburg PA
CBHW071327210326
41597CB00015B/1372